COMMENTARY

on the

SONG OF AWAKENING

COMMENTARY
on the
SONG OF AWAKENING

Kōdō Sawaki

A Twentieth Century Japanese Zen Master's Commentary on
the Seventh Century Poem by the Chinese Ch'an Master
Yung-chia Hsüan-chüeh (Yōka Genkaku)

Foreword by Shohaku Okumura

French translation of Japanese original
by Janine Coursin
English translation from the French
by Tonen O'Connor

Consultation on Japanese text
by Shohaku Okumura and J. Thomas Rimer

MERWIN

ASIA

Portland, Maine

MERWIN

ASIA

Distributed by the University of Hawai'i Press

Library of Congress Control Number: 2014940598

978-1-937385-61-3 (Paperback)
978-1-937385-62-0 (Hardcover)

Printed in the United States of America

The paper used in this publication meets the minimum requirements of
the American National Standard for Information Services—Permanence of
Paper for Printed Library Materials,
ANSI/NISO Z39/48-1992

Contents

Acknowledgments

First and foremost, deep gratitude to Janine Coursin, who undertook the considerable challenge of bringing Sawaki's Japanese into French. Gratitude as well for her graciousness in supporting the English translation before her untimely death in 2001.

Thanks also to l'Association Zen Internationale, the thriving network of European Sōtō Zen temples in the lineage of Sawaki's student, Taisen Deshimaru, for their permission to publish this translation of Mme. Coursin's work.

Special acknowledgment must be given to Shohaku Okumura, Sawaki Roshi's dharma grandson and abbot of Sanshinji in Bloomington, Indiana, who checked the entire English text against the Japanese original, clearing up linguistic, historical, and cultural confusions.

Gratitude as well to Prof. J. Thomas Rimer, scholar of Japanese theater and good friend through numerous adventures in the United States and Japan having to do with the Milwaukee Repertory Theater's bilingual dramatization of Shusaku Endo's novel, Silence (Chinmoku). In the early stages of the work, Tom helped out on numerous occasions by going to the Japanese original when I found the French translation uncertain.

Acknowledgments

Back in 1999, my teacher, Tōzen Akiyama, kindly took the time to vet my translation of *Shōdōka* against the Japanese version and encouraged the reading of the first draft of the work by the book discussion group at the Milwaukee Zen Center.

And, finally, my appreciation goes to my sons, Ian and Doug, for their continuous support of my adventures in the world of Sōtō Zen.

—Tonen O'Connor

Foreword

As a disciple of Kōshō Uchiyama Roshi, who took over Antaiji from Sawaki Roshi, I was honored to be asked to write a Foreword to this English translation of Kōdō Sawaki Roshi's talks on *Shōdōka*. For Sawaki Roshi's Dharma descendants, this is an historic publication in English as we approach the fiftieth anniversary of Sawaki Roshi's passing away in 1965.

Kōdō Sawaki Roshi was one of the most important and influential Sōtō Zen masters in twentieth-century Japan. For a half century, he continuously traveled all over Japan and taught people in his unique way. He visited any place he was invited, from Hokkaido in the north to Kyushu in the south, and taught both priests and lay people. Even after he became a professor at Komazawa University, the Sōtōshu university, and the gōdō of Sōjiji, he continued to travel. He taught at the university, monasteries, temples, schools, lay people's homes, even at prisons. He taught numberless Sōtō Zen priests and also thousands of lay people, making Sōtō Zen practice and Dōgen Zenji's teachings accessible to innumerable people outside the traditional monastic system. He called his teaching activity a "moving monastery." Because he never had his own temple or monastery and was always traveling, his nickname was "homeless" Kōdō.

Sawaki Roshi's Dharma legacy has now been transmitted to many parts of the world. At the end of this book, three masters are mentioned who contributed to the transmission of Sawaki Roshi's Dharma through their teaching activities for Western practitioners either in Japan or in the West.

He himself wrote no books, but many of his talks were transcribed and more than twenty books were published, including this record of his talks on *Shōdōka* (The Song of Awakening), one of the most popular classics of Chinese Zen literature, a beautiful long poem composed by Yung-chia Hsuan-chueh (Yōka Genkaku), an eminent disciple of the Sixth Ancestor Huineng.

Sawaki Roshi created many unique and humorous expressions using colloquial language and Japanese dialects. He was not a poet like Dōgen Zenji, but was in his own way a genius of language. For example, in the last several sections of this book, he often uses the expression "below zero." It might be difficult to understand the exact meaning of this expression, particularly for American readers who are not familiar with Centigrade. He coined this expression during his visit to Manchuria, quite probably in the winter. "Below zero" means below $0°$C, the freezing point in Centigrade.

What does this mean in the context of Buddhist or Zen teaching? In Hakuin's Song of Meditation (Zazen Wasan), we read:

> Sentient beings are primarily all Buddhas:
> It is like ice and water,
> Apart from water no ice can exist;
> Outside sentient beings, where do we find the Buddha?
> (translation by D.T. Suzuki in Manual of Zen Buddhism,
> p.151)

Here Hakuin says that ice is deluded human karmic consciousness that is nothing other than frozen buddha-nature. The world of "below zero" means the world of karmic consciousness in which we are always self-centered. Going beyond zero means the ice of karmic consciousness melts, becomes water, and functions as buddha-nature.

In Section 20 of this book, Sawaki Roshi talks about the four wisdoms, a concept of that comes from the Yogacara school, according to which human consciousness is analyzed into eight layers. The first five are the consciousnesses caused by the five sense organs. The sixth is our usual thinking mind. The seventh is called manas consciousness, or in English ego consciousness. And the eighth and deepest is called the alaya consciousness. Alaya means storehouse. All of our karmic experiences are stored in the alaya consciousness. And the seventh, the ego consciousness, clings to the seeds stored in the storehouse as "I" and influences and controls the first six consciousnesses. According to Yogacara, this is why our way of viewing things and behavior is always self-centered. This is ice.

According to Yogacara, after a long period of bodhisattva practice the eight consciousnesses will be transformed into four wisdoms. The alaya consciousness begins to function as the great mirror wisdom. The seventh consciousness functions as the wisdom that sees the equality of all beings. The sixth consciousness functions as the wisdom that marvelously observes things. The first five consciousnesses function as the wisdom that enables us to achieve activities. Once transformed, the eight consciousnesses function as the Buddha's wisdom. This is when the ice melts and becomes water.

In the case of the Yogacara system, it takes millions of kalpas to completely transform our karmic consciousness into wisdom. But the Zen teaching of sudden enlightenment insists that this transformation is possible in an instant. When the ice melts, it functions as water. This is what "going beyond zero" means in Sawaki Roshi's talks. In the case of Hakuin's Rinzai Zen this point of transformation is called kensho or an enlightenment experience. But in the case of Sawaki Roshi's teaching, just as we immediately become a thief when we steal something, when we sit following Buddha's example our zazen is itself Buddha.

Here, I would like to introduce another longtime lay student of Sawaki Roshi who became a priest after Sawaki Roshi's death. His name was Tosui Ohta Roshi. Ohta Roshi received Sawaki Roshi's eyeglasses as his keepsake. When I met him, he was wearing the glasses and said, "Sawaki Roshi's eye glasses are beginning to fit my eyes."

Probably Ohta Roshi himself did not have Western disciples, but Tozen Akiyama Roshi was first ordained by Ohta Roshi in 1974. When Akiyama Roshi started to practice under the guidance of Ohta Roshi, he was told, "For two years, read only Sawaki Roshi's Zendan (Talk on Zen) and his commentary on *Shōdōka,* practice zazen with me and listen to my talks. That's enough."

Akiyama Roshi, who inherited Sawaki Roshi's spirit and practice style from his first master, came to the United States in 1979 and became Resident Priest at the Milwaukee Zen Center in 1985. Rev. Tonen O'Connor, translator of this book, is Akiyama Roshi's Dharma heir. Even though she is not officially in Sawaki Roshi's lineage, she inherited Sawaki Roshi's spirit through Akiyama Roshi. I am deeply grateful for Rev. O'Connor's efforts to translate Sawaki Roshi's teachings from the French version.

In conclusion, there is one other comment I would like to make. Sawaki Roshi was born in 1880 and I was born in 1948. He was sixty-eight years older than I. This age difference covers deep changes in the history of Japan. Three years before I was born, Japan lost World War II. The Japanese educational system was changed by the Americans, and Japanese culture as a whole was Americanized. Because of this generational difference, some points of Sawaki Roshi's teachings are difficult for me to accept. One of them is his appreciation of the idealized way of warriors (samurai). Sawaki Roshi talked about the virtue of many samurai who were glamorized in fiction. I don't think these kinds of stories show the historical actuality of samurai life. Not only because of the generation gap, but also because of my upbringing as a descendant of merchants in Osaka, it is difficult for me to appreciate the way of warriors. I don't think the samurai's way of sacrificing themselves for the sake of their lords or their institutions came from the bodhisattva spirit and practice of no-self or from being free from self-clinging. Fortunately, I don't believe that praising the way of the samurai mars the essence of Sawaki Roshi's teaching.

—Shohaku Okumura

January 2014

Preface

This translation of Kōdō Sawaki's Commentary on *Shōdōka* is an attempt to fill a gap in the English-language availability of a revered twentieth-century Japanese Zen master's teachings. Kōdō Sawaki Roshi is a legendary figure within Western Sōtō Zen, thanks to the teachings of his disciples, Kōshō Uchiyama Roshi in the English-speaking world, and Master Taisen Deshimaru in France. However, although we may have heard a great deal about the vivid personality of this straight talking, erudite yet iconoclastic teacher, beloved in Japan, only one slim volume of his sayings has been available in English.

To my surprise, it was in Japan that I made the discovery of a beautiful French translation of Sawaki's Commentary on The Song of Awakening (jpn. *Shōdōka*), a renowned Ch'an poem from seventh-century China. I was spending two weeks of practice, including a sesshin, at the Keisei Zendo on Shikoku Island. The practice place, a farmhouse converted to a zendo through the efforts of Rev. Ryodo Yamashita, had a small library. On one of the shelves stood Le Chant de l'Éveil. With growing enthusiasm, I read Sawaki Roshi's Commentary cover to cover and then asked my hosts how they'd come by this book in French. The reply was that the French translator had practiced with them during a stay in Japan to conduct her research. And, yes, they could give me her address.

With Janine Coursin's gracious permission, I then did a rough translation for use in the book discussion group at the Milwaukee Zen Center. And in 1999, the matter rested there. I became exceedingly busy as the Resident Priest at the MZC, Janine died in 2001, and although in 2003 I was given permission to seek publication by l'Association Zen Internationale, who hold the rights to her work, the material lay fallow for the succeeding years, circulating occasionally in manuscript. When I stepped down as Resident Priest at the MZC in 2011 and my schedule became more relaxed, it seemed time to revisit the book. In all that time, only an English translation of Homeless Kōdō, short sayings of Sawaki Roshi with commentary by Uchiyama Roshi, had appeared.

A word here about The Song of Awakening. This classic Chinese poem is a well-known and important Zen text, and available in several excellent translations. However, despite the remarkable work being done today within the world of academia to bring us translations of classic texts, little is available of the teachings of twentieth-century scholar-monks, actual practitioners of Zen. This makes the appearance of Sawaki Roshi's Commentary doubly important. This book is based on lectures he gave in 1946.

It is important to note that the Commentary is drawn from recordings of Sawaki's actual talks. It was not created as a literary effort, with everything edited and smoothed out to present a sanitized view of the author. Here we find Sawaki Roshi at his most feisty, most personal, and occasionally most opinionated. This is not a picture of the perfect teacher, such as can happen when all we have from a renowned master are his best sayings. It allows us to engage with

Sawaki Roshi's personal perspective in 1946 that, while not surprising given his background, may ring a bit oddly or even unpleasantly today. Here he is, warts and all, giving brilliant teachings.

This book is, of course, a translation of a translation, and prey to the possible weakness of such a process. And yet, it is but one more step in the transmission of the Buddha's teaching via translation. The Dharma has arrived in the twenty-first century via early oral transmission, translation into Pali on palm-leaf books, into Sanskrit and via the Silk Road into Chinese, the language of Yung-chia Hsuan-chueh (Yōka Daishi), into the Japanese of Sawaki Roshi, the French of Janine Coursin, and now into my English. Over thousands of years, hundreds of individuals have expressed the Dharma in their own language.

Indeed, this personal expression is imperative. To quote Sawaki Roshi: "What we call the Way is the imprint of the footsteps of the sages of the past. That is to say, the traces sages have left on the road they have taken. To take this Way is to make it one's own and make it one's own lifeline. To put it another way, in realizing our true nature we ourselves become the Way, each one all the while walking it in his own manner."

Yōka Daishi sang a powerful song of his awakening to an awareness that one's entire being is Buddha, that we and the universe are one. In direct, informal, and forceful language, Sawaki Roshi's Commentary illuminates The Song of Awakening for us, while also imparting an astonishing degree of information about Zen Buddhism, its philosophy, and its history.

It is my hope that through Sawaki's Commentary Yōka Daishi's realization may become the reader's own.

—Tonen O'Connor
Resident Priest Emerita
Milwaukee Zen Center

Information on Forms Used

Typographical Forms

Standard

> —Zen when used as an adjective, i.e. Zen practice or part of a name, such as Sōtō Zen

Italics

> —*zen* when used to speak of the philosophy

> —titles of sutras and shastras in Sanskrit, Chinese, Japanese

> —traditional chants for Sōtō services, *Hokyo zanmai.* etc.

Other Forms

References to Buddha

> Individual or distinct—capitalized: "a Buddha," "the Buddha," "Buddha"

> General or adjectival—lower case: "buddhas and ancestors," "buddha nature"

Honorifics

> *Daishi*—"great master." Sawaki refers consistently to the

author of *The Song of Awakening* as Yōka Daishi

Roshi— "an elderly master." Term of respect for senior monks in general or for one's teacher. **Never** used with reference to one's self.

Orthography for Romanized Chinese

The Wade-Giles system is used throughout, as it was in the French translation.

Temple names

In Japanese, *–ji* as a suffix means "temple." Thus *Eiheiji* or *Eihei-ji* mean "Eihei temple." Though redundant, for clarity's sake it is common to add "temple" thus: "*Eiheiji* temple." This translation sometimes adds "temple," sometimes not. The important thing is that a place with the suffix "–ji" is a Japanese temple.

Western teachers' Buddhist names

It is common for Sōtō Zen priests in the West to use their Buddhist names as their first name. In some cases, such as the translator's, it has actually become their legal first name. **These names are not titles**. In many cases, an American priest will, when necessary, adopt "Rev." as a title. Nor are these Japanese names translated. Tonen is known as Tonen, not "burning cave."

Biographical Note on Kōdō Sawaki

Kōdō Sawaki was born June 16, 1880, near Ise Shrine, into a well-to-do and happy family with seven children. His name was Saikichi. When he was five years old his mother died, and at the age of eight he lost his father. He was adopted by Sawaki Bunkichi, a friend of his uncle who had meanwhile also died. A professional gambler, Sawaki Bunkichi was a weak and lazy man believing only in "tobacco and sex," and who had had eleven wives. The one of the moment was a prostitute given to attacks of hysteria.

At thirteen, Saikichi had to work to eat, and in this sleazy quarter he became a lookout in the pay of gamblers. After witnessing the death of an old man in a brothel, he became brutally aware that he didn't want to finish his life in so dishonorable a manner. This incident put him on the road to Buddhism. He regarded his manner of living with horror. He then encountered the Morita Soshichi family, honest and pure people who had received great education, and the aid he received from this family was a window opening onto the truth. He began to frequent a Shin Buddhist temple, and when he was tempted to become a monk to escape his family, a Shin priest counseled him to orient himself toward Zen. In 1896, he departed for Eihei-ji. Arriving there and being unknown, his difficulties commenced. He could not become a monk and had to accept a place as a servant, which enabled him, despite everything, to learn to practice zazen. Finally, in 1897, he received tokudo (ordination) from Sawada Kōhō Oshō in a temple in Kyūshu and became a monk under the name of Kōdō. He remained there for two years.

Later, he met another master in the person of Fueoka Ryōun Oshō, who taught him the correct approach: don't search for satori or anything else, simply sit down in zazen. This master-disciple relationship lasted for a year and was interrupted by his induction into the army in 1900. In 1904, during the Russo-Japanese War, he was sent in the infantry to the Chinese front, where he was seriously wounded. He then returned to Japan to be treated and to remain in convalescence. In 1905, he was sent back to China until the end of the war.

In 1908, at the age of twenty-nine, he entered the school at Hōryū-ji in Nara and there studied philosophy, never neglecting zazen or the study of Dōgen's Shōbōgenzō.

In 1912, he became tantō, the first assistant in the dōjō, at Yōsen-ji.

This was followed by a period of solitude concentrating on the practice of zazen in a little temple in the province of Nara.

In 1916, he quit this retreat to become a lecturer, kōshi, at the Daiji-ji Sōdō. Then, in 1922, he left Daiji-ji to go live with a friend.

In 1923, he began traveling around Japan to give lectures and conduct sesshin.

In 1935, he became a professor at the University of Komazawa, where he gave lectures on Zen literature and directed the practice of zazen, and then was appointed the gōdō at Soji-ji. In 1940, just before the attack on Pearl Harbor, Kōdō Sawaki also led a group of practitioners at Daichū-ji, a big temple in the mountains.

It was after the war that he became particularly celebrated in Japan through organizing sesshin and summer camps in various places. He taught lay people as well as monks, gave lectures as often in prisons as in universities, and participated in the foundation of numerous dojos. He was nicknamed "Homeless Kōdō" because he refused to install himself in a temple and he always traveled alone. He brought a breath of fresh air to moribund Zen by reintroducing the universal practice of zazen.

In 1963, at the age of eighty-three, he fell gravely ill and withdrew to Antai-ji (a temple he had transformed into a place of pure practice). From his bed he spent long moments looking at Mt. Takagamine, and three days before his death he said to a female priest: "Look! Nature is magnificent. I understand the problems of men. In my whole life, I have never encountered a person to whom I could have submitted and whom I could have admired. But this Mt. Takagamine always watches me from on high, saying: "Kōdō, Kōdō." These were his last words. He died December 21, 1965, at 1:50 am.

Kōdō Sawaki's Zen

This book is a commentary on the nature of Zen practice and enlightenment. The question naturally arises: what is *zen*? And, specifically, *zen* as Sawaki Roshi understood it.

What we know today as *zen* began in China in the sixth century, known eventually as Ch'an, a word signifying "meditation" and derived from the Sanskrit term dhyana. Meditation and direct experience of enlightenment came to surpass in importance the study of texts. (See Verse XLV of The Song of Awakening). Yōka Daishi (665–713) lived at the beginning of what has become known as The Golden Age of Ch'an that flourished from the seventh to the ninth centuries in China, and his poem offers a seminal understanding of the nature of enlightenment that even today influences our understanding.

Of the two major streams of Ch'an—the Lin-chi (Jp. Rinzai) and Ts'ao-tung (Jp. Sōtō)—that made their way to Japan, Kōdō Sawaki was a devoted adherent of the Sōtō tradition established in Japan by Eihei Dōgen (1200–1253). Dōgen traveled to China in search of what he came to call the true Buddhadharma and found his teacher in the Ts'ao-tung master Ti'en-tung Ju-ching (Jpn. Tendō Nyojō). He returned to Japan in 1227 determined to offer his new insights, with special emphasis upon shikantaza, "just sitting," silent meditation without object, letting go of thoughts to sit quietly in the state of hishiryō ("that which is immeasurable by thought," no-thought).

It is the practice of shikantaza that dominated Sawaki Roshi's practice and his approach to understanding the teachings of the Buddha. He was renowned for his fierce dedication to shikantaza and for leading groups all over Japan to practice in this form. Quotations from Dōgen's writings abound in his Commentary. (See Suggested Readings for translations of Dōgen's works.)

Today, the Japanese Sōtō organization has thousands of temples in its home country and hundreds of practice centers elsewhere in the world. For a complete overview of contemporary Sōtō activities, the reader is directed to the web site of the Japanese Sōtōshu: SOTOZEN-NET.

In addition to a wealth of information, this web site offers an outstanding Glossary of Buddhist terms. If the reader has questions unanswered by context or the extensive Notes in this volume, please visit the Glossary on the Sōtōshu web site.

Introduction by Kōdō Sawaki

Genesis of The Song of Awakening (*Shōdōka*)

In Shākyamuni's time there were no Buddhist writings. The teachings of the Buddha[1] rested solely upon the physical presence of the man Shākyamuni. He expressed himself clearly and unequivocally and his message was perfectly understood. At that time, they didn't expect flawless doctrine from him, they merely desired his presence. But Shākyamuni died. A man's absence makes all the difference. In fact, the fundamental problem is precisely that such a man existed. His teaching was perfectly adapted to the realities of life. To everybody's satisfaction, he rejected no aspect of it, accepting at one and the same time the bitterness and the sweetness. This is why Shākyamuni was a unique being.

After Shākyamuni died, all that remained to his disciples was the memory of his words. They had no better solution than to record them to perpetuate his teachings. Thus the sutras[2] appeared. It is said in the *Yuikyōgyō*:[3] "After me, my disciples will make the Wheel of the Dharma turn by practicing it. Thus the Tathagata's Dharma body will live forever and for eternity." After the man has disappeared, the only master that remains is the teaching. Eventually, a considerable number of sutras saw the light of day.

They were translated into Chinese and soon into Japanese. No matter the era or place, when a new culture appears in a country, persons with learning in this strange tongue enjoy great prestige. Long after the completion of the translation of sutras coming from India, scholarly linguists specializing in Sanskrit continued to be the object of admiration regardless of their moral worth or their personality. They were venerated as Buddhas, even if, although monks, they did not observe the precepts. People conferred upon them the title of Master of the Tripitaka [Three Baskets[4]]. In order for the Chinese translations to be read in Japanese, they had to be annotated and accompanied by commentaries. Thus appeared the interpretations of the sutras.

The translations were difficult, so the scholars undertook to dissect the sutras in order to comprehend their sense, which gave rise to all sorts of interpretations with psychological or philosophical tendencies, ever more complex and more abstract. Their authors won fame by giving courses and lectures on all these complicated things. These days, this method is called research in Buddhology. The insufficiency of these studies comes from the fact that what is important appears neither in the words nor the letters of these Scriptures. Only direct contact from person to person can transmit what no text can express.

Direct transmission is to encounter Shākyamuni and genuinely touch him. It is the encounter between two individuals, master and disciple, whose vision is identical, with no shadow separating them. Two persons correspond in nature, in perfect agreement as if they were joined one to the other.

Manzan Oshō[5] has expressed it poetically in a collection entitled Myōdō nishidan ni ge o atau: "On the zagu, no space separates us; though separated by an immense ocean, our eyelashes would remain intermingled." The zagu is the rectangle of cloth that the monk extends before himself to make prostrations. The border of the master's zagu is placed over the border of the disciple's and they prostrate together, face to face. This signifies that from now on they are one and no obstacle separates them.

"Though separated by an immense ocean . . ." I am in Kyūshu and you are in Hokuriku. Although we are separated in space, we are one, our eyelashes intermingle and our spirits are linked by indissoluble bonds. Direct transmission is the intimate fusion of two spirits.

Poetry gives off subtle tones that prose cannot express. The resonance of a verse awakens mysterious emotions in us. It's a matter of a direct and personal understanding, an immediate and intuitive apprehension or, according to the expressions of *zen*:[6] "transmission from my mind to your mind," "a special transmission outside of instruction," or again, "beyond words and letters." The personality of its author flows from a verse. A Zen monk who teaches the Way must be like a deaf-mute. His clumsiness matters little; what counts is the radiance he gives rise to; resonances must flow from his person. The deaf-mute expresses himself through gestures and mime, and if we had to make ourselves understood in the same way, we would certainly be much more creative and original. In truth, a Zen monk's transmission is situated somewhere else than in words.

The direct transmission of the spirit of the teaching of the Buddha takes very special forms of expression. Let's say it is the originality of *zen*. They always say that in *zen* one has need of neither sutras nor literature, but if one consults a bibliography of Buddhist writings, one is surprised to ascertain that works of *zen* are by far the most numerous. The reason for this abundant production lies precisely in the creativity and originality of Zen thought. It is truly very interesting and worth the effort to uncover it, if only by the reading of a single sentence. But the words that express it will remain empty shells if one is unaware of its substance. The historical linguist is a blind man who contemplates the cherry trees in bloom. He hugs the trunk in his arms and asks himself if it is a cherry tree he's clutching. There are those who see and those who do not see, and in the case of cherry trees in bloom, that makes all the difference.

Through study one can know everything there is to know about the five aggregates, six roots, and twelve causalities that lie at the origin of the illusions which engender our actions, causes of our suffering in the past, present, and future. This mountain of learning will perhaps be useful for passing an exam, but what does it have to do with our own self? *Zen* is not that. The transmission from person to person is an electric current that passes between two beings. From Shākyamuni, the current has passed to us. Conventional words are powerless to transmit the spirit of Buddha. Only poetic language can stir resonance in us. The first Zen poem that appeared in China is the *Shinjinmei*[7] of the third patriarch.[8] The second text in verse is the *Shōdōka*. The poem is in Chinese, but in order to render it accessible to the Japanese reader, I have introduced kana[9] and restructured the phrases in the Japanese order.[10] Nevertheless, I advise the reading of it in Chinese to better appreciate its extraordinary flavor.

We know the quality of the Indian dharani,[11] of the Japanese haiku[12] and waka,[13] but the resonance of Chinese poetry is completely exceptional. *Zen* was introduced into China at a time when the writings of Lao-tzu were in vogue and Taoism had exercised a profound influence. I am not an historian, and I cannot say if it's due to *zen* or to the Chinese, but the poetry of this epoch sounds clear to the ear and crackles on the tongue. The highly subtle verses are sharpened like a razor. For whatever reason, a new literary genre with unique resonances was brought to life.

The verses of the *Shōdōka* sound clear and strong when read aloud. The rhythm of the verses and the modulation of the sounds render their recitation easy. In addition to the *Shōdōka*, numerous Zen songs belong to the same genre, such as the *Shinjinmei, Sandōkai*,[14] and *Hōkyō Zanmai*,[15] or also the poems to recite, Senshi and Shinpō,[16] as well as the poem Sōan[17] by Sekitō Daishi.

These long poems antedate the Hekigan.[18] They were put to music and gave birth to the music of ceremony. The Chinese poems are rhythmic and melodious; their impact is still greater when one chants them. It is not a didactic poetry aiming at touching the intellect. Rather, it is like playing an instrument or listening to music. One experiences a religious feeling simply by reciting them.

Fūgai Zenji had three disciples: Ekidō, Mukan, and Tanzan. Fūgai was, they say, big enough to strike fear in those he encountered. He was an excellent calligrapher and talented musician. He also painted with elegance. I have a Parinirvana Buddha[19] of his that I value highly and consider as my treasure. I would give it to no one, even if I were begged. For decades, inspired by this Parinirvana, I have celebrated an annual ceremony in honor of the Buddha.

Fūgai's first disciple practiced only zazen, the second consecrated all his time to deciphering manuscripts under a magnifying glass, the third did not practice zazen and never cracked a book. He was an impudent being who did nothing but swagger about. Fūgai said to the first: "This is fine. Your posture is very good. Nothing is more important for a Zen monk than zazen. I saved up for a long time to get this zafu.[20] I give it to you." Ekidō was filled with grateful confusion. At that time, kapok was rare and expensive. A zafu cost from three to

Fūgai Zenji

five ryō,[21] which represented a considerable sum. They say that from then on Ekidō practiced zazen with even greater fervor.

To the second disciple who devoted himself to study, Fūgai said: "This is fine. You are carrying on a work of deep research. A Zen monk who passes his time in blowing his horn or in doing zazen is worth nothing if he doesn't have knowledge. Here is a book that I annotated when I was young. I give it to you." Mukan's ardor for study was even greater.

To the third disciple, the impudent braggart, who beat his own drum and blew his own horn, Fūgai said: "This is fine. You are intelligent and you have talent. One can always do zazen and accumulate learning, but if one is not intelligent, that means nothing. Then Tanzan bugled even higher and more strongly. The first disciple who did only zazen became Ekidō Zenji.[22] Tanzan Oshō,[23] the braggart, taught Indian philosophy at the beginning of the Meiji era at the imperial University of Tokyo. He had a beard and wore an o-kesa[24] over his Western clothes and blew his horn more than ever. As for Mukan Oshō, he published an arrangement of the *Shōdōka* for recitation. He added to the text some notations permitting it to be sung and, thanks to him, *Shōdōka* became included in the repertoire of ceremonial music. The text was preceded by an introduction by Fūgai.

The *Shōdōka* is much simpler and more stripped down than the Hekigan, the Shōyō-roku,[25] or the Mumonkan.[26] Comparing them to Japanese literature, the *Shinjinmei*, the *Shōdōka*, the *Sandōkai*, and the *Hōkyō Zanmai* are nearer to the Man'yōshū[27] in their formal, direct, and spare simplicity. The Hekigan and the Shōyō-roku are more sophisticated and more intellectual. They are closer to the literary refinement of the Kokin-Waka-shū [28] than the simplicity of the Man'yōshū. From the point of view of genuine contents, the spare and sober esthetic reveals itself to be the more effective. The *Shinjin-mei*, the *Shōdōka*, the *Sandōkai*, and the *Hōkyō Zanmai* are the jewels of Zen literature. The *Shōdōka* has been nicknamed "The Mahayana sutra that resolves all problems."[29]

Kōdō Sawaki's Biographical Notes
on Yōka Daishi

The oldest sources we possess on the life of Yōka Daishi are the Dentō-roku[31] and the *Rokuso Daishi Hōbōdangyō*,[32] the essentials of which I will cite here (direct quotes are *italicized*):

Zen Master Yōka Genkaku was born to the family Tai in the province of Unshū. The family name Tai is a local name that one still finds today on numerous grave markers.

At a young age, his parents entrusted him to a monastery, meaning at five or six years, the age of the kouan[33] when the hair is still tied at the top of the head.

He studied deeply the Tripitaka, or Three Baskets, which is the Buddhist canon of Scriptures that are divided into three parts: rules of discipline, sutras, and commentaries.

He also perfectly mastered the Tendai method of concentration and cessation, and realized to perfection the Four Behaviors. Cessation is total immobility, and concentration is the means to arrive at it. The Four Behaviors are the four attitudes of man: walking, standing, sitting, and lying down. This expression indicates that he practiced concentration in all the activities of his daily life and never allowed himself to be shackled by his illusions. Today we would say that he was always perfectly centered in his actions.

Genrō Zenji of Sakei encouraged him to pay a visit to the patriarch of Sōkei. He departed in company with Shūsaku Zenji. Sōkei was where Hui-neng, the Sixth Patriarch, resided.

Upon arriving, he shook his pilgrim's staff and carried a gourd in his hand.

The pilgrim's staff is not that used by monks for going begging. It's the travel staff that was part of the monk's equipment when he departed on his wanderings. Crossing the mountains, he also blew a conch shell. The staff was covered with metal from which were suspended metal disks that rang when one walked. This staff is invested with different religious meanings, but besides the symbolism, its purpose was to scare off savage animals. In the Himalayan region, villagers frighten away tigers by beating on tin boxes and shouting. In the same manner, the monk rattled his staff and blew on his conch shell. The gourd he carried in his hand was also part of a traveler's equipment. These days, we buy a lunch box and some tea on the train.

He walked three times around the patriarch and stood motionless before him.

A Japanese who does zazen can't get up and walk in a circle, but in China one could. Yōka wore his traveling clothes, straw sandals and a robe pulled up behind by a belt.

The patriarch said: Monk, you who certainly practice the three thousand precepts and the eighty thousand minor rules, where do you come from and why so much pride?

Life and death are the great matter. Life is impermanent and passes so quickly.

The question was nothing extraordinary, but Yōka's response was vehement and unexpected. We don't know when death will come.

There's no time to lose. If the breath goes out and doesn't come back in, it's over. Each day is a new encounter. If we must waste our time, good-bye! While waiting, I keep my sandals on, ready to leave again. If I hurried to come here, it's to find the Way.

Why don't you realize that if there is absence of production, there is absence of swiftness?

In truth, if there is no production, there is no movement.

That's so! That's so! said the patriarch.

The chain of logic was flawless. It's evident that to understand the impermanence of life, the essential is to realize the un-born, the un-produced, the un-conditioned.

The whole assembly was struck with astonishment. Yōka prostrated as formality prescribed and immediately made the customary salutations before taking leave.

Aren't you departing too quickly? demanded the patriarch.

If fundamentally speed doesn't exist, how could I depart too quickly?

Who knows that movement does not exist?

It is yourself who creates a distinction.

You have understood very well the notion of the un-born.

One can't have a notion of the un-born, remarked Yōka.

If there is no notion of no-birth, who can make distinctions?

The notion of distinction does not exist either, responded Yōka.

Excellent! Excellent!, exclaimed the patriarch. Delay your departure and spend the night with us.

Such is the direct and personal transmission between two men: perfect accord between two spirits that coincide. The same wave length.

From that time on, his contemporaries called this conversation: "The Awakening of one night's stay." Shūsaku remained at the monastery, but the next day Yōka descended the mountain and returned to Unkō.

Men in ancient times didn't squander their time for nothing. Yōka had attained what he came in search of, so bye-bye!

Later on, a great number of students flocked to him, and after his death they conferred upon him the name of "Great Master of the Awakening to the Truth."

Yōka was truly an uncommon man.

Yōka Daishi is also the author of a collection entitled Yōka-shū. He was a remarkable man of the Tendai school and disciple of the sixth patriarch of Zen. The *Shōdōka* is the song of the realization of the Way, the song that makes the Way understood. He gives us the essential; all the rest is superfluous. What we call the Way is the imprint of the footsteps of the sages of the past. That is to say, the traces sages have left on the road they have taken. To take this Way is to make it one's own and make it one's own lifeline. To put it another way, in realizing our true nature we ourselves become the Way, each one all the while walking it in his own manner.

Even in applying make-up, one must not imitate others. The make-up must be adapted to each person's physiognomy. A snub-nosed person will make the ridge of the nose more noticeable and tone down the wings; a forehead too high will be hidden under bangs; a pointed chin under a beard and a bald cranium under the hair at the temples folded back onto the top. Each man is unique, all the while having the characteristics common to all beings. In the same way, the present moment is unique and eternal at the same time. The spot where I exist is unique and simultaneously the universe. It's thus that the Way must be understood.

To follow the Way is like holding a steering wheel. It is not because you imitate your friend that you drive well. Each one has his personality. We don't ride on rails laid down in advance. We must improvise at each instant and go forward. Turning the wheel, we determine our direction. We must be ceaselessly alert or, in other words, hold ourselves at the ready.

Notes on Sawaki's Introduction
and Yōka Daishi's Biography

1. **Buddha** (skt., pali) lit. "awakened one." (1) A man having attained perfect Awakening, that is to say, total deliverance (nirvana). (2) The historical Buddha Shākyamuni (566 or 563 to 483 bce. (3) The "principle of the Buddha" that manifests itself under the most diverse forms. The Hinayana admits of the existence only of a single earthly Buddha per era who teaches the truth to men. The Mahayana recognizes innumerable transcendental Buddhas who are so many incarnations of the varied aspects of one unique principle. (4) Symbol of the Absolute, of Ultimate Reality, truth eternal, timeless, lacking form, color and quality. *Empty*

2. **Sūtra** (skt.) lit: "conducting thread." Shākyamuni's sermons. Tradition has them going back to Ananda, one of the disciples of the Buddha who is thought to have memorized his words and recited them after his death. Sutras are prose texts introduced by the words: "Thus have I heard." Chants (gathas) accompany certain texts.

3. *Yuikyōgyō*: "Sūtra of the Teachings of Transmission." Translated into Chinese by Kumarajiva (344–413). It would have been preached by Shākyamuni to his disciples just before his death. It

establishes that one must observe the precepts in order to control the sense organs and to regulate one's mind.

4. **Sanzōhōsshi**: Sanzō (skt. Tripitaka): lit. Three Baskets, that is to say, the three sections of the Buddhist canon: (1) The doctrinal teachings of Shākyamuni (2) the rules of monastic discipline. 3) The commentaries on the sūtras. Hosshi: lit. "Master of the Law," comes from the tenth chapter of the Lotus Sūtra, entitled "Hosshi," which treats of the practice and propagation of the sūtra after the death of the Buddha. It mentions the five practices of the sūtra: to believe, read, recite, teach, and copy it.

5. **Manzan Dōhaku** (1635–1714) Japanese monk of the Sōtō school. Author of poems, including "Myōdōnishidan ni ge o atau" (The Song of Myōdō Offering the Zagu).

6. *Zen*: abbreviation of the word zenna, Japanese transcription of the Chinese term chan'na (abbreviated to ch'an), itself derived from the Sanskrit dhyana, which designates concentration of the mind.

7. *Shinjinmei* (Chn. Hsin-hsin-ming): lit: "written down on faith in mind." Work of Seng-ts'an (Jap. Sōsan) (died in 606), third patriarch of Ch'an (Jpn. Zen) It begins with a phrase that remains celebrated: "The perfect Way knows no difficulty, save that it resists all preference." In this poem appears for the first time the fusion, so characteristic of all later Ch'an, between Taoism and Mahayana Buddhism, neither of the two doctrines dominating the other.

8. **Patriarch of the line of Zen transmission**: a great master having received transmission "outside of the Scriptures," which he then transmits to a successor whom he deems worthy. There are twenty-eight patriarchs in the Indian lineage succeeding Shākyamuni and

six in China. Bodhidharma is both the twenty-eighth patriarch of the Indian lineage and the first of the Chinese lineage. The sixth Chinese patriarch, Hui-neng, did not transmit the patriarchate to any successor. Nevertheless, many disciples succeeded him in the Dharma.

9. **Kana**: a system of writing that permits the phonetic transcription of Japanese; utilized for the reading of Chinese characters, suffixes, grammatical particles, and morphological modifications.

10. **Japanese order and Chinese order**: for example: Chn. "to see-deep-mountain" (3 characters), Jpn. "deep (ki) mountain (o) to see (ru)" The three characters are Chinese, but the position is inverted. They are read in Japanese, and between the characters kana have been added to indicate their grammatical function : fuka(ki) yama(o) mi(ru). The Chinese is constructed like French and English.

11. **Dharani**: brief sutra comprised of syllables of symbolic content, charged with energy. They can equally well represent the essence of a doctrine or a certain state of consciousness, renewable at will by the repetition of the dharani. They play an important role in tantrism. Cf. *Hannya shingyō*: " Gyatei, gyatei, haragyatei, harasogyatei, bo ji so wa ka." ("Go, go, go all together, go beyond the beyond, on the shore of satori.")

12. **Haiku**: short poems of 17 syllables in 3 verses (5-7-5) " Sort of a light scar traced in time." (Roland Barthes) For example, this haiku of Ryōkan: "Repairing the roof/my scraggly golden balls/ the cold wind of autumn." (French trans. Joan Titmus-Carmel)

13. **Waka**: poem of 31 syllables in 5 verses (5-7-5-7-7) A waka of Ryōkan: "Just as the water, passing over the moss, follows its course among the rocks in the shadow of the mountain, I become

clear imperceptibly." (trans. Michiko Ishigami-Iagolmitzer)

14. *Sandōkai*: (Chn. Ti'an-t'ung-ch'i): lit: "Harmony between Difference and Identity". Song of Ch'an Master Shih-t'ou Hsi-chien (Jap. Sekitō Kisen) (700–790). It celebrates the state of Awakening that transcends all dualities.

15. *Hōkyō Zanmai*: (Chn. San-mei k'o) lit: "Samadhi of the Precious Mirror," written by Ch'an Master Tung-shan Liang-chih (Jap. Tōzan Ryōkai) (807–869) It celebrates the experience of "thusness" or manner of being of things—their True Nature—during the state of awareness in meditation.

16. **Sesshi**: (Child of Snow), Shinpō (New wealth) by Tōzan Ryōkai

17. **Sōan**: (Grass Hut) by Sekitō Kisen

18. **Hekigan-roku**: (Chn. Pi-yen-lu) (Blue Cliff Record): the oldest collection of kōan in Ch'an literature. It was drawn up in its current form in the twelfth century from a collection of one hundred kōan established a century before by the Ch'an master Yuan-wu K'o-ch'in (Jap. Engo Kokugon). The Hekigan also includes praises and poems in classical Chinese verse that belong to the summits of Buddhist-inspired Chinese poetry. It is also one of the most complex writings in all Zen literature.

19. Buddha stretched out at the moment of his death and his entry into nirvana.

20. **Zafu**: lit. "cushion." Round cushion covered with black cloth and filled with kapok upon which one sits during zazen. A celebrated Zen saying: "You must first die on the zafu." Here, the death is not that of the body, but of the ego's illusions, and of blindness, in order to reach Awakening.

21. **Ryō**: gold piece from the Edo period. 15 g. of pure metal.

22. **Zenji**: lit: "master of Zen." Honorific title signifying great, cel-

ebrated master of Zen. Generally given posthumously.

23. **Oshō**: (skt. upādhyāya): Buddhist master, spiritual guide.

24. **Kesa**: part of Buddhist monastic garb. Large rectangle of cloth fastened on the left shoulder, leaving the right shoulder free, that monks wear over their koromo (under robe.) It symbolizes transmission.

25. **Shōyō-roku**: (Chin. Ts'ung-jung-lu): "The Book of Serenity". Collection of one hundred kōans composed in the twelfth century by the Zen master of the Sōtō school, Hung-chih Cheng-chueh (Jap. Wanshi Shōgaku). The work draws its name from the master's hermitage, called "Cell of serenity." More than a third of the examples are identical with those in the Hekigan-roku. This example proves that Sōtō Zen also uses kōan as an effective means of training.

26. **Mumonkan** (Chin. Wu-men-kuan) lit: "The Gateless Barrier." One of two principle collections of kōan in Zen literature, the other being the Hekigan-roku. Numerous masters prefer it to the Hekigan-roku, due to the fact that it is less sophisticated. When the master Daie Sōkō perceived that his students had a tendency to intoxicate themselves with the sonority of the Hekigan-roku texts, rather than trying to experience their contents, he had all the texts of the Hekigan collected and burned.

27. **Man'yōshū**: "Collection of ten thousand leaves." The oldest preserved collection of poems in Japanese. Compiled at the end of the eighth or the beginning of the ninth century, it includes 500 poems in 20 volumes. The poetry is characterized by clarity, vigor and simplicity.

28. **Kokin-Waka-shū**: "Collection of ancient and modern poems." Compiled in 905, it includes 1,100 poems.

29. *"Daijyō Ketsugi kyō"*

30. Yōka Daishi (Chin. Yung-chia Hsuan-chueh, Jpn. Yōka Genkaku) (665–713)

31. **Dentō-roku**: (Chin. Ch'uan Teng-Lu): the oldest work in the history of Chinese literature, compiled by the Chinese monk Tao-hsuan (Jap. Dōgen) in 1004. The work is composed of short biographies and innumerable anecdotes on the life of the first monks.

32. *Rokuso Daishi Hōbōdan-gyō*: (Chin. Liu-tsu-ta-shih Fa-pao-t'an-ching) "The Platform Sutra of the Sixth Patriarch"—fundamental Ch'an text that gathers together the biography, teachings, and statements of Hui-neng (Jpn. Enō)

33. **Kouan**: three months after birth, the baby's hair is cut, with the exception of a tuft at the top of the head which is divided into two locks and tied in the form of horns.

COMMENTARY
on the
SONG OF AWAKENING

The Song of Awakening

Yōka Daishi (Yung-chia Hsuan-chueh)

(Translator's note: This long work is actually a series of individual poems, or statements about the nature of reality. Many should be read as self-contained utterances, although some may be seen as a continuation of the previous verse. As a whole, they are Yung-chia's hymn to his profound awakening.)

I

Friend, don't you see
This tranquil man of the Way, who has attained awakening and ceased
    studying and acting?
He doesn't set aside illusions and no longer seeks the truth.
The true nature of our ignorance is no other than our buddha nature.
Our empty and illusory body is the Dharma body.
When we awaken to the Dharma body, there is no longer anything.
Our own original nature is the true and intrinsic Buddha.
The clouds of the five aggregates float here and there in vain.
The bubbles of the three poisons rise and burst, empty.

II

When one establishes the reality of things, neither man nor Dharma remains.

The avichi karma is instantly annihilated.

If I lie to deceive you,

May my tongue be torn out forever!

III

Suddenly, at the moment when one realizes the *zen* of the Buddha,

The six great virtues and the ten thousand practices are perfectly accomplished within us.

In our dream, we clearly distinguish the six destinies.

After awakening, all is empty, not even the universe remains.

IV

There is neither unhappiness nor happiness, neither loss nor gain.

In the peace of extinction, there is nothing to seek.

Up to this moment, dust has accumulated on the mirror.

Today it is time to restore its brightness.

V

Who is no-thought? Who is non-born?

If non-birth is true, not even no-birth exists.

To learn when one becomes Buddha by accumulating merits,

Question a marionette.

VI

Abandon the four elements, retain nothing.

In the peace of nirvana, eat and drink as you please.

All phenomena are ephemeral, all is empty.
Such is the great and perfect awakening of the Buddha.

VII

You recognize a true monk by his resolute speech.
If you don't agree, check it out for yourself.
The sword of the Buddha is for cutting to the root.
What good is it to pluck the leaves and search the branches?

VIII

Man doesn't recognize the precious mani pearl
Deep within his buddha nature.
The marvelous faculties of the six senses are both empty and not
    empty.
The perfect light of the pearl is a form devoid of form.

IX

It's through purifying the five visions that one obtains the five powers.
He who has realized awakening knows the inconceivable.
It is not difficult to see a form in a mirror,
But how can one seize the reflection of the moon in the water?

X

Going always alone, walking alone, these are
The accomplished ones who together travel the road of nirvana.
From ancient times, their purity of spirit accords with a natural
    nobility.
Faces emaciated, bones protruding, they pass unperceived.

XI

The sons of Shākyamuni call themselves poor.

In truth, though poor in body, the way they follow is not.

Wearing coarse clothing, they are poor.

Possessing within themselves an inestimable treasure, they are rich.

XII

They use this treasure without ever exhausting it,

Lavishing it on others, each according to his need.

The three bodies and four wisdoms are perfected in their body.

The eight liberations and six discernments are engraved in their mind.

A superior mind cuts through with one blow and attains understanding of all things.

A middling or inferior mind studies much and questions much.

Just strip your mind of its dirty clothing,

But don't brag of your progress to others.

XIII

Accept criticisms and slanders.

Their intent is to enflame the heavens, but it comes to nothing.

I hear them and savor them like sweet nectar.

They melt into me and instantly I enter the inconceivable.

XIV

Meditate on slanderous words and make them into friends

That will guide you on the way of the good.

If a slander brings up hate in you,

How can you manifest the wisdom and compassion of the non-born?

XV

Penetration of original reality and penetration of the teaching go
  hand in hand.
When concentration and wisdom are perfectly clear one does not
  stagnate in the void.
But I am not alone in understanding this.
All the buddhas, innumerable as the sands of the Ganges, are as I.

XVI

The lion roars the fearless doctrine
That shatters the skulls of the beasts that hear it.
Fleeing, the elephant loses his dignity.
Only the dragon, delighted, listens to it in silence.

XVII

I have crossed rivers and oceans, traversed mountains and waded
  streams.
In search of the Way, I have questioned masters and practiced *zen*.
Now that I have found the path of Sōkei
I know that birth and death do not concern me.

XVIII

To walk is *zen*, to sit is *zen*.
Speaking, remaining silent, moving, being still, the body is at peace.
Facing the blade of the sword, the spirit is tranquil.
Facing poison, it remains calm.
My master has encountered the Buddha Nentō.
He was the ascetic Ninniku during numerous kalpas.

XIX

How many times have I been born? How many times have I died?
Birth and death come and go without end.
Yet, suddenly, when one understands the non-born
One doesn't rejoice at praise, one is not distressed by blame.

XX

Entering the deep mountain, I live in a hermitage
Under a great pine on a steep peak overhanging the abyss.
I sit tranquilly and without care in my humble abode.
Silent retreat, serene simplicity.

XXI

When we awaken, we understand that merits do not exist.
Everything is different from the conditioned world.
A gift motivated by the desire to be reborn in heaven
Is an arrow shot into the empty sky.

XXII

Its force spent, it falls back to earth,
Risking provocation of an undesirable rebirth.
How can this compare with the gate of unconditioned reality
That one clears at a leap, entering the land of the Buddha?

XXIII

Seize the root, don't worry about the branches,
Just like the transparent jewel swallows the light of the moon.
I know now that this wish-fulfilling jewel
Is an inexhaustible treasure for myself and for others.

XXIV

The moon glistens on the river, the wind plays in the pines.

Pure twilight of a long night, why all this?

Buddha nature, jewel of the precepts, is inscribed in the depths of our
    being.

Drizzles and dew, mists and clouds, clothe our body.

XXV

The bowl has subdued the dragons, the staff has separated the tigers.

Its suspended metal rings sound loud and clear.

We do not carry these emblems in vain.

We intimately follow the imprints of the Buddha's staff.

XXVI

Do not search for truth, do not cut off illusion.

Understand that both are empty and devoid of character.

The absence of character is neither emptiness nor non-emptiness.

It is the true reality of the Buddha.

XXVII

The luminous mirror of the mind illuminates without obstruction.

Its immense radiance penetrates innumerable worlds.

It is here that the innumerable phenomena reflect.

It is a jewel of perfect life, with neither inside nor outside.

XXVIII

Suddenly revealed, emptiness eliminates the chains of cause and effect

That provoke confusion and disorders that attract misfortune.

Yet, to reject the existing and attach your self to emptiness is also a

disease,
Like throwing yourself into the fire to avoid drowning.

XXIX

Abandoning illusion to seize the truth
Reveals a mind of preference that leads to fallacious choices.
The student who practices in this spirit suffers from a lack of discernment
That allows him truly to mistake a thief for his son.

XXX

We squander the riches of the Dharma and destroy its merits
By relying on discriminating thought.
This is why the Zen disciple rejects this,
To enter immediately into the non-born through the power of direct recognition.

XXXI

The great man seizes the sword of wisdom,
With its adamantine flame and point of prajna·
He not only shatters the heretical mind,
He reduces to nothing the boldness of Mara.

XXXII

Beating the drum, he activates the thunder of the Dharma.
He spreads a cloud of compassion and rains a torrent of ambrosia.
Dragons and elephants frolic and trumpet his infinite blessings,
Awakening all beings of the three vehicles and the five families.
Unadulterated, the hini grass of the snowy mountains

Yields the pure clarified butter that alone nourishes me.

One nature perfectly penetrates all natures.

One phenomenon contains all phenomena.

A single moon appears in all waters,

The myriad reflections emanating from a single moon.

The Dharma body of all the Buddhas penetrates my nature,

My nature and Buddha forming one nature.

When one stage is passed through, all are.

There is neither form, nor mind, nor karmic act.

A snap of the fingers and the eighty thousand teachings are accomplished.

And in an instant the three great kalpas are destroyed.

Numbers and words are neither numbers nor words.

What do they have to do with my wonderful awakening?

XXXIII

Neither laudable nor subject to blame,

Like space without limits, its body is empty.

It is always right here, clear and tranquil.

But, friend, if you seek for it you will not see it.

XXXIV

It can be neither seized nor rejected.

It may be grasped only within the heart of the ungraspable.

XXXV

When speech is silence and silence is speech,

The door of the great gift opens of itself, without obstruction.

If someone asks me upon what principle I stand,

I answer: "The power of prajna."
What are good and evil? No one knows.
Progress or regression? Even heaven cannot measure.
My practice began very early and extended through numerous kalpas.
I am not some joker who speaks lightly.

XXXVI

To raise the banner of the Dharma, establishing the teaching of our
    school,
The clear-sighted Buddha designated the monk of Sōkei.
Kāshyapa, the first, transmitted the lamp.
His line numbers twenty-eight generations in India.

XXXVII

Now, crossing rivers and seas, it has entered our land.
Bodhidharma was our first patriarch.
We know that six generations have transmitted the robe.
Innumerable are their successors who have attained awakening.

XXXVIII

Truth is without foundation and illusion is empty from the outset.
If we simultaneously dismiss existence and non-existence, non-emp-
    tiness is emptiness.
The twenty gates of the void are without foundation.
The nature of Buddha is unique; just so his essence.

XXXIX

Activity of mind is the base, it creates phenomena as dust.
Both leave traces on the mirror.

Wiped clear, it regains its original brilliance.

No longer obscured by the dust of mind activity and phenomena,
true reality appears.

XL

Alas! The Dharma is in decline, evil reigns in this age.

Beings lack virtue and control their passions with difficulty.

The more distant the Saint grows from us, the more profound the
heresies.

Demons are powerful, the Dharma weak, and hate wreaks havoc.

When Buddha's doctrine of sudden awakening makes itself known,

Their frustration is that they cannot smash it like a tile.

XLI

Actions arise from the mind, spawning retribution upon the body.

There's no point in complaining or blaming others.

To avoid creating a karma of uninterrupted suffering,

Do not slander the teachings of the true Buddha Dharma.

XLII

The lion makes his home within the thick foliage of the sandalwood
forest

In which no other trees grow.

Alone, he prowls in the silence and tranquility of the forest.

All other animals, having fled, stay away.

XLIII

A band of lion cubs follow him.

At three years of age their roar is already powerful.

Even if a hundred thousand jackals wished to pursue the king of the
    Dharma,
These monsters would yap in vain.

XLIV

The sudden perfect doctrine is without human inclinations.
If you have unresolved doubts, you must struggle with them.
Humble mountain monk that I am, I have no personal point of view,
Fearing that my practice might fall into the rut of nihilism or eternalism.

XLV

Right and wrong are neither right nor wrong.
But be off by a hair and you are a thousand miles distant.
Right, one becomes Buddha like the daughter of the naga king.
Wrong, one is thrown living into hell like Zenshō.
During long years I have amassed learning,
Studied the commentaries and consulted the sutras.
Without rest I have analyzed words and signs.
Counting the grains of sand in the sea, I have exhausted myself in vain.
The Buddha has severely reprimanded me,
"What good is it to count the treasures of others?"
I have gone astray on dead-end roads and experienced the futility of
    my efforts.
So many years wasted for nothing, wandering in the dusts of the world!

XLVI

When a spiritual line becomes corrupted, knowledge and compre-
    hension become mistaken.
We cannot gain access to the perfect awakening of the Buddha.

The Two Vehicles have energy, but do not have the mind of the Way.

Heretics have intelligence, but do not have wisdom.

One who is foolish or naïve is fooled by an empty fist or an index finger.

He takes the finger for the moon and makes an effort for nothing.

He forges strange chimeras from the phenomena his senses perceive.

The one who does not perceive a single phenomenon is identical with the Buddha.

He truly merits being called Kanjizai.

With clarity of understanding, the emptiness of karma's shackles appears.

Without it, karmic debts remain due.

XLVII

Though hungry, they do not eat the royal feast they are offered.

Sick, they consult the King of Physicians, but do not follow his prescription.

Within this world of desires, it is the power of seeing and knowing that permits the practice of *zen*.

The lotus that blooms in the fire is indestructible.

Though having committed a capital crime, Yuse realized the unborn,

Became immediately a Buddha, and remains so now.

XLVIII

The lion roars the doctrine without fear.

Alas! How pitiful are these confused and limited spirits!

Comprehending only that grave faults are an obstacle to awakening,

They are incapable of penetrating the Buddha's secret.

Two monks became guilty of lewdness and murder

And Upali, no more enlightened than a firefly, merely aggravated
     their guilt.
The great Vimalakirti immediately melted their doubts
Like frost and snow beneath a blazing sun.

XLIX

The power of deliverance is inconceivable,
With limitless marvelous functions as numberless as the sands of the
     Ganges.
Would one dare renounce offering it the gift of the four possessions
When ten thousand pieces of gold would not suffice?
Grinding our bones to powder or cutting our body in pieces could
     not repay it.
A single word well understood surpasses ten thousand words.

L

It is lord of all existences, none surpass it.
All buddhas, as numerous as the sands of the Ganges, bear witness to
     it.
Now I understand the nature of the mani jewel.
It accords with all those who receive it in trust.

LI

One perceives clearly that there's nothing at all,
Neither man nor Buddha.
The myriad universes are bubbles in the ocean,
The saints and sages, lightning flashes in the sky.
Even if our heads were crushed below a turning iron wheel,
The perfect light of concentration and wisdom would not vanish.

LII

Though the sun may cool and the moon warm,

Mara's hordes cannot destroy the true teaching.

The high chariot drawn by an elephant tranquilly advances.

How could a praying mantis deflect it from its course?

The great elephant does not frequent rabbit runs.

Great awakening is not concerned with little details.

Do not calculate the vastness of the sky by peering at it through a
straw.

Friend, if you have not yet clearly understood, I have given you here
the key.

Commentary by Kōdō Sawaki

1

Friend, don't you see
This tranquil man of the Way, who has attained awakening and ceased
*   studying and acting?*
He doesn't set aside illusions and no longer seeks the truth.

The Universe at Work

All zen monks are familiar with the poem *Hōkyō Zanmai* by Tōzan Ryōkai.[1] Like *Shōdōka*, it's a song, and both of these works speak to us directly. The first stanza of *Hōkyō Zanmai* calls to us: "Now you have it; preserve it well." Tōzan and Yōka intend to forge an intimate relationship with the reader. From now on, we will no longer be anonymous, distant, and impersonal members of the crowd. The pronoun kimi (informal version of "you") appears at the head of the first verse and again in the final verse. It is through the medium of kim*i* that Yōka addresses his message to us. As the main through line of the work, it is kimi (you) who practices zazen and studies the Way.

Shōdōka is Yōka Daishi's testimony to his personal awakening. It is here that he expresses his own spiritual process. In modern terms, we might say that it's an examination of consciousness, an intimate reflection on his experience of awakening. In any case, Yōka Daishi's personal testimony is of concern to all of us who practice zazen.

Friend, don't you see? If he hadn't been composing a poem, he might have said to me: "Hey, buddy, how can you possibly not see? Ok, let me explain it to you. What you aren't seeing is that the tranquil man who has attained awakening has ceased studying and acting. He doesn't set aside illusions and no longer seeks truth." To put it another way, "You don't see the principle that the universe fills all things." Yōka's experience is based upon the fact that no gap, no discontinuity, exists between self, Buddha, the universe, and all existences in the ten directions.[2]

Our religion is a good religion because each of our actions is that of all buddhas in the ten directions and three times.[3] This means that, considered as an individual, I am not as negligible as it might appear. Certainly, men love to think deeply about great matters, matters about which the person with the least little bit of reputation immediately cries to the four winds so that everyone can know about it. Each one also thinks deeply within his self, but what these men do not know is that at this very moment they are themselves the entire universe. When I sneeze, the entire universe sneezes.

Our every action, however secret or intimate it may be, resounds in the universe. This is why a person doing zazen generates once more the awakening of all buddhas and gives new vigor to the study of the Way. Conversely, committing a bad action is to insult the entire universe and outrage all buddhas and living beings in the three times and ten directions.

It degrades the entire universe to think that each of us, as an individual, can permit himself to do no matter what. On the contrary, when working for the universe, an accomplished action becomes eternal. *Shōdōka* brings forth the fundamental principle that our actions are not separated from the universe.

Our downfall is to cut ourselves out of the universe. The fall occurs when the "I" solidifies and places itself outside of the universe. Conversely, when one carries the universe within oneself, seeing it as one's personal responsibility, that is when one experiences what Shinran Shōnin[4] meant when he wrote: "The more I reflect on the vows Amida[5] made after meditating for five kalpas,[6] the more I am convinced that they have been made exclusively for me and my salvation."

Realizing that these vows were formulated for him, Shinran understood that he carried all humanity within himself and, in consequence, he took upon himself the practice of all living beings. However, we don't need to roam the world to find men living with illusions, it suffices to merely close our eyes. After a bit, we will see them abounding in serried ranks within ourselves. Everyone can understand this; without even thinking about others, let us simply look within, where they teem. Each of us is a small-scale model of the universe.

This fusion with the universe is precisely what one calls becoming Buddha. All, absolutely all, becomes Buddha: living and non-living beings, plants, trees, lands and planets; without distinction all is Buddha. To understand that I am Buddha is to contain within myself the entire universe. You don't see this principle, any more than you see *"this tranquil man who has attained awakening and ceased studying and acting."*

However, if we are aware that we are living in illusion we are in the situation of a poor man who knows he is poor. Still, this is reasoning applied after the fact, like rouge. A baby doesn't know he's poor. Moreover, a rich person who's conscious of his wealth is a mere poseur, he wasn't aware of it as a baby.

It is also insupportable to hear someone say: "I have satori.[7]" One knows neither that one has satori, nor that one lives in illusion. The correct state of consciousness is hishiryō,[8] thinking without thinking, or thinking beyond thinking. In this state there is neither consciousness of satori nor consciousness of illusions. It's also said that it's thinking in the absence of concepts and self-will. Nevertheless, we shouldn't think that our mind disappears into the clouds like a balloon.

Of Life and Death

The *Shijūnishōgyō*[9] poses a question: "To whom must one make an offering to obtain the greatest merits?" The response is that there is greater merit in nourishing a good man than a bad man. You might say that it counts more to offer a meal to a cop than to a gangster.

It's profitless to lend money to a poker player. Presumably, if there is more merit in assisting a good man than a bad one, the investment in a man of satori is still better. Now, there are many levels in satori and the further we climb up the hierarchy, the greater the profits, and there, right at the top, without superior or equal, resides the Buddha. Consequently, rather than make offerings to a million men of satori, I would make them to the Buddha. But there is something still better: the man without thought, without attachment, without practice, without satori. My gift would go to him, because through him I would obtain the greatest merits. This man, without thought, without attachment, without practice, without satori, is "*the tranquil man who has ceased studying and acting.*"

This tranquil man is a man whom nothing and no one can disturb. A wooden man or a stone woman. Atop the Gōjō bridge in Kyōto, there is the image of a Zen monk menaced by a saber poised to cut off his head. The monk stretches out his neck as though to say,

"Go to it!" This monk named Daitō Kokushi[10] had converted the emperor Go-Daigo, and his attacker was an Ashikaga who wished him to change his alliance: "Will you be one of ours?" "No." "Then I'm going to cut off your head." "Go ahead!" and Daitō offered his neck. An inscription on the image says: "Like a wooden puppet, the monk is unaware of the icy breath of the saber." This man is unshakeable, indifferent to death. Here is truly the man without thought, without attachment, without practice, and without satori.

The problem lies not in the fact of accepting death, for that anyone can do, depending on era and circumstances. As far as that goes, Kunisada Chūji[11] and Banzuiin Chōbei[12] risked their lives many times without being Buddhist patriarchs. We, as well, though far from being hot heads, put our life at stake doing zazen. If he does zazen, even a fellow whose deepest nature is corrupted becomes intimate with death. That's not the difficulty. Dōgen Zenji[13] writes in Gakudōyōjinshū:[14] "There are numerous men who from ancient times have ground bones and broken bodies, but among them very few have transmitted the Dharma; equally numerous are those who have practiced austerities and rare those who have realized awakening." There is something still more difficult than sacrificing one's life or practicing mortifications; it's accomplishing an action without feeling that one is sacrificing one's life. Keizan Jōkin[15] wrote in Zazen Yōjinki:[16] "The great man whose mind does not think is a great corpse." We say he is like one dead, for no adjective could qualify him, he is incommensurable. This great dead man is in union with the universe.

The tranquil man who has ceased studying and acting doesn't let himself be led around by the nose. He doesn't give way to either the charms of satori or those of a beautiful woman, never mind a plain one. Would this great man of no-thought, like a corpse and in union with the universe, flee a plain woman? It is illusion that discriminates, fantasizes and elaborates concepts, and he doesn't even know what illusion is. To be Buddha is to be the awakened person who has ceased studying and interfering. He neither rejects nor seizes phenomena. He rejects nothing because there is nothing to reject, he seizes nothing because there is nothing to seize. He's the entire heaven and earth, and there's no longer anything either to flee or to pursue. I endlessly repeat: "Hold your fire!" for people constantly resort to this bizarre word "satori," misusing it and thereby brazenly making it ridiculous. It is an illusion to believe that one has satori. There's nothing more absurd.

"*He doesn't set aside illusions and no longer seeks the truth.*" Men are astonishing. Those who think themselves better than others are not, and those who put themselves down are not as bad as they think. Likewise, realizing that one lives in illusion is proof that one doesn't have so many. There's no need to either reject illusions or search for truth. You don't have the objective of becoming a Buddha. You don't even think about it.

After these introductory verses, let us enter the heart of the matter.

2

The true nature of our ignorance is no other than our Buddha nature.
Our empty and illusory body is the Dharma-body.

The Buddha and the Devil

Ignorance is at the root of illusions, and ignorance and satori are not as different as one might imagine. The Buddha and the devil can have the same face. The devil is not on one side and the Buddha on the other. Sometimes it's Buddha, sometimes it's the devil. Empress Shōken Kotaikō[1] wrote in a poem: "According to the heart of the one who possesses it, gold is a treasure or an enemy." We see parents sweat blood to put money aside for their children, but this money rarely creates happiness for those who inherit it.

Then, wouldn't it be better to be poor? Yes, I think so, if one enjoys good health and one's deep nature isn't corrupted by it, nor the heart filled with bitterness. Poverty is good; so is wealth, provided that it doesn't go to your head. I am also aware that money is convenient. In short, according to the individual, money is an enemy or an ally. If poverty embitters some, it can also strengthen character, reinforcing a spirit of independence. It depends on the heart of the one experiencing it. A child detests a father who scolds him for doing something stupid, but when he needs him and the father isn't there, he feels very alone. And yet, it's the same father. Our own blindness is at the root of our illusions.

The Way of Independence

Miyamoto Musashi[2] wrote Dōkukōdō,[3] a code of conduct for warriors. The title was borrowed from a verse[4] in *Shōdōka*: "*Going always alone, walking alone.*" The warriors receive military training, but bushidō[5] goes beyond the practice of arms. It's a code based upon fidelity to the bonds of kinship and upon *zen*. When we study the so-called "Zen of the samurai" we see that their understanding of the Buddha Way is astonishingly accurate and profound.

1. Don't go against the customs of your time.
2. Don't seek pleasure.
3. Remain impartial in all things.
4. Make little of yourself and much of others.
5. Throughout your life remain unaware of desires.
6. What's done is done; do not regret it.
7. In both good and bad fortune, envy no one.

8. Whatever your road may be, depart without sadness.

9. Reproach neither others nor yourself for anything.

10. Don't keep attachments in your heart.

11. Don't covet anything.

12. Don't wish for a dwelling for yourself.

13. Don't seek refined food.

14. Don't acquire old things with the idea of selling them.

15. Don't practice rites of abstinence.

16. Be attached to nothing in the world, except your weapons.

17. So long as you practice the Way, do not fear death.

18. Don't desire wealth for your old age.

19. Venerate the gods and buddhas, but ask nothing of them.

20. Surrender your life, not your honor.

21. Never swerve from the Way of the Warrior.

12th day, 5th month, 2nd year of Shōhō era

Shinmen Musashi, for Lord Terao Magonojo

"Don't seek pleasure" because the search for pleasure belongs to man's illusions. "Make little of yourself and much of others." Normally, one shouldn't take oneself lightly and should consider life with seriousness, but for the ancient warriors, when there was no way out it was correct to end one's life by committing hara-kiri. Dagger in hand, they reviewed the situation and if irremediable, hup! They plunged the dagger in. That's what it means to make little of yourself and much of others. Today, we sacrifice the others, not ourselves. We think only of ourselves and of filling our pockets. The person who meets failure complains about his fate, totes up his grievances and takes off. This is someone who makes much of himself and little of others.

The sixth item is amusing: "What's done is done, do not regret it." The warriors of old had good sense. Musashi died in 1645, one week after having written Dōkukōdō. The manuscript is preserved in Kumamoto.

One day I had a visit from a man with bloodshot eyes, exhibiting signs of great nervousness. He told me he was afraid he wouldn't pass the chief civil service exam. I speculated that he wanted to practice zazen in order to cure his depression, so I answered him: "If you fail, it will be because there are stronger candidates and you must rejoice at that. If you succeed, it will be because you are the better, and you must be distressed because there are so many mediocre people in our country." My response surprised him. You must understand this kind of thing or you will only regret what you've done. It's better to say to yourself: "If I fail the exam, it's because there are stronger candidates than I. As the proverb says, 'The old river doesn't run dry. Even if tainted, it still glitters golden." There are still many valuable people in Japan. That's good and I can rejoice." That's what one should think, but few people understand. What's done is done, yet the majority live in regret.

The seventh item: "In both good and bad fortune, envy no one." The warriors weren't jealous of others. Today everyone envies his neighbor. The Dōkukōdō is very short, but it hits the mark in every sentence.

A Luminous World

Ignorance is an obscuring of the self by the self. We deprive of light our own life and that of all beings. He who goes from darkness into darkness is an ignoramus.

The ordinary man consumes his life in the service of ignorance. That is to say, in the service of illusions. He lives in darkness. In the poorly lit quarters of the city, ravishing creatures drift by like phantoms, seeking to seduce you. Speaking truthfully, I'm not the type of man they're attracted to, but a handsomer man would be hopelessly caught, escaping only when his wallet was empty. This is how you waste your time when you live in the darkness of ignorance. Days annihilated in vain.

The "Great Dharma Wheel"[6] is the Wheel-Jewel that conquers our imagined world and pacifies it. With a terrifying noise, it rolls before the Tenrinjōō [7] kings, crushing all enemies in its path as though leveling high mountains. These enemies are not warriors armed with swords; the enemies it reduces to dust are illusions. Ponderously, slowly, it opens a luminous world. Where the Dharma Wheel is found there is light and where ignorance is found there is darkness. Rich or poor, the ignorant man lives in shadow. He cannot even escape the night through learning, for he takes roads without light; if he doesn't study, the obscurity is worse. When he eats, he eats too much. When he drinks, he drinks too much. To eat and drink are good, but it depends on the manner in which you do so.

An object is an object, a moment a moment, one is no more favorable than another for becoming a Buddha. Any moment is good, no matter which. Good and bad days don't exist when practicing the Way. Each day is a good day, whether rainy or windy. For the ignorant, even the day when one receives a gift is an unlucky day. If someone gives him money, he'll lie around all day. Why work when he's got something to eat?

During the Russo-Japanese War, a soldier learned that he'd been mentioned for the order of the golden Milan.[8] He immediately borrowed a huge sum of money, to be repaid when he received his pension. While waiting, he took up the high life and squandered in dark places everything he'd borrowed. (In truth, bright or dark doesn't change anything.) When his pension arrived, he succeeded in obtaining new loans that he immediately spent on geishas. He continued in this way until the day came when it was impossible for him to pay off his debts. His family fell into poverty, when he could have used the money for the good of the country, of the Way, of society, of others. A thing is a thing, neither good nor bad; the difference lies in how we utilize it.

Dōgen wrote in the Busshō chapter of Shōbōgenzō: "No moment exists that is not propitious, no moment exists when the buddha nature does not manifest." What remarkable words! Let's rejoice whether we eat grilled eel at a picnic or barley rice after zazen. You can be unhappy about eating rice gruel; you can also be happy. A haiku poet, long bedridden with a grave illness, lamented: "How happy one is when one has good health! What misery to be ill!" He began to write poems again and little by little his spirits raised. One day he composed this poem: "Oh, it's more than I merit! More than I merit! Today, regarding the morning glories, I again drink rice broth. Wife! I want to live a long time." He could have written: "O cursed! Cursed! Today I again endure the jeers of the healthy morning glories while swallowing rice water. Wife! I no longer want to live!" In the same circumstances, at the same moment, for the same thing, we can feel gratitude or feel sorry for ourselves.

The Secret Transmission of Buddhist Practice

"Our empty and illusory body is the Dharma-body.[9]" Our physical and material human body is not separated from our mind. We are not composed of two opposing principles, body and mind. The essence of mind is life. Does life really exist only within us? The fact that we must die doesn't necessarily mean that life finishes at our death. Yoshida Shōin[10] was only thirty when he died. Though he had lived but a brief

life, the noble and luminous essence of his mind will shine forever in a secluded corner of the Setagaya district of Tokyo. He wrote in a poem: "The spirit of Yamato, conscious of its acts and their consequences, never gives up." He never gave way to despair, even as he died, his head struck off. No matter what anyone says, when this empty and illusory body, liable to disappear at any moment, accomplishes an immortal work, death is not death. That said, many people destroy their digestive system through over eating, or abuse alcohol, are drunk two days running. Others bungle their work yet demand a salary. It is truly strange that the empty and illusory body that can accomplish actions of universal consequence can equally well commit acts with no tomorrow, remembered by no one, or that cause evil.

The fundamental principle of Buddhism is simple, answering the question: "How can we lead our life for the greatest good?" The intent of Buddhism is to give sense to our life. How can we accomplish an immortal action with this empty and illusory body, liable to die at any moment? It's an important question. What must we do?

My answer is that we must find the true practice and correct teaching and become the Dharma-body.

Do you know how to resolve Jōshū's kōan[12] "mu"? One response that was permitted was to get down on all fours and bark "Bow wow!" Can there be anything more stupid? It means that they do not understand the origin and history of "mu." Or again, "on the night when you hear the soundless caw of a crow, can you tell if it's male or female?" This time, you cover your ears, close your eyes and cry "Caw! Caw!" Utterly stupid!

These kōans pose the problem of emptiness: How to become the eternal self within this moment? How to live this moment fully and perfectly? The answer is that our empty and illusory body is the moment and the Dharma body is eternity. Such is the true practice and teaching of the Buddha Way. It's precisely what one means by secret transmission.

The Buddha himself had a life, a birth, and a death. I don't know whether a celestial dragon made it rain sweet nectar or whether springs gushed from the earth. Perhaps he said: "Above heaven and below heaven I alone am the honored one."[14] I don't know, but I do know that if he had a death, he also had a birth. I care little whether he died from eating poisoned mushrooms, salt bacon, or something else. The fact is, he is well and truly dead. If we examine his life, we find there no shadow, not the slightest blemish, each moment was lived fully. Thus we say that Shākyamuni is perfect and his virtues infinite. At each moment, his self was one with the universe, each of his acts filled the universe, his self was time eternal. *The true nature of our ignorance is no other than our Buddha nature. Our empty and illusory body is the Dharma-body.* These two verses must be read with attention, otherwise the deep meaning escapes us completely. They signify that the ignorant one, the ordinary man, is Buddha. Exactly "as he is," he is Buddha.

At first glance, one might think that though this may sound very grand, in reality there's nothing to it. This kind of perspective is extremely compelling, because men pass their lives within the limits of birth and death. Yet Buddhist practice offers irrefutable arguments that, though limited by birth and death, one need not live trapped in an impasse. Our vision clears and luminous perspectives open before us when we realize that our self is unlimited and eternal.

When they limit themselves to immediate facts, men's actions are as disordered as a day on the stock market. There are stories that at the beginning of the Meiji era one individual tried to sell the five-tiered

because what are believed to be "facts" are not, they are ideologies — or they are false inferences — we jump to conclusions or grasp

pagoda of Hōryūji for fifty yen and that another tran
the same lacquer statue of the Buddha before which
every day. Man finishes by confining himself with
limits.

In his old age the poet Issa[15] wrote this poem: "Man is equal to
a drop of dew, do you understand this?" The one who doesn't understand it lives in illusion and irremediably wastes his life. As we
become aware of our true nature, we realize that man has no reason
to live unless he recognizes this truth: *The true nature of our ignorance
is no other than our Buddha nature. Our empty and illusory body is the
Dharma-body.*

Illusion and awakening do not have different natures. We must
grasp the origin of that which so completely blinds our self that we
see dualism where none exists. We must become conscious within our
most profound depths that our body, as it is, is one with our mind and
that it is identical with the essence of the universe.

To discover the ultimate reality that constitutes the grandeur of
our life and consecrate all our efforts to it, we must find it within the
nature of our ignorance and our empty and illusory body. When we
comprehend the essence of the universe, we understand that living
beings, plants, minerals, absolutely everything in the universe has
buddha nature and that it's good thus. Things "just as they are" is the
natural condition and therefore it's appropriate.

To Seize the Vital Energy

The first three verses of *Shōdōka* constitute the introduction,
and the following two verses summarize the entire work. These are
constructed as counterparts and form a couplet. Similarly, an elder
has said:

at the quietest, easiest answers

The mind in its essence comes and goes without substance
The empty and illusory body is born and dies.

Ordinary persons and Buddha are one. The essence of our mind and our empty and illusory body are not separate. The duality between body and mind does not exist. The essence of the mind is the empty and illusory body.

The teaching of Buddhism does not lie within the domain of academic studies. No doubt a time will come when recordings are made of Buddhist learning, but the direct, authentic relationship between master and disciple that gives life to the teaching of the Way cannot be put on a phonograph record. The transmission of *zen* "from my mind to your mind"[16] is special. It happens outside of all books or oral teaching and could never be the subject of a broadcast, even if a radio program were created on the teachings of Buddhism. For example, in Hagakure,[17] a work dedicated to the Way of the Warrior, we find this phrase: "To do well is to endure."

We can debate endlessly about the meaning of "do well" in terms of morality and psychology, but it will become so complicated that the ideas are completely muddled and no conclusion will be reached. In the final analysis, isn't the response, "To do well is to endure." simpler and easier to understand? Such is the principle of the secret transmission of *zen*. It happens outside of texts or words or writing. *The true nature of our ignorance is no other than our Buddha nature. Our empty and illusory body is the Dharma-body.* It's simply that.

Isn't that what Yamamoto Tsunetomo, author of Hagakure, felt when he wrote: "The mountain cherry tree, how many leagues from our ephemeral world?" The distance is very great between our empty and illusory body and the Dharma-body, as great as between life and non-life, as far as the limits of the universe. Upon his master's death, according to custom, Yamamoto should have committed hara-kiri, but he chose to remain alive and withdraw from affairs. In truth, he seized life. People who don't perceive the breath of life can't understand the profound sense of "The mountain cherry tree, how many leagues from our ephemeral world?" Such people are interested only in money and other trifles. This poem expresses not only the spirit of *Shōdōka*, but also the very substance of *zen* and the essential meaning of the Buddha Dharma. It's truly a poem of great subtlety.

3

When we awaken to the Dharma-body, there is no longer anything.
Our own original nature is the true and intrinsic Buddha.

Gold Is a Venomous Serpent

To awaken to the Dharma-body is to catch hold of life. It's to plant our feet firmly on the ground, understanding that a human being is a product of the universe and in no way separate from it. If we don't perceive that our self and the universe form an indivisible unity, we become prey to our individual egos, duping ourselves. But when this deception ceases, we see that there is no longer anything.

Predictions foretell fortune and misfortune, good and bad luck. But is it luck to get something? Is it bad luck to lose money? Wouldn't your load be lighter? Can one really know what is good luck and what is not? If we investigate things a bit we realize that there's just as much good in one case as in another.

Personally speaking, I greatly dislike receiving gifts; I can't help it. On the other hand, to give brings me great joy. I adore giving gifts. If I had inherited a fortune, I'd be in a hurry to run through it. For better or for worse, I possess nothing, so each day is a new battle. This is neither good nor bad luck.

Buddha has said that gold is a venomous serpent. Once there was an old man and an old woman who were extremely poor. One day when Shākyamuni[1] and Ananda[2] were passing, a rock suddenly pulled away from the mountain and streams of gold coins poured from the depths of the earth. Seeing this, Shākyamuni said to Ananda: "There are venomous serpents here." Ananda answered, "Certainly there are venomous serpents," and they continued on their way. The old man said to the old woman, "How about we have a look?" They approached and sifted through the gold coins that sparkled in the sun. "I wouldn't mind if there were thousands of venomous serpents like these," said the old man. He snatched up one and they treated themselves to a banquet. He caught another and they bought beautiful coats. He took another, and another, until there were no more. The authorities traced the coins, which were stamped with the seal of King Ajase[3] and the two were arrested. They convinced themselves that if they confessed, the serpents that they'd hidden would be taken away, so they agreed not to confess no matter what happened. As their heads were put on the block, the old man said to the old woman, "It truly was venomous serpents." "Yes, it surely was venomous serpents," the old woman responded. When asked to pronounce their last words, both said it was venomous serpents. This statement was so strange that a decision was made to question them anew and the old people finally confessed the truth. This story is the origin of the saying, "Gold is a venomous serpent."

Lao-tzu said, "Beauty is not good luck." If it's good luck to be beautiful, the implication is that it's bad luck to be ugly. That's a completely arbitrary human judgment. People never stop lamenting, "You're beautiful, I'm ugly." Nothing is ever as clear and final as that. They exaggerate the value of a passing and ephemeral state, envying others.

People are strange creatures. The rich look upon the poor with complete arrogance, a beautiful woman gives herself airs, and someone with a little bit of talent takes himself for a genius. What does all that matter? Nothing remains after death. There is nothing before birth. All that is only an ephemeral appearance. We humans are merely mold secreted by the warmth and humidity of the terrestrial globe. Truly, we develop exactly like mold. Who hasn't seen those strange mushrooms that in one night spring up from nowhere? That's what we are: thinking and talking mushrooms. Mushrooms whose thoughts contain an infinite number of illusions and who rarely attain satori. Violent and cruel mushrooms that talk of bizarre things like civilization, progress, thought, philosophy.

What then is this civilization we talk about so much, when human nature has made no progress? It is proof that Shākyamuni remains unique. No man comparable to Bodhidharma or Dōgen has appeared again. Even if you rummage everywhere, you find only types like me, pretty insignificant. Is eating chocolate proof of civilization and progress? Is it so extraordinary to wear rubber sandals? No, truly not. It would be much more extraordinary to wear straw sandals.

When we become aware of the Dharma-body, we link ourselves in uninterrupted connection with the universe. We have life because we belong to the universe. We must act in concert with it.

In Ibaraki Province there is a place called Makabe. In the old days a servant named Heishirō lived there. On a very cold day when his master had withdrawn to his quarters and Heishirō had carefully placed the lord's geta[4] inside his kimono to keep them warm, his master suddenly returned. Heishirō hurriedly pulled the geta out of his clothing, but he'd had no time to put the cords back on and presented them as they were. Not for a moment did the lord consider that his servant had been taking great care, but said to himself that he'd been sitting on them, a good–for–nothing like the rest. He grabbed a geta and struck Heishirō on the forehead. Heishirō blanched with anger, thinking to himself, "He hit me when I was keeping his geta warm!" He vowed to avenge himself, and that night left the castle, carrying with him a geta. Thinking, "I will find a way to avenge myself," he decided to become a monk so he could pray for the death of his master. He practiced with fervor and later even went to China to stay at a famous monastery called Kinzan.

But the more his practice strengthened, the less he prayed for his master's death. Finally, he forgot about it. He returned to Japan at a time when the emperor fell ill and had the honor of being chosen to perform kito[5] for the cure of his majesty's illness. His effectiveness was such that he became celebrated throughout the country. As thanks, they offered him a position as head of the temple in Makabe, vacant at that time. Thus he found his old master again. When Heishirō came to pay his respects, he carried with him the half-decayed old geta. This astonished the old lord, who wondered, "Could this old geta be some sort of kōan?" Heishirō revealed that he had once been a servant in the household and reminded the lord of the day that he had unjustly struck him on the head.

This story is the source of an old saying, no doubt spoken in the local dialect: "When we awaken to the Dharma-body, there is no longer anything. Hold on, here's Heishirō of Makabe." The old master remained what he was, but Heishirō was another man.

Our own original nature is the true and intrinsic Buddha: there is no gap between ourself and the universe.

4

The clouds of the five aggregates float here and there in vain.
The bubbles of the three poisons rise and burst, empty.

One Night's Mushrooms

The five aggregates[1] are: form, sensation, perception, formation, and consciousness. Form is the physical aspect of life, the material and concrete world. It includes the six sense organs, or six roots,[2] and their respective objects. That is to say, the eyes and sight, the ears and sound, the nose and odor, the tongue and taste, the body and touch, and the mind. Form also includes those things we can see only with a microscope or telescope, or hear only with a radio. That's to say, all physical phenomena that manifest through the senses. Perception is the psychological effect of the information received: pain and pleasure, insupportable cold or agreeable soft warmth. It is also the imagination. For example, one may imagine that a certain monk is great and another very kind.

The character gyō, which expresses mental activity, is rich in substance. One finds it in the expression shogyō mujō, "All phenomena are impermanent," where it means ""phenomena," but the aggregate gyō can also present other aspects. It can mean time, time being a strange notion, neither mind nor matter. Or again, direction, also strange, for it gives the impression that it exists yet doesn't have a fixed character. Gyō can also signify social position. We say someone is "an eminent person," yet don't know what is eminent in him. When we don the robe as monks, we reject all distinctions of social rank. We are not concerned with whether a man is important or not. We have friends equally among the stable boys and the generals. This doesn't mean that social classes do not exist. A great man is a great man. But do we estimate the greatness of a man by the level of his salary or the level of his talents?

The notion of quantity is also imprecise. We say "much," but starting from what quantity do we calculate "much?" Below what level is there "little?" Gyō includes at once the physical phenomenon and its conceptualization.

Consciousness is the function of discernment that we currently think of as the grasp of consciousness. That is why the verse states: "*The clouds of the five aggregates float here and there, in vain.*"

In a work entitled Isan no keisaku[3] there is this phrase: "Illusory body, home of the dream, form of emptiness." Again it's a matter of mushrooms. With an important air a mushroom says: " Please, don't make me lose face." And another responds: "Who do you think you are? You're nothing but a mushroom face, you're not something extraordinary! You have the arrogance to wish to protect your prestige? You're only a mushroom, with a mushroom's life, and you won't live to be a hundred!" If we step back and take a look at it, within universal life our longevity isn't even comparable to a one-night mushroom. Truly not much.

There was once a monk who practiced zazen. A demon arrived with a corpse on his shoulder and let it fall in front of the monk. At that moment another demon arrived unexpectedly, shouting: "Give me this cadaver!" The first demon replied, "It's mine! I brought it," and they commenced to quarrel. They couldn't settle the affair and decided to refer it to the monk. "Master, it's me who brought this cadaver here!" said the first demon. "Yes, in effect, it was certainly you," responded the monk. The second demon, furious, tore off the monk's arm and devoured it. Seeing this, the first demon cried, "Poor monk, it's my fault he's suffering!" and pulled an arm from the cadaver and replaced the monk's missing arm. The second demon then seized the monk's other arm and devoured it. Next he detached one leg, then the other, until the head and the whole body vanished in this manner, while the first demon progressively replaced the pieces. In this way the monk lost everything that was his while seated in zazen. What he now possessed belonged to the cadaver. Nothing remained of his original person. Isn't this body a corpse? Isn't this body mine? At bottom, who am I?

Strangely, when we think about it, we are born in complete ignorance of the self. Before we are born, there is the time in the uterus. Some microscopic sperm, shaped like little spoons, swim upward—these are the father's mushrooms going to meet the mother's mushrooms—and then, bang! a unique cell is created. It is sucked into the uterus where the metabolic process is completed and it is born. It suckles the mother's breast and grows. It swallows nutrients and lets the residue fall into the toilet where a demon seizes it. Then it once again goes to the restaurant where another demon corrects the situation. Sweat flows in the bath, at the hair dresser's hair falls. Thus from metabolic transformation to metabolic transformation we arrive at the dawn of today: *The clouds of the five aggregates float here and there, in vain.*

The mind functions in precisely the same way: *the bubbles of the three poisons rise and burst, empty.* The three poisons are greed, anger and ignorance, foam on the ocean. Shokusanjin[4] wrote long ago: "Are we not bubbles adrift on the river of our passions?" Whether we weep about it or laugh about it, whether we like or do not like, whether we are for or against, *when we awaken to the Dharma-body, there is nothing,* because *our own original nature is the true and intrinsic Buddha.* That's the truth.

5

When one establishes the reality of things, neither man nor Dharma re-
main.
The avichi karma is instantly annihilated.
If I lie to deceive you,
May my tongue be torn out forever!

To Look at the World through Colored Glasses

The aim of the practice of Buddhism is to make us discover true reality. It immediately awakens a pressing need to know what it's like. Now, the true character of reality has but one characteristic: an absence of character. It's neither this nor that. All existence in the universe, all phenomena without exception are the true nature of reality. It is said in the *Hannya Shingyō*[1]: "All dharmas are marked by emptiness ; they neither arise nor cease, are neither defiled nor pure, neither increase nor decrease." Such is the true nature of reality: without beauty, without filth, without birth, without death.

We can't see this reality from our human point of view. The men of our time, especially the intellectuals, those people who make it a habit to pass exams and fill a copy book no matter what the subject, try hard to push their pens to describe it, but the more they seek it, the more it hides, and whatever their papers produce resembles a tiny little turd. Due to the very fact that we are human beings, it's impossible for us to see the true nature of reality. We men can see only our world of men. A fish sees only its world of fish. A thief sees only thieves. Someone told me that a judge remarked, "I see a criminal in every man," no doubt a true statement. As he was an expert in lies, it's normal that he should think in terms of guilt.

If you are an antique dealer and revere a Buddha, you begin by estimating its value: "How many yen is it worth?" As soon as you see a Buddha, you put a price tag on it. This is the reason all the Buddhas have disappeared.

Regarding the world with the eye of Buddha, everything is buddha. Demons no longer exist. All beings, sentient and insentient, are the Way: grass, trees, land, planet, all is buddha. Our body, just as it is, is buddha.

An ordinary man of this world will say that I am not a Buddha, just a man like any other, because he sees me through ordinary-man-colored glasses. When he wears blue glasses, he sees the world in blue. If they have the color of desire, in this world he sees only objects of desire.

We must then comprehend true reality. Still, it is not an easy task, since the human condition is opposed to it. Here, all is illusion. In everything in the world, nothing exists besides illusions. Everything without exception is illusion. Let's just say that it's all karma.[2] A man has stolen something, is afraid, and runs away. A policeman pursues and stares at each passerby, wondering if the guy in front of him might be the thief. In consequence, the pursued and the pursuer each goes along in completely different worlds. This is why it's so difficult for us to understand. To discover the true nature of reality is to embrace the panorama of the universe in a single glance. When we have vision like this, we have comprehended the teaching of the Buddha.

It's not necessary to use a telescope or bend over a microscope to contemplate the spectacle of the universe. There's no need to take so much trouble. It's sufficient to refuse to perceive as true all the illusions that blind us. We must say to ourselves:

"My ideas are false: this one, that one, all is false. I reject them." If we chase them all away, nothing exists in us any longer. It is written:

"In cutting the bonds of karma, one finds calm in all things. One no longer thinks in terms of good or evil, one no longer distinguishes the true from the false." In short, one has a total and immediate vision of the real. Thus it best serves our purpose to look over our glasses or, better yet, to take them off.

Seizing the universe at a glance is a problem of quality, not quantity. Even when the distance to the limits of the universe is measured in thousands of light years, beyond that remains the unknown. In the Lotus Sutra[3] the duration of the universe is estimated as five hundred cosmic cycles. Whether infinitely large or infinitely small, the world is unlimited. The true problem is neither time nor space, but the essence of the universe.

We do not embrace the universe with a single glance and so we weep and we laugh. When our vision is total there's neither attraction nor repulsion: things are simply what they are, that's all. This is only this; that is only that. Yet we can't comprehend that social work, whose purpose is to do good, may not make the beneficiary happy. As a matter of fact, by giving charity to the man who suffers from being poor we thus augment his humiliation and leave him more unsatisfied than before. I always say that one ought to beg from the poor. The indigent person thus thinks: "They can still ask something of me," and he instantly rediscovers his dignity as a man. This is why Shākyamuni sought alms of the most miserable of the miserable. When one gives, one is not poor. The proof is that a rich man abhors being given alms, for it devalues his most important attribute, money, without which he no longer exists. He loathes receiving as a gift his most valued possession, money. In this example we've seized at a glance the essence of the universe. So lucid a gaze is not explicable: it's to have the eye.

In the old days, there were no glasses for regarding the sky, nor X-rays, nor microscopes. None of these existed, so you had to equip yourself by yourself with eyes capable of seeing well without instruments to assist you. Then one day an eye perceived reality in its totality. This extraordinarily piercing eye saw itself, as well as others. It penetrated happiness and unhappiness. Regarding all things with his prodigious eye, for the first time a world appeared to Shakyamuni in which nothing existed.

One day in the outhouse a worm fell on a sheet of ice. A compassionate soul saw this pitiable worm in great danger and deposited it in a place where it could be warm all night. The next morning it was dead. What the man thought of as good luck was not good luck for the worm. We're wrong to think that what makes for the happiness or unhappiness of some does so for others as well.

We must develop the power of our eye to see with a single glance rich and poor, man and woman. If we consider only the happiness of one or the other, we see nothing at all. When we embrace all things at a single glance, we have mastery over the universe. However, we can't do things by half or stop along the way. We can't remain suspended in confusion. We must go to the end to the point where we awaken to true reality.

When one establishes the reality of things, neither man nor Dharma remains. One perceives simultaneously the emptiness of man and the emptiness of the Dharma.

Now, illusions have their root in that which gives man his specificity, his self. That's to say that man's point of view is subjective and personal. Or to put it another way, he doesn't go beyond human subjectivity. He is not in a continuum with the universe, he is in a continuum with himself. It is written: "Abandon the ego's notions, abandon also the dualism of empty man and empty Dharma." When one awakens to the emptiness of all things, man's ego no longer exists. Nothing any longer hinders him.

A poem says: "Birth and death come and go, Man's reality. For him the four elements[4] and five aggregates are indestructible." We wrongly consider birth to be a happy event, for one can be born crippled or an idiot. So birth must not be systematically filed under the category "good luck." We are also accustomed to speaking of death as an unhappy event. In truth, one should rejoice at it. The engine driving our suffering ceases to turn over. You see a beautiful woman, a passion arises, you look at a tasty dish, and another passion springs up. Whatever we may say, our body produces these and on the day it disappears we should heave a sigh of relief: "Ouf! I'm finally rid of my body and the suffering of life!"

There Is No Impasse

One day when it was snowing, a student at the Kyōto Imperial University sent this letter to a friend: "They say that a snow-covered landscape delights the soul, but it doesn't engender any cheery feelings in me. The moment I go out I slip at every step. What a relief it would be if the snow covering the mountains in the ten directions would melt! The sight of this snow makes my teeth grind."

His friend in Tokyo wrote back: "There are people who admire snow, flowers, the moon and welcome them even though there's nothing special about them. As for me, I find it most agreeable to admire the snow while sitting in a corner by the fire, drinking sake´ in the company of a pretty girl. I also think of the postman, who must distribute mail even on snowy mornings. Where is the truth? You tell me you hate watching the snow fall, something that is after all a normal occurrence in the winter." When one sees the universe at a glance, birth and death come and go, the five aggregates are without

42

substance. The *Fugen-kyō*[5] says: "All karmic obstacles originate in illusions. If you wish to repent,[6] sit down in zazen and think of true reality." To awaken to true reality is to have a gaze that penetrates all things, an instant total vision of the universe.

Long ago, they categorized the various obstacles and hindrances[7] that impede practice and explained that our mistaken vision came from our illusions. In modern terms, we'd say that we're trapped by our illusions, and according to our dispositions each of us is held in a considerable number of traps. The term sange (to repent) makes you think of some formula for exorcism, but there's nothing magical about it. It is by doing zazen that we do away with obstacles and it is by embracing the universe with a single glance that we discover the true identity of phenomena.

So, would our happiness be identical to that of the worm in the latrine? No, whatever his happiness may be, it's not ours. Each of us carries within himself his own happiness, which he must discover. There are many who, seeing a down and out bum, think they are happier than he, but this bum also has his happiness. At the end of his day he staggers tipsily home in a good humor. He curls up in the corner of his hovel and goes to sleep a blissful man. That's his happiness!

When we see the universe at a single glance, there's no more impasse. It's also said in the *Fugen-kyō*: "All our faults are drops of dew on the grass." The fault that binds us exists nowhere. This is this and properly so; that is that and also proper. The head is the head, the feet are the feet, each plays its role. "All your faults are like dew on the grass, they will disappear under the rays of the sun of wisdom." If we have the wisdom to embrace the universe, doesn't this wisdom also melt away the errors through which we fall into the trap? We are captives of our faults: our concepts, our received ideas, and our prejudices. Many people envy others' happiness. "How I'd love to be in her place!" But what creates your happiness doesn't create mine. You yourself must discover your happiness within yourself.

When one awakens to true reality: *the avichi karma is instantly annihilated.* At one time they thought that he who committed a capital crime fell into the avichi[8] hell where he suffered without a moment's respite. In Buddhist terminology, an instant[9] is truly short: the time it takes to bend an index finger, divided by sixty-two.

What we generally understand as suffering is not some ready-made product out of a box. According to our character, each of us has his own suffering. And fundamentally speaking, if suffering did not exist, neither would pleasure. Thus, if we come to our senses about suffering and pleasure, as though waking from a dream, instantly we have an accurate vision of true reality and seize the universe.

It's written in a sutra: "He who awakens to all the buddhas of the past, present, and future sees naturally the essence of the world of the Dharma where all things form one." To see naturally the essence of the Dharma is precisely to embrace the universe with a single glance. Multiplicity becomes unity. I love. Very well, I love! I detest, so I detest. I am me, just as I am. You are you, just as you are. Yamaoka Tesshū[1] has written concerning a painting of Mt. Fuji: " Whether in clear weather or under clouds, Mt. Fuji is beautiful, her shape does not change." Such is true reality.

If I lie to deceive you, may my tongue be torn out forever! Yōka Daishi is swearing that his testimony is true. If not, may he fall into liars' hell[11] where those who con people have their tongues torn out.

6

Suddenly, at the moment when one realizes the zen of the Buddha,
The six great virtues and the ten thousand practices are perfectly accomplished within us.

Counterfeits of *Zen*

Satori makes you think of a feat of sleight of hand, or a lamp that lights in the mind, always you have the impression that something has changed. This is why it's important to thoroughly investigate this phrase: *Suddenly, at the moment when one realizes the zen of the Buddha.*[1] An unnatural practice leads to aberrations, just as much in the Buddha Way as in business. Even the practice of zazen can become diabolical or greedy, so we must know how to discern counterfeit practices in order to grasp the true *zen,* the *zen* of the Buddha.

It seems that when I make a circuit of the dōjō, stick[2] in hand, and pass behind the rows of "clouds and water,"[3] icy shivers run through their backs as though I were a serpent. The postures immediately straighten, but as soon as the danger moves on, they slump once more. I also hit strongly when they sleep, but it always begins all over again! This is what I call "hell *zen.*" If zazen is so painful, why did these guys become monks? I don't get it.

To practice zazen to cure an illness appears to me to be less aberrant. The other day, a monk came to tell me that he had gotten rid of his beriberi thanks to zazen. He added that it took two or three months. I don't know if he's recovered his health, but he's acquired a beautiful posture, very dignified. They say that you become ill when you have nothing to do, so it's a good opportunity to practice zazen and at the same time take care of stomach ills. After all, you're packed in like sardines and can't indulge your temptation to nibble in secret or eat too much—habits that are often the cause of stomach maladies.

Moreover, there's no time to indulge in idle thought when you hear the stick whistling, and your mind, rid of all other preoccupations, doesn't go wandering off.

Although the objective of zazen is not curing sick bodies, I'm convinced that zazen constitutes an infallible therapy for psychic troubles, provided they are mild. One truly lacks the time to concentrate on little woes.

Some time ago I had boils under my buttocks, two in a row. At that period I didn't have time to call a doctor because I was leading two sesshin,[4] one at my place and one on the outside. It was very painful to remain seated motionlessly, and when the pain became unbearable I got up and walked around the dōjō. When I apply the kyōsaku it's my nature to hit will all my strength, so even if I'm only passing I provoke a tension that immediately straightens backs. Thus I told myself as I walked that thanks to these boils I would obtain infinite merit! I had a salve intended to resolve the matter, but I gave up on it since I ceaselessly had to move about. I let things take their course, and the boils opened without my noticing it.

Might zazen be a sovereign remedy for boils? In the old days, the sage Daie Sōkō Zenji came down with anthrax and when they told him he would probably die, he answered that in that case he must absolutely continue practicing zazen. And so he did, with even more enthusiasm, and they say he recovered. In our day, we think that when our life's at stake that's not the time to do zazen. The ancients, on the contrary, knew that while doing zazen the abscess was going to open of itself, release its pus, and heal. To sum up, if you consider zazen as suffering because you get hit with the kyōsaku, you're practicing a hellish[5] *zen*.

Next comes greedy *zen*.[6] Like hungry ghosts, we always want something, and as soon as one desire is satisfied, another comes along: "How I would like to have that dress! How I wish I had those cosmetics!" say the women, and the men: "If only I had his salary!" Among the hungry ghosts, we find few who are tormented by an insatiable desire to do zazen. On the other hand, certain among them desire satori. In short, we want everything that's good, everything that's beautiful and ardently aspire to possess this object and yearn for that object.

A greedy spirit who does zazen to get satori isn't worth very much. The moment he has it, he'll lose his head over a woman and even the word "satori" will go up like smoke from a cigarette. Furthermore, the greedy spirit is never satisfied. As soon as he has something he loses interest in it. When he has money, he wishes power. When he has power, he wishes glory.

Following greedy *zen* is animal *zen*.[7] This one is particularly stupid. Nothing interests him outside of sex and food, and it's the biologists who know him best. He's the focus of their research, given the fact that the survival of the human species depends on sex and food. And we can add those who sleep during zazen. The Lotus Sutra says: "They know only water and grass, unaware of all the rest." During zazen, they speculate whether there'll soon be some cake, and what the vegetable will be tonight, or how the rice will be prepared. They think only of eating and at the first moment of leisure fall into bed and sleep, indifferent to what is going on around them.

Next comes bad-tempered *zen*. This is competitive *zen*. One wishes to speedily overtake the others and win the satori marathon. Among this sort, nothing exists except the desire to be tougher than others.

Human *zen*[9] also includes some bizarre folk. They are overcome by the desire for a beautiful appearance. Some part their hair, others grow a beard or wear kimono on top of their city clothes, which makes them sweat profusely. And on top of their affectations and love of money they have strange superstitions.

Heavenly *zen*[10] is the *zen* of ecstasy. One adores zazen. Seated immobile, one feels good, happy.

Up to this point, even while doing zazen we have been living in the common world of mortals. We have turned the wheel of life along the six roads or conditions of existence as if we've been doing zazen while rotating round and round a traffic circle without ever exiting. Whether a person uses the zazen posture to strengthen his hara, find ecstasy, live better or eat healthily, all that isn't even worth discussing. It is outside our purpose. Since the time of the Buddha's teaching, ninety-six errors of practice have been recorded, and that covers a great many things.

Now let's enter into the Buddha's teaching. Beginning at the bottom, one finds shōmon *zen*[11] and above this, engaku *zen.*[12] Here we're dealing with people who have taken a one meter square box and after filling it with a synopsis of Buddhist learning they say: "There, that's the Buddha Dharma—it's one meter square!" Let's immediately leave this box behind in the baggage room and climb toward the heights to discover the vast horizons of the bodhisattva.[13] At this level, there are two possibilities: an inferior way, the Hinayana[14] and a superior way, the Mahayana.

The *zen* of the six roads or conditions of existence is situated outside of the Way, but shōmon and engaku *zen* are inside the Way. Such practitioners are absorbed by the teachings of the Buddha, yet still remain ordinary men. When they become bodhisattvas, they will join the ranks of the saints, because they will have broken free from within the walls of the fortress of ordinary men.

I've enumerated all these *zens* of bad quality so that you can clearly distinguish the *zen* of the Buddha. As soon as you understand it, all the others will disappear. The *zens* of hell, greed, animality, anger, human beings, heaven, and even the shōmon and engaku, these states of consciousness will no longer exist. When zazen is strong, suddenly at one stroke you realize the *zen* of the Buddha. That is to say, you grasp that you are Buddha.

Daily Life and Religion

The "six perfections" are also called the six paramitas.[15] These are the virtues practiced by the bodhisattva to attain the other shore. They are: giving, precepts, patience, diligence, concentration, and wisdom.

Today, when we think of giving we think of a sum of money given to a monk or to a temple. But here it rather signifies practicing without anticipating personal profit, whether in material terms such as money or others such as satori or paradise. Not only does one not desire paradise, one does not fear hell. Giving transforms daily life. It gives rise to a new man who needs nothing, not even life itself. This is a formidable individual: free, relaxed, open, and unconventional.

It's wrong to think of the precepts as interdictions. It is written: "In the precepts, the notion of eternal punishment does not exist." It is not a problem of interdiction. The precepts are the fundamental virtues that lead a man to do what is just.

Patience is not the result of an effort of will. You don't force yourself to endure or to persevere. You live like a man who forgets his ego, a man free of the fetters of his personal views, concerned about neither satori nor practice. It makes no sense to speak of mastery of the self, since fundamentally the self does not exist. Thus there is no self to conceptualize as showing forbearance. This is patience.

Diligence[16] means to not stuff oneself with kōyadōfu (freeze dried tofu), nor eat soybeans like a horse, nor snort like a bull. The Japanese word shōjin is composed of two characers, shō, which means excellent, pure, subtle, and jin, which means to progress, advance. Shōjin is thus the opposite of passivity or vulgarity. It means to progress toward the good and renounce the evil, to progress without holding back, to have proper behavior without associating with evil. This does not mean that it's essential to follow the straight and narrow, pure and without stain. But when one decides to stop, one stops. For example, it's shōjin to stop smoking. It's also shōjin to not drink to excess. It's really not easy to practice shōjin.

We're less tempted toward lavish indulgence when we need to untie our own purse strings, but when someone else offers free drinks, we need vigilance and the practice of shōjin. Someone once said, "I'd like to be celibate, but am not sure I can persevere." On this topic, I'd like to say that if one can't control oneself, it would be better to go to prison where only celibacy is possible. A prisoner for life must practice celibacy. Aside from stallions, even horses live alone. If these animals can endure their life without physical and psychic troubles, why shouldn't man, king of creation, be able to?

Concentration is to live in conformity with the Dharma, without adulterating it, without soiling it, without contradicting it through one's activities.

Wisdom is to conduct oneself with lucid attention to all things.

In reality, the six perfections are only one. If we actualize them in our daily lives, they include all of our physical and psychic activity. For example, when one practices giving, one eats just what is necessary without desiring more, and one behaves the same as an invited guest. Charity means that you get up in the morning without procrastinating. You don't cling to your bed until your wife scolds, because that would be greedy. All this is a question of good sense, clarity, wisdom. You must grasp the essence of the six perfections without separating them. To grasp the essence is to understand the *zen* of the Buddha and to understand the *zen* of the Buddha is to become Buddha.

In reality, the most difficult thing to comprehend is how one can, at a single stroke, become Buddha. But let's take the example of the man who says, "Well, well, someone's left out his watch!" and—pfft—he slips it casually into his pocket. Suddenly, he's become a thief. Just as suddenly, we can become a greedy spirit or a brute.

The Secret Charm of the Oral Tradition

It is the most efficacious of all methods of teaching. One can study alone for a lifetime without profit. Handling a sword, for example, is just like any practice. It's not enough to just strike or cry "Yaa! Yaa!" without reason, for you are surely chasing your ruin. But if you conform to the rules, if you put yourself on guard and your posture is correct as you aim: "Yaa!"—then you hit your opponent. The whole secret is in the posture. Your master has inherited it from his ancestors and whether or not you follow his teaching makes all the difference.

I knew an old woman who taught her grandchildren sewing, tea ceremony, the koto, and all sorts of things. I had the opportunity to see her do it. When you wash a collar of Japanese crêpe by scrubbing it too hard with soap, it shrinks. The grandmother called to her grand-daughter: "Watch me do it!" She heated water in a pot to a rolling boil and asked her granddaughter to take hold of one end of the cloth. Holding it over the steam, each pulled from their side to stretch it and then let it dry.

This example of know-how shows exactly what I mean by the oral tradition. Everything you hear me say about the teaching of the Buddha is an illustration of the oral tradition. It alone permits us to grasp the secrets and understand them well, even if we end up writing them down in a notebook. The reason the secret transmission is so important is that it makes you see in the moment.

The secret of the Buddha's teaching that since ancient times masters have strained to transmit to their disciples is zazen: "Stretch the muscles of your back!

Push the sky with your head! Push on the intestines! The chest sticks out, that's normal! Let the shoulders fall . . ." If you're not familiar with the oral tradition, then come sit even just three days of sesshin and you'll be stupefied by it to the point of tears! Within the practice, there are loads of experiences like this. They make up the secret transmission and are taught from generation to generation. Dōgen Zenji's Fukan zazengi[17] and two chapters of his Shōbōgenzō, Bendōwa[18] and Zanmai ō zanmai[19] as well as Keizan Jōkin's Zazen Yōjinki[20] belong to this tradition.

Once you've been taught a good posture, you feel gratitude and spontaneously do gasshō.[21] You feel good and want to sit in zazen, but if your posture is bad, your mood is as well. Some priests excuse themselves, saying, "I shave my head in spirit," and grow bushy hair. Like this, they do not experience the spirit of a priest. When we shave the hair from our head, impurities are shaved from our mind. When we wear a layperson's hakama, our mind becomes that of a layperson. This is why *I* venerate the okesa. *Suddenly, when one realizes the zen of the Buddha,* one shaves one's head and dons the okesa—one is precisely in the spirit of *zen.* If not, it is not the *zen* of the Buddha.

With head shaved and wearing the okesa, if you do zazen with correct posture, no illusion can enter. But if there's the slightest chink, you allow animal *zen* or greedy *zen* to penetrate and you open the gates to a flood of human desires. Since human desires are illusions, if you stop up all the chinks while doing zazen, you will be protected from them. When you are sitting simply in shikantaza[23] with correct posture, nothing can infiltrate.

A master asked a young monk who was doing zazen, "What are you doing?" The young monk answered, "I'm doing nothing." "What! You're not engaged in doing zazen?" "No, I'm doing nothing, not even zazen." This young monk practiced a very strong *zen.* He breathed. Nothing else penetrated him. He didn't do zazen to obtain satori or anything else. He was simply sitting in zazen. This is what we call shikantaza: to be completely engrossed in the act.

One day a sly type said to me: "I understand that the life of a monk is shikantaza, but how about me, can I be shikantaza while drinking a glass of whiskey?" There are certain people who logically deduce that one can practice while sleeping, eating, or amusing oneself. Certainly, a person can, but it will not be easy for someone who has not experienced it to live shikantaza at the table, in bed, or in the latrine. That's where the whole problem lies!

On this topic, Dōgen wrote in Fukan zazengi: "What does the position of the body matter, seated or lying down." Further on in *Shōdōka* there is this phrase: "To walk is *zen*, to sit is *zen*. Speaking, remaining silent, moving, being still, the body is at peace." When you understand the *zen* of the Buddha and realize it in daily life, *"the six great virtues and the ten thousand practices are perfectly accomplished within us."* Zazen becomes our daily life. It's certainly not a matter of remaining frozen indefinitely in zazen. Even Bodhidharma didn't do that. In his case, the legend has outstripped the historical truth. It's truly stupid to imagine, as certain literary or mystical types do, that he stank because he remained nine years without budging. If he ate, he drank, and also went to the toilet. He probably read. He got dressed and he washed his clothing. Moreover, no organism could have endured nine years of immobility without atrophying or decaying. It's obvious that he had other ways to spend his time. Zazen was the backbone of his life and his activities. He slept at night, did kinhin,[24] prepared his food, and commenced again every day. He realized the *zen* of the Buddha in each of his acts. It's what I call "always being on the same wave length as the Buddha."

In the Zanmai ō zanmai chapter of Shōbōgenzō, Dōgen wrote: "Zazen instantaneously transcends this world. It causes us to penetrate into the secret of the patriarchs and become Buddha. Passing over erroneous or heretical practices, it gives us access to the dwelling place of the Buddha. Zazen alone allows us to attain the perfect awakening of the Buddha." Which comes back to saying that to do zazen is to realize the *zen* of the Buddha.

I prefer to use the word "perceive,"[25] rather than "understand," since awakening is an intuitive perception. Keizan also employs it in Zazen Yōjinki: " When the perception of awakening arrives, one is naturally in harmony." To put it another way, if your muscles are in a position of harmony and peace, you awaken. Your body is then in accord with Buddha; you "feel" that your nature is Buddha's.

They recount that once someone did zazen while balancing an iron stupa twenty-five centimeters high on his head, and someone else a ball like those that decorate the parapets of bridges. No question that they remained motionless! When I was young, I myself had occasion to do zazen with a tea cup full of water on my head, so that if I budged the slightest bit it slopped over, which certainly leads to a taut posture. The buttocks pull up, the knees push the ground, the muscles of the neck lengthen. The zazen posture that permits reaching the Buddha is extremely rigorous.

To Base His Practice within Illusions

Dōgen wrote in Gakudōyōjinshū: "To base one's practice within illusions, to obtain the mind of awakening before perceiving it." In the practice of the Way, illusions have been compared to a "precious clot of blood." The practice of the Way implies many things, but zazen always rests at the heart of daily life. It's said that to practice is to block entrance to illusions. Men are men and although we tell them that there is no miracle, still they hope that their wishes will be fulfilled and they will retain a reward for their efforts. Since man is made this way, the zazen of the ordinary man is to wish to stop illusions, although the practice of the Way must be pursued in the midst of illusions. During zazen, out of his desire to stop them, this man fixes the clot of his illusions in place, when on the contrary the good method is to let them go by. Let us pose to ourselves only this question: "Does my action serve the Way, or illusions?" If we act blindly, without discernment, we are exactly like a cat with its head in a paper bag that can't distinguish east from west in the middle of the Ginza and so dies without knowing what to do. Someone said, "Until I was fifty I went from darkness to darkness." That's a very hazardous life!

These days, I always repeat the same phrase: money is made to be spent. However, in our era far too many people allow themselves to be manipulated and enslaved by money. If they inherit a fortune from their parents, they become a slave to it and lead the life of the guardian of a strongbox without ever doing anything else.

In the Sōtō branch of *zen*, children learn the Gakudōyōjinshū by heart. As adults they still have this text in their memory, but since the substance of daily life has not been restored to the words, they fail to understand it. They see the words without comprehending the meaning. One must truly live the words.

To simply transmit words, recite names, count the treasures of others from morning to evening, all that's worth nothing. "The word is green, the word is not ripe." How accurate these remarks are! *"Suddenly, when one realizes the zen of the Buddha"* is, as Dōgen says, to "base his practice within illusions, to obtain the mind of awakening before perceiving it." To become Buddha is to be seated wholeheartedly in zazen. Just as it is, the body in the posture of zazen is Buddha.

To recognize the Way is to follow it. Practice and awakening are one. There is no awakening without practice.

In practicing, that is to say practicing in the midst of illusions, awakening is produced before being aware of it. Isn't this a marvelous practice? Then, each moment of practice gives off a gentle light that illuminates the fundamental awakening. This is what one means by realizing the *zen* of Buddha. It's certainly obvious that to just read books without practicing is of no assistance in the Way.

I'm always asked what book to read to understand *zen*. If I'm stretched out lying down, I answer without moving: "I'm busy. Come do zazen every day." This form of concern is to be classified under the heading of the passions. *Zen* is "to do." The problem is, above all, not to commit an error in "doing." Most often, I give explanations by taking people by the hand and showing them how to sit. I am extremely severe about the posture.

There are always two hundred students in the dōjō at Komazawa University, and it has always astonished me that with so many people such a profound silence reigns. Although in the ordinary way all these youngsters are noisy and unmannerly, I have never seen a single one come into the dōjō humming or with a cigarette in his mouth. They all look as though they wouldn't hurt a fly. They enter in silence, do gasshō and sit down. Those who wait at the exit and haven't yet practiced zazen are astonished.

A group functions just like a charcoal fire. If a single lighted coal is not fanned, it goes out by itself. A big pile of coals becomes a hot blaze. A person who coughs, blows his nose or changes his leg must do so discretely. When there are many, each one must take it upon himself to not disturb the others, and by virtue of this a unified atmosphere is obtained. This doesn't depend upon me, but upon each member of the group.

In Zen temples, giving way is hindered by the large number of participants. It's thanks to the students that I myself hold firm, and it's reciprocal. When there are fifty of you, that's fifty to take it. When there are a hundred, there are a hundred to take it, and the pervading mood is indescribable! It's precisely through this ambience that one recognizes a dōjō of the Way of the Buddha. In living this experience, the experience of zazen, we incarnate the six perfections. "The moonlight pierces the water of a heart without stain. Even if the waves break it up, it continues to shine." Daily life becomes transparent like pure water. When zazen has been unclouded, it's impossible to leave the ambience of the dōjō singing at the top of your lungs, or go drink a glass of alcohol, under pain of falling on your face.

Zazen is to sit down desiring nothing. We speak of eternity, but according to the Way of the Buddha, eternity is to practice here and now. If I succeed in making you understand this in the deepest part of yourself, you will not live in darkness until you're fifty! But unless you grasp this essential point you cannot follow the Way of the Buddha. Zazen is also to practice the precepts here and now. Now! Now! Now! Life is a succession of "now."

When doing zazen, you are an integral part of the universe and the essence of all things, and consequently you are without ego. When you abandon your ego, you incarnate patience and it comes back to saying that zazen is patience. You must do that which is in the Way, that which gives a solid foundation to your daily life and demands great diligence. By living in conformity with the Buddha Dharma, you produce lucid judgments full of wisdom. It's thus that *the six great virtues and the ten thousand practices are perfectly accomplished within us.* "Within us" means within the body of the *zen* of the Buddha. It boils down to saying that the *zen* of the Buddha contains the six perfections and ten thousand practices as well as all the practices of the Way of the Buddha. These two phrases of this verse are extremely important. I think they are the heart of the poem.

7

In our dream, we clearly distinguish the six destinies.
After awakening, all is empty, not even the universe remains.

Ephemeral Mushrooms

When one conceptualizes the Buddha, one imagines that to become Buddha and to have satori are two different things. Novices don't understand and are amazed: "As soon as I sit down in zazen, passions arise!" For it to be justified, this remark must be made on the condition that one has already experienced zazen. If passions come during zazen, very well, let them come! No matter how numerous they may be, our intention is not to chase after them. It's through the practice of zazen that we realize the obvious fact that all things are equal, zazen as well as phenomena.

When zazen opens us to the transparency of ourselves, all things—satori, teachings of the Buddha, even zazen—all become the fabric of delusion. This is what is meant by the phrase, *In our dream, we clearly distinguish the six destinies.* The six roads or destinies are the conditions of existence on the wheel of life: states of hell dwellers, hungry ghosts, animals, fighting spirits, humans, and heavenly beings.

Dōgen wrote in a poem: "Stupid man, you waste time in the six roads instead of going straight to the goal!" How can one thus go in circles through the six states all the days of one's life without ever stopping? It's incomprehensible. The truth is that man is nothing at all. Considered from the perspective of biology, a man's existence is as ephemeral as that of a mushroom. Each one is imposing to his neighbor: one is a high-level functionary, another is rich. Each of them establishes a hierarchy of value to suit himself. Yet all that is merely trifles! A slight breath of wind and everything flies away! One night's mushrooms! Let's go further and say that everything belongs to the world of the dream. Even truth does not exist and the concepts formed by our mind are also in the realm of dreams.

In an ancient Buddhist text it says, "To realize that good and evil are precisely dreams is to immediately transcend the law of causality and realize emptiness, the absence of characteristics." Consequently, the concepts that human life gives rise to within us each day are dreams. What I love today, I will detest tomorrow. Whatever else this love may be, it is not eternal; apathy soon arrives. Life is a dream. A bubble. A lightning flash. A dream. The six destinies belong to the world of this dream, and if we ask ourselves if they will still belong after awakening, the answer is no: *After awakening, all is empty, not even the universe remains.*

On the point of death, Takuan Oshō had written a poem on the dream, but when one of his disciples begged him to pronounce his last words, he answered: "I don't have any." "What! You have nothing . . . nothing to say?" He then pronounced a single word, "Dream," and died. Here is Takuan's poem. The calligraphy is preserved at Tōkaiji in Shinagawa.

> One hundred years, thirty-six thousand days.
> Are Miroku and Kannon good? Are they bad?
> Miroku is a dream; Kannon is also a dream.
> Good is a dream; evil is also a dream.
> Buddha said, "All things are precisely thus."

It's thus that we, too, see them. One hundred years, thirty-six thousand days . . . it can't be said that he was a whiz at doing sums on his abacus!

8

There is neither unhappiness nor happiness, neither loss nor gain.
In the peace of extinction, there is nothing to seek.

Tranquil Truth

When we become aware of reality, there is no longer anything there: *neither unhappiness nor happiness, neither loss nor gain.* In our society, according to the circumstances, killing a man is considered to be either an abominable crime or a remarkable act of heroism. *In the peace of extinction, there is nothing to seek.* This signifies that everything is annihilated: self and other, love and hate, dualism, relativity. When we speak of the peace of extinction, we think of death, but that has nothing to do with it. Choosing between what he loves and that which disgusts him, man chooses what he loves. However, pleasure is an illusion. You love satori, you don't love illusions, so you chase after satori like a game of blind man's bluff. And what happens? You catch an illusion. You need courage and composure to get rid of the scarf blinding you. Nevertheless, keeping your composure does not suggest you should have the audacity to remain indifferent to your creditor's recriminations as though they were no more than a nightingale's song. I'm speaking about a composure that is the tranquil strength of a man sure of himself, for whom there's neither good nor evil, no Buddha, no satori, nothing to seek, nothing to flee.

We always compare ourselves to others: "Him, he deserves respect because he has money. Me, I'm insignificant because I don't . . . " Him, he's strong, but me, I'm nothing but a shrimp and even eating enough for four doesn't make me grow." Long ago, Gankai,[1] renowned for his exceptional intelligence, lived for more than twenty years by begging. If he'd been like those folks who complain even when faced with a groaning table, he'd have to have been the unhappiest of men, which was far from the actual case. No matter their fortune or their knowledge, men are always unsatisfied and complaining. History gives countless proofs. In the chronicle of the Taira,[2] a great counselor declares, "Whoever does not belong to our house must be judged to be less than a man!" Taira no Kiyomori wished absolute power and obtained it, yet he wasn't particularly satisfied with it. This was also the case with Taira no Masakado and Minamoto no Yoritomi, who seized more than sixty provinces without being in the slightest appeased. All these powerful men arouse my pity.

One day when the nun Teishin went to pay a visit to Ryōkan, she found him dying, eyes rolled back by the illness. Hearing her, he murmured, "Sometimes they fall on the back, sometimes on the front, the maple leaves." They spin from one side to the other, but that changes nothing: they fall. What I mean by "composure" is Ryōkan's imperturbable calm before death, taking as his example the maple leaves. He neither hoped for nor desired anything and he fled nothing, not even suffering.

A samurai said, "I am a warrior even if I earn only one go."[4] If he'd said, " Me, too, I'd like to earn a thousand koku,[5] it makes me furious to have only one go, " he wouldn't have been able to take pride in belonging to the warrior class. This is exactly the same sense of rancor as the worker who says of his boss: "The bastard! He offers himself the best wines!" The expression, "I am a warrior even if I earn only one go" is identical to "Just as I am, I am Buddha.[6]" This is why in the peace of extinction there is nothing to be sought. There where there is nothing, nor anyone to beg, if we try to obtain or to find something, we rush into a blind alley.

Accordingly, in all places, at each moment, and in all circumstances, one is calm, assuaged, tranquil. It is also written: "Within the body of the world of the pure Dharma, phenomena neither appear nor disappear." Even assuming that they do appear, the infinite compassion of Kannon[7] manifests and comes to the aid of those who appeal to it. However, it comes only provisionally and its role is limited to identifying with all human beings and sharing their tears and their laughter. I don't think it's good luck to be born. If that were the case, why would parents suffer such pain to amass a nest egg for their children? Even supposing that one is born poor, that's bad luck at the beginning that later transforms itself into good luck. Infinite compassion manifests itself to those who invoke it . . . Is our passage on this earth good luck or bad luck? Speaking truthfully, I don't know, but *in the peace of extinction there is nothing to seek.*

9

Up to this moment, dust has accumulated on the mirror.
Today, it is time to restore its brightness.

To See Clearly

We've barely discovered the absolute calm of extinction, where there's no need to seek for anything, when someone comes along to tell us, *"up to this moment, dust has accumulated on the mirror."* This is something truly annoying. It's got to be done, certainly, but we've just barely arrived at a state of calm and our carcass is refusing to make one more move.

They often say to me: "Allow me to congratulate you, your sermon was excellent . . ." What they're finding excellent is only the words, nothing but intellectual comprehension! Certain people also say: "I don't like zazen, but what you say is fine." Sometimes by dint of speaking I lose my voice in an attempt to say interesting things, so as not to be boring. What else can I do? I hope by this means to point out the way of zazen. Despite that, there are fish that escape me. The other day, the moment zazen was over a student came to see me and said: "What you said is powerful. Very interesting." Let's say that this one had swallowed the hook.

We must polish our own mirror and it's only by wiping it that we give it back its brilliance. If it's not clean it reflects inaccurate images. When it is polished and brilliant, it does not distort Buddha. Polishing it allows it to reveal in all clarity that the sky and the earth have a single root and that all things are one.

We possess a beautiful mirror, but it's steamed up by the mists of our illusions. *Today it is time to restore its brightness.* Here and now, with courage and energy, let's reject concepts and categories, seat ourselves firmly in zazen, and suddenly the *zen* of the Buddha will be realized. It is written: "In cutting the bonds of karma[1] we find peace in all things, we are unaware of good and evil, we no longer distinguish the true from the false." And also in the *Yuikyōgyō*[2] the monks are reproached: "All these idle disputes bring confusion to your mind." And in another passage: "Even if you have put on the robe, you have not yet exterminated the passions; this is why you must immediately cease these vain discussions that corrupt the mind." Consequently, hold yourself apart from these conceptual fabrications, practice zazen with application and in accordance with the Dharma.

It's the same for archery. It's not enough to do exercises and have a posture in accordance with the rules, the mind must also be perfectly steady, for the quality of the shooting depends upon the mind's attitude, whether sure or in error. We, too, are in some way archers. We train this five-foot mass of flesh to acquire the proper posture and the correct mind of Buddha. When our mirror is polished and without tarnish, we distinguish clearly and distinctly where illusion lies and where satori, the way of man and the Way of the Buddha. *Today it is time to restore its brightness.*

To put it another way, we must clear it of the crust of dried gelatin that covers it.

10

Who is no-thought? Who is non-born?
If non-birth is true, not even no-birth exists.

Eyes and Eyebrows Do Not Know One Another

Who is no-thought? Who is non-born? The first stanza gives us the answer: *This tranquil man of the Way, who has attained awakening and ceased studying and acting. He doesn't set aside illusions and no longer seeks the truth.*

The question could have been framed differently: "Who is this tranquil man of the Way who has ceased studying and acting? Who doesn't set aside illusions and no longer seeks truth? Who doesn't desire wealth and doesn't fear poverty? Who doesn't seek pleasure and does not flee pain?"

One day, a disciple of Sōzan Daishi[1] asked him: Do the eyes and the eyebrows know one another?" Sōzan responded: "They do not know one another." Is it that the eyes have a lower IQ than the eyebrows? Are the eyebrows more fools than the eyes? We cannot rank them. The eyes rest in silence below the eyebrows and the eyebrows rest in silence above the eyes: they have no illusion.

It is written in the *Kegōnkyō*[2] : "The cause knows not the effect." We aren't "no-thought and non-born" when we tell ourselves that we deserve a big bonus at the end of the month. Man generates things of great power, and among them are the mental fabrications that in our modern language we call "concepts."

When your pals go off to party with a gourd of saké under their arm and you don't join them, you feel uneasy because that gives a bad impression. Or again, if they go to a hanami party to admire the cherry blossoms, and you don't go because you don't have any money, you're ashamed. So you pretend to go to a party, but just eat a cheap sweet potato under the cherry blossoms and go home early. Just because others enjoy something, it doesn't mean you need to. On the contrary, it might cause suffering for you.

What is happiness? Some say it's to inherit a fortune. I ask myself if becoming the guardian of a strongbox is happiness. I grew up inside my stepparents' "Number-One-Japan-Poverty" but, though today I am poor, I cannot become poorer than they. They got along thanks to the pawnshop, but although I am poor I have never pawned anything or borrowed money from others. Only men of little capacity think that happiness resides in taking care of inherited wealth. Not only didn't my parents leave me a penny as inheritance, I found myself with a load of debts to be paid off by working during my studies. Yet I will go so far as to say bluntly that it's worth more to inherit debts and pay them off, than to run through a fortune by drinking.

The tranquil man of the Way who has ceased studying and acting is without thought and without birth. Although the expression "without consciousness-without thought" is also employed, that doesn't mean falling into a trance. On the subject of zazen, I often hear it said: "As for me, I can't succeed at being "no consciousness-no thought." It's a mental idea to believe that our ego can escape itself and project itself into the fundamental universe, given that the sky and the earth have the same root and that all things are one. My self is included and cannot be disassociated. Consequently, when one acts, one does not act for oneself, or for others. One simply does what is true, simultaneously for oneself and for others.

One day someone asked me, "Is your goal to save all living beings?" As far as I'm concerned, I just go straight ahead, doing what must be done. Whether I help people or not is something to be judged afterward by each as they please. I do what must be done, quite simply and without ulterior motive. Consequently, I'm not acting for the sake of society or for anyone in particular. I don't seek to achieve something. I let myself be carried along by the current of the ancients, I stay in their footsteps. I walk in their footsteps, that's all. Just as one day I left my native province on foot and step by step I arrived in Tokyo. To be without thought is to act for nothing, without any intervening intention, without a goal.

Non-born signifies that it has not had birth and therefore cannot have death. To be born implies to die, just as production implies destruction. It is thus with our mental constructions. Ideas, however beautiful they may be, are fabrications of the mind and inevitably perishable. All that is created must die, without exception. What we're aiming at is a life without birth that in consequence is indestructible.

To Lift Off the Scarf

Nonomiya Sontoku[3] wrote this poem: "Without sound or scent, the earth and skies repeat without end a sutra without words." It is an unproduced sutra, a sutra that has not been written. Mice make their nest in sutras fabricated by man. Returning from a trip six months long, I was discouraged to discover that termites had devoured thousands of yen worth of books. The sutras are human products, so it's normal that they perish. In India, in ancient times they engraved them on copper plaques and still they perished. What is called the unproduced is uncreated. It is not an invention of the mind, but true reality.

If non-birth is true, not even no-birth exists. If the word "born" doesn't exist, obviously neither does the word "not-born."

Satori exists only by virtue of its opposite, illusion. For the one who is truly awakened, the dualism illusion/no illusion no longer has reality.

Likewise, the expression "nouveau riche" applies only to a poor man who has recently made a fortune. It cannot be utilized for a man who has always been rich. In a country where money does not exist, the word "poor" does not exist. In a rich country you are unaware of your wealth. You say you're poor when your bank account is overdrawn, but that's merely a figure of speech. Consequently, where there is truly no production, there is neither product nor producer. "Without sound or scent, the earth and skies repeat without end a sutra without words." The sky, the earth, the entire universe are no-thought and unborn, and since they are unborn, "no-birth" has no meaning for them.

If ever we lift the scarf that covers our eyes to contemplate the reality of the true world, it is magnificent. One discovers so many things there! But it's absolutely impossible to discuss it with men. There is no other solution than to kill the man who resides in us and once that man is dead there's no more problem.

The Zen dōjō is the place where one kills men. We also call it the "hall of dead trees." It's true that when we're all lined up in zazen we resemble a forest of dead trees. Mujū Zenji[4] wrote: "It's because there is death that there is life, if you wish to live, you must die." If the man doesn't perish, the life of this world does not appear. As long as the man lives in us, our world will remain a world of illusions and chimeras. Man laughs, cries, loves and hates, rejoices and despairs, without even understanding what happiness or unhappiness are a question of. All his values are arbitrary.

To contemplate the world, it is essential to die. The spectacle of the world is interesting viewed from within the shroud. Numerous are those who dictate their last wishes before dying. Among these final words, some are excellent and some particularly stupid. For example: "How to divide my possessions on the seventh day after my death . . ." "I want my tomb to be of natural stone . . ." "I want to be buried at such and such a spot . . . " "I leave this sum to So-an-So . . ." There are innumerable nonsensical statements like this. In contrast, Toba Sōjō,[5] our ancestor of the comic strip, who died when he was over eighty, left a truly original will. He had converted an emperor, I no longer remember which, and enjoyed great prestige at court, through which he received considerable donations. They say that, without particularly wishing it, he amassed a considerable fortune. In any epoch, material wealth is always appreciated and Sōjō's disciples were no exception. The money interested them more than the Buddha Dharma. Within the Buddha Dharma desire no longer exists, so there is no need to make a will, but here below, the situation becomes extremely tense when money is in question.

The problem became urgent when Sōjō's illness worsened. The disciples no longer had anything in their heads but the fortune: who was going to inherit it? "It's surely me, it can't be that guy . . ." Some even went so far as to think that if the fortune didn't fall to them, they'd seize it at sword's point.

At last Sōjō definitively closed his eyes and the disciples of the Dharma all began to search for something resembling a will. They ultimately discovered it and, upon reading it, remained frozen in stupor. He'd written: " As far as the division of my wealth is concerned, fight among yourselves and may the best man win!" He had a sense of humor. The disciples hearts were deeply touched and the quarrel faded away of itself. It's said that the whole business was regulated in an amiable manner. Had Sōjō drawn up a conventional will he would have unleashed chaos. Those who have not yet understood the sense that Mujū gave to the word "life" should reflect deeply on this phrase: "It's because there is death that there is life, if you wish to live, you must die."

One day a man was crossing a river on a tree trunk when he was overcome by an epileptic fit. He fell into the water in the middle of the river and was carried away by the current. At dawn, he opened his eyes, not knowing where he was. Where had the waves carried him? He had run aground on a sand bar, his body half in the water. "Where am I? In the hereafter or here below? I must be on the road to hell. How cold it is!" Then he perceived that he was still in the water. Little by little he remembered . . .he was born in the year . . . in the month of . . . on the day of . . . in the Hijoi family . . . he took a wife in . . . and in the year . . . the month of . . . the day of . . . he went to his work in the neighboring village . . . he crossed the river . . . then nothing. "Ah! This has happened to me before, I remember that a monk told me: "It's because you are dead that you have life. If you wish to live, you must die." This is the humorous tale that Mujū Zenji tells in *The Collection of Sand and Stone*.

Who could give us information about this world that we cannot know unless we die? Let's look at the world of men. What do we find? Warm-blooded animals made up of a mass of cells. They smoke and drink alcohol. They are vain and are liars, imposters, and hypocrites. There's nothing to hope for from that direction. Even monks renowned for their learning have sexual desires, appetites, and yearn for one thing or another. It's the height of stupidity to believe that one comes to something in this world.

11

To learn when one becomes Buddha by accumulating merits,
  question a marionette.

The Vicissitudes of Life

If we can't make inquiries of men, useless eaters of rice, then to whom should we address ourselves? *Question a marionette,* we are told. In puppet shows for children, they often call on Jizo,[1] for he knows the truth.

When would you become Buddha if you sought it in doing meritorious works? If you say "I wish to become Buddha," you will not become Buddha. To be Buddha is to not seek Buddha. Man may very well think that happiness is a state well separated from unhappiness, but happiness has limits. Everything changes ceaselessly in this world. Thus the poem *Iroha*[2] says: "Once past the high mountains of this ephemeral world, there are no longer intoxicating dreams." To put it another way, once past the high mountains of cause and effect, there are no longer illusions or gratifications. Over there, absurd dreams do not reappear and one can no longer get drunk on the poisoned wine of illusions.

To seek Buddha is of no use, it's to dance in a circle in the midst of the vicissitudes of existence. Formerly they said, "Even if you shift the load to the other shoulder, you still carry it." Today we talk about worries, anguish, torments, and we go to the temple to get rid of our load. One day a visitor said to me, " No matter what religion it is, they all impact suffering like alcohol. If I marry the woman I love, I'll have no more need of religion." I said to myself that if the love of a woman is sufficient for his happiness, well then, may he marry her and may he be happy! Given that unhappy people evade their torments by reciting *amen* and *namu amida butsu,* if one marries the woman of his dreams, has good health, eats well and thinks that is happiness, then I consider religion to be completely useless.

I knew a person like this in Kumamoto. She ran a farm that produced more than a thousand sacks of rice. Her elder son was a brilliant businessman in Saga, and the younger, who had passed the administrative exam, was an attorney in Hiroshima. One day she said to me: "Mister Sawaki, this world here below is enough for me. I am in good health, I suffer from no pain, my elder son earns a lot of money and the younger is succeeding in a fine career. We live well, the price of rice is up, the hens lay and the mandarins ripen." That took place in 1919–1920, during the period of prosperity that followed the World War in Europe. At that time, a farmer who produced a thousand bags of rice was considered a prosperous man. Yet it's very naïve to say that this is happiness. Three years had barely passed when this woman died, and in the two or three following years the stormy winds of economic crisis began to blow. Unquestionably, the hens lay and the mandarins ripen, but in a world full of vicissitude.

They say that even heavenly beings suffer from the five declines[4] and their sparkle fades, their feather robes becomes soiled. In short, the light of happiness goes out.

Accordingly, if you make efforts to become Buddha, you will not become Buddha. One must neither wish to become Buddha nor covet happiness.

It's written in the *Kongō Hannya-kyō*[5]: "He who sees my face, hears my voice or seeks me, practices in a heretical way. He places himself outside the Way and cannot realize the Buddha." If we conceptualize the Buddha, we are internally fabricating a form—he's like this, he's like that, we see his face, we hear his voice. In seeking Buddha thus, we follow a false path. To see true reality, we must look in another direction.

We must not name as Buddha that which is not Buddha. The *Kongō Hannya-kyō* tells us that to be Buddha is to "attain understanding of the supreme wisdom."[6] To put it another way, it is not in seeking Buddha that we will find him. He will be there when you have ceased searching for him, when you are no longer anything other than one with him and you have forgotten him, when you've stopped forcing your poor incompetent brain to function and you go to the dōjō to practice under a master to understand that which cannot be explained in words.

When I was a young monk, I often asked for explanations, and they always answered that one cannot talk about it. Now I know that one says nothing. However, there's a big difference between saying nothing and not being able to talk about it. When I was young, I got myself entrapped once by an old saké brewer with an audacious and innovative spirit. One day he asked me, "Sawaki, what's *zen*?" I answered, "You can't explain it with words." Then he said to me, "It's the same for saké. I studied physics and chemistry and research on the fermentation of alcohol. Now I apply my knowledge and I make good saké. I can explain the technique of manufacture, but that's not sufficient. One can explain only that which is explicable. In addition to that, there's all that one cannot explain with words. It's in doing this that one understands." This intelligent man had given me a good lesson. What cannot be spoken can be expressed otherwise. Even a mute can express himself when it's a question of a physical experience.

No matter what quantity of words is absorbed by those who don't practice with their bodies, it will all come to nothing. Consequently, if you seek the Buddha without practicing, you cannot find him. You can neither visualize him, nor call out to him, nor seize him with the mind, nor seek here or there. So Buddha, where are you? Where are you?

The master with whom I practiced when I was young once said to me, "You're like a person with shit on his nose asking everyone else "Who farted? Who farted?" He said this to me because I was extremely eager to get satori or find the Buddha. Sotoba[7] spoke in more poetic terms:

> *Drizzling rain on Mt. Lu*
> *The waves of the Zhe river.*
> *Before visiting there, I felt discontented in many ways.*
> *Having visited there and returned,*
> *There is nothing special.*
> *Drizzling rain on Mt. Lu.*
> *The waves of the Zhe river.*

We go to seek very far away that which has always been near.

12

Abandon the four elements, retain nothing.
In the peace of nirvana, eat and drink as you please.
All phenomena are ephemeral, all is empty.
Such is the great and perfect awakening of the Buddha.

My Heart Has Changed Dwelling Place

Abandon the four elements, retain nothing. In Buddhist terms, the four elements— earth, water, air and fire—are the principle constituents of matter, including our body of flesh. Our body is the temporary union of these four elements. *Abandon the four elements, retain nothing,* because our own body deceives us. In the same spirit a poet sang, "In this same world, merely changing my way of life with my mind, it becomes easy to abandon my body."

In the peace of extinction, eat and drink as you please. The peace of extinction is the utmost bliss, nirvana. Man behaves incoherently: he wants to eat fugu[1] but he's attached to life; he wants to have a career, but hates to study; he wants praise but sleeps late; he desires satori but doesn't want to do zazen. In the absolute calm of extinction, satori is useless and one doesn't detest zazen. Even if one breaks one's bones in the task, one needs no praise. One doesn't eat fugu, yet is unafraid of dying. Most often, a man deprives himself of fugu because he wants to live a long time, studies to get good grades, and works to receive bonuses. He wants to be paid in return for everything he undertakes. In the absolute realm of extinction, if one estimates that a thing must be done, one simply does it, neither waiting for nor hoping for recompense.

The peace of extinction is an extraordinarily vast idea. When it rains, it rains in the peace of extinction. The sun shines in the peace of extinction, the moon, too. They don't say, "I dance a kagura[2] or I sing a poem because I shine." They shine in silence.

This is also the response of the marionette in the preceding verse. Then there is also this poem: "The wooden man sings, the stone woman gets up and dances." When one becomes a wooden man or a stone woman, one is in harmony with circumstances, one drinks, one eats, completely naturally.

All phenomena (gyō) are ephemeral, all is empty. Gyō here expresses the instability of phenomena and includes a great number of ideas, such as duration, level, quantity, direction. Viewed from a great distance, "west" is a very curious thing since the sun also shifts. Fundamentally, if "west" and "east" have no intrinsic existence, direction and all things related to it are based only on relationships. It's the same with "small" and "large." We speak of a big flea and a little elephant. Which is the more remarkable, the big flea or the little elephant? Both are remarkable. Starting from how many millimeters can we determine the existence of big or small? They are variables just like our perception of duration: an hour of zazen is long, while four or five hours passed partying with your buddies or playing *go* until dawn is short. And let's consider the social scale: starting at what level is one important? The elaborations of our mind are ceaselessly fluctuating and ephemeral: all phenomena are impermanent.

The five aggregates that constitute an individual are also gyō. Form, sensation, perception, mental formations, and consciousness are all linked and interdependent. The universe, the body, the mind, and the heart unite in an inseparable whole. Large? Small? Long? Short? Warm? Cold? We hang names on phenomena that do not have self-existence. It's clear that we must not allow ourselves to be duped by our impressions, for everything is relative and depends upon our point of view: a large thing is large compared to a small one, something is long compared to something short and the reverse is also true: *all phenomena are ephemeral, all is empty.*

When we approach reality from a partial and relative point of view, we place our self in a perspective where we don't apprehend the totality of things at a single glance.

If you cut out a photo of me shivering at the age of one, you can't say that this is Sawaki in his totality. His "totality" is made up of the instant when his mother's egg was fertilized, of the day when his head was shaved and he donned the okesa, of daily meals and the day of his funeral. Only through these elements can one contemplate a biography of Sawaki. No matter how precise the camera may be, a snapshot cannot express the totality of an individual and a portrait sketched via some images means nothing, because in reality the one called Sawaki is composed of many Sawakis.

Today I can't even to begin to believe that it was I who shouted, "Fire! To the attack!" during the Russo-Japanese War. Obviously, I have become a monk and fifty-seven years have passed since a ball pierced my neck, but the fact remains that I fought during the war. However, it would be ridiculous to isolate this episode of my life and say that this completely represents me.

There is truth and falsehood in all things, because *all phenomena are ephemeral, all is empty.* Well, a lucid glance perceives simultaneously the part that is false and the part that is true, the positive and negative aspects. It is the mind of hishiryō, the mind beyond the mind, the absolute mind, that of the *tranquil man of the Way, who has attained awakening and ceased studying and acting.* When one perceives the non-duality of positive and negative, one doesn't take love and hate for two separate states. At a single glance one takes in the universe in its totality. From the depths of infinite space, nothing escapes this regard. *Such is the great and perfect awakening of the Buddha.* It's the marionette's response.

13

You recognize a true monk by his resolute speech.
If you don't agree, check it out for yourself.

Urgent Problems

By abandoning the four elements and seizing nothing, you liberate yourself from the fetters of the self and it becomes easy to live life on this earth. Our perception of the world is erroneous because we view it through our self when, on the contrary, we should see our self from the standpoint of the world. Because we are prisoners of our emotions when we look at it, according to our mood the moon appears melancholy one day and joyous the next. If we could see our self with the eyes of the moon, we wouldn't commit these errors. That is the peace of extinction.

I say again and again that in embracing the universe at a single glance, reality becomes true reality. Awakening cannot become the object of a desire. The awakening of the Buddha is absolutely not something that one applies to the skin. The Buddha, like a woman's beautiful face, disappears under tattooing. The true reality is that *all phenomena are ephemeral, all is empty.*

A definitive explanation expresses an obvious fact, an undeniable truth such as "When it rains, the sky is not clear," or "My older brother is older than I." It does not express itself in vague and ambiguous language such as "it's without doubt that . . . perhaps that . . ." Children do not have an ambiguous language, but when they become adults they lose themselves in conjectures about heaven and hell. Am I Buddha or am I not Buddha? The problems raised by the after life are merely the pastimes of the idle. Will I go to heaven or hell after my death? How can we make such a fuss about this when we're assailed by immediate problems? Man has the sufferings of man, woman that of woman. The poor have the sufferings of the poor, the rich those of the rich. A beauty has the sufferings of a beauty, a plain person those of a plain person. These innumerable sufferings are our immediate problems, they descend upon us full force. He who does not take a beating is either an imbecile or a fool. If we don't take into consideration these urgent questions, the Buddha Dharma is just a jam jar full of established dogma.

Shinran has said correctly: "I really do not know whether the chanting of Amida's name (nembutsu) may be the cause for my re-birth in the Pure Land, or the act that shall condemn me to hell."

The first time I presented myself at Eiheiji[1] they asked me: "Why do you want to become a monk?" I answered, " I want to become a monk for nothing." My interrogator didn't understand. Only a great man of letters, or even better, a great orator, would have known how to express the feelings that had pushed me to make this decision. I was orphaned at the age of eight and from the age of ten or eleven I had only one thought: to escape the sufferings of my miserable life. And I must say that the sole place on this earth where I could have found refuge was with the monks. I arrived at Eiheiji with twenty-seven sen[2] in my pocket, after having traversed two hundred seventy-five kilometers barefoot. In such circumstances, was it possible to explain in one word how my desire to become a monk came to me for the first time? I could only respond to the Eiheiji monk, "I don't know why . . ." "You don't understand why you've come here to be a monk? Didn't you tell me that you lost your parents? Well then, it's for the repose of their soul that you've come."

As far as I was concerned, I didn't have time to waste with the soul of my parents or any other nonsense of that ilk. I replied to the monk, "No, it's not for the repose of their soul." The monk was stupefied. "Don't utter stupidities! From now on, whenever anyone questions you about this, you will answer that it's for the repose of the soul of your parents." He wished to force me to say it was for my parents.

It was truly not my problem. For me, the repose of the soul of the deceased lies in the little cakes that one places on the family altar. My parents, like so many others, had followed in turn the six roads of the wheel of life. For me, the problem does not rest over there, it's here with us. These are things one can't explain in one word.

Each time, I answered him, "No, it's not that," so well that finally he got angry. At the time, I was seventeen and he forty. I have become a monk and he has reached the age of eighty-three without ever changing his opinion. He was truly stubborn as a mule! To not understand that all those are ideas fabricated by the mind seems to me to be the height of stupidity.

Even Shinran Shōnin never recited a namu amida butsu for the repose of the soul of his parents: "I, Shinran have never even once uttered the nembutsu for the sake of my father and mother." One recites namu amida butsu exclusively for Amida Buddha. As for Dōgen, he also considered practice for the sake of the repose of one's parents to be too narrow. If we single-mindedly practice zazen as a more fundamental, a more decisive, statement, this in itself helps the repose of one's parents.

In the *Daichido-ron*[3] we find this expression: "The serpent's path is well known to the serpent." A Japanese proverb also says, "The serpent's path is for the serpent," and in the same sense, the Lotus Sutra says, "Only between Buddhas." If I become Buddha, the Buddha Dharma is my way. If I do not become Buddha, I do not understand the Buddha Dharma. The ordinary man regards the Dharma like the poet the horizon: "Beyond the river I see distant mountains. Is it a cloud or a mountain? Is it the land of Wu[4] or the land of Yue?" He understands nothing; everything is blurred and indistinct. They speak to him of "satori," but that doesn't help him to see more clearly, even less so "the peace of extinction." These words disquiet him more than they reassure him. If they wish to reassure and calm him, isn't it preferable to say things simply?

In Gakudōyōjinshū, Dōgen wrote: "Practitioners of the Way must first of all have faith in the Way. Those who have faith in the Buddha-way must believe that one (the self) is within the Way from the beginning; that you are free from delusive desires, upside-down ways of seeing things, excesses or deficiencies, and mistakes." Here's something not hard to understand. You are you: have confidence in yourself. Otherwise, you do not know yourself; you are not you. When you are you, it matters little whether others watch you or not. If you do what ought to be done, you do it well. Thus, during zazen you hold yourself very upright when the kyōsaku is behind you, and you don't become a limp rag when it has passed. Why act otherwise? Isn't it our own body? Since it's our own body, it must be treated with dignity.

Those with faith in the Buddha Way must have confidence in themselves. You must believe that nothing differentiates you from the Buddha. My basic material could have been put to other uses. I could have been, for example, a professor and become a leading figure in the field. Or again, a politician, although actually, what do you become when you are a politician? How many times do you get sent to the clink? Perhaps a clown in a chindon-ya orchestra? I think I would have liked that. Or better yet, a gangster, though I'm not sure one acquires prestigious titles on that road. In any case, whatever one does, one inevitably becomes something. During the Russo-Japanese War, I departed for the front as a private first class. "Private first class Sawaki—Present!" Then I became a corporal and even got as far as the rank of sergeant, but the career of soldier Sawaki stopped there.

When I'm angry and the blood rushes to my head, my face is angry. When I laugh, it laughs. I am not another man when I become Buddha; I become myself. My raw material, with nothing hindering it, becomes Buddha.

I'm often asked: "Can a poor type like me have buddha nature?" I answer, "Idiot! What are you talking about? Aren't you at the very heart of buddha nature? If you kick your illusions out the door, you are at the very center of zazen! The problem is not to "have or not have" buddha nature. When you do zazen, your entire body "is" zazen. This is absolutely true. If you drink alcohol, each joint, each muscle, the least cell, your entire body "is" drunk. This is what I call an incontestable truth and what I mean by a definite statement.

Let us now take a look at this doctrine at the core of the Buddha Dharma. Kanzan Kokushi[6] said: "In this world, there is neither birth nor death." That is to say that the world of the awakened man is not that of the ordinary man. The awakened man has a complete vision of the universe. From this perspective, all things, sentient or insentient, become the Way: plants, trees, earth, and planets are Buddha; mountains and rivers its manifestation. In the world of the ignorant man, one hears only remarks of this type: " I lack time for zazen these days . . ." or again, "I'm too busy to do zazen right now . . . " Viewed from the world of zazen, the entire world is zazen. The song of the wind and rain is zazen. Thus, viewed from the world of the Buddha, everything in the world is Buddha. For the one who is not Buddha, nothing is Buddha. This is why one can practice the Way no matter where, with nothing getting in the way.

Any site can become a dōjō. To attract students and practice zazen, all that's required is for me to put up a notice. After I leave, it will again become some habitation or other. This is how a man may transform things by his actions. If we understand that our own action can change the world, we are forced to feel respect and consideration for ourselves.

Such is the clear and precise doctrine that reveals the true monk. There is no place in this doctrine for beating about the bush. You fire at the bulls-eye without hesitation. *If you don't agree, check it out for yourself.* Whether an escaped bull charges or the sky falls, we do not budge. What exists, exists; what does not exist, does not exist. What one can do, one does; what one can't do, one doesn't do. One does what should be done and doesn't do what should not. Thoughts and actions are clear and distinct. This is what's meant by a precise and specific doctrine. It's the profound conviction that what one says is the truth and that this truth is eternal.

14

The sword of the Buddha is for cutting to the root.
What good is it to pluck the leaves and search the branches?

An Artificial Life

One commentary on the *Shōdōka* has been titled: "To cut directly to the root." The choice of such a title demonstrates the interest aroused by these two lines.

I often hear it said, "I'd like to stop drinking, but I just can't get there." Here we have people who most certainly don't cut the evil at the root! If women and alcohol are their enemies, why do they always run after them? Without doubt they'll never stop. It's necessary to cut without hesitation and without the least regret.

Formerly, there lived a very beautiful nun named Ryōnen, renowned for her profound spirit. The monks gaped in admiration of it. One day one of them secretly declared his love for her. She answered him: "I will grant what you desire, but I beg you to be patient for a few days." The day celebrating the enlightenment of the Buddha arrived. A crowd was present and the monks entered the imposing Buddha Hall in close file, grave and dignified, according to the protocol for great ceremonies.

Once the room was full, Ryōnen stripped naked and approached the monk. "Forgive me for having made you wait," she said to him, "here and now you can accomplish your wish." The monk fled precipitously and no one has heard of him since. To use vague, hesitant, half-way terms like "It's possible that . . . eventually. . . I wouldn't go so far as to say . . ." is not to speak truthfully.

To cut to the root is to be your self, authentically your self. A novice is not an abbot, he must behave like a novice, and should he become an abbot, he will harmonize with his new estate and make the necessary adjustments to be an authentic abbot. Each stage of life must be true and lived authentically. A young girl must be a true young girl and prepare herself to be a true woman, then a true grandmother, and a true widow who will prepare herself to truly die. Life is an eternal becoming. What was yesterday has definitively disappeared today. Thus turns the wheel of life.

We must always seize the present moment. Always one must seize oneself. The present contains eternity; eternity is a succession of "now." At each instant, we must be fundamentally ourselves, realizing our own Buddha nature. At each instant, we must find ourselves in harmony with the characteristics of our present state. True young girl, true young monk, true abbot.

What good is it to pluck the leaves and search the branches? If I don't seize the whole, I miss the target. Yōka Daishi goes straight to the point. Insignificant things and minor details don't interest him. Not embracing the whole is exactly as if someone tore out one of my eyes and said, "Here's Sawaki," but an eye is not Sawaki. *To pluck the leaves and search the branches* is to fixate upon the particulars of a detail. For example, studying the texts of the Buddha Dharma by making an in-depth analysis of each word when a few notes of commentary would suffice, even jotted rapidly in the margins of the book. To understand what the text is saying to us, we must strike to the heart of the matter, seizing the original root, the true source.

15

Man doesn't recognize the precious mani pearl
Deep within his buddha nature.

The Box for Passions

The mani pearl symbolizes the buddha nature. In English, we have the word "money" and in Sanskrit "mani," a magic pearl. I don't know the origin of these two words, but they resemble one another. Where, then, is this treasure? It is in your hands and nowhere else. If your thumb and forefinger make a circle, it signifies "money," but that's not precisely what we're talking about here. Nevertheless, the treasure is truly in your hands.

Daichi Zenji[2] tells us: "The sublime treasure is hidden in Mt. Gyōsan."[3] Gyōsan is an image signifying our material body. The poet Ninomiya Sontoku[4] sings of it in his way: "The solar star spreads its inexhaustible treasure; cultivate it with the hoe, harvest it with the sickle." However, when we search everywhere, where is the treasure? Where is the buddha-nature? Yōka Daishi chooses the image of a pearl to express the same thing.

Buddha nature is fundamentally inside us, but *"man doesn't recognize the precious mani pearl."* All the masters say repeatedly: "Stop seeking after words, pursuing words, seeking to know it!" Men accord value only to words, yet there is nothing in the words. "Turn away from the reflections and echoes!" You must yourself practice the Buddha Dharma. Only our practice is important. Even if we were to write the word "fire" for an unlimited period of time, even in gothic script, we would never obtain a flame. Not long ago, while visiting the great sanctuary of Izumo, I saw the "fire cypresses." They introduce a stick into a cavity of the tree, rub vigorously, and fire shoots out. Without evoking fire, nor even naming it, they make fire. It's enough to rub with the appropriate stick. Thus it is with the practice of the Buddha Way. The magic pearl possessed by man reposes within his buddha nature like the fire in the cypress. It's obvious that one must rub to make the flame spring up.

16

The marvelous faculties of the six senses are both empty and not empty.
The perfect light of the pearl is a form devoid of form.

Mysterious Relations

The six sense organs—eye, ear, nose, tongue, body, consciousness—each has its own domain: form, sound, smell, taste, touch, and mental objects. What the eyes see, the nose knows nothing of. If a repugnant odor wafts by the ears, they understand nothing about it, but the nose recognizes it. The functioning of these organs is truly strange. Equally surprising are the relations that exist between perception and the object of perception or, to use Buddhist terminology, between the six roots of perception and their six fields of activity. The *Hannya shingyō* says: " Form does not differ from emptiness, emptiness does not differ from form; emptiness is form, form is emptiness."[1] The problem isn't trying to know whether things exist or do not exist: they are empty and yet they are not empty.

    Earlier we have seen that *in our dream, we clearly distinguish the six destinies. After awakening, all is empty, not even the universe remains. There is neither unhappiness nor happiness, neither loss nor gain.* From the Meiji era through today, our culture has retained traits from the Tokugawa era. Along with the good in our native culture, we have now seen what is of value in other cultures around the globe, but it's not as though there is a strong distinction. It's not that city people are intelligent and country people are not. This dualistic vision is an error; it emerges from the garbage dump of our passions.

Without exception, all men suffer because of their passions and their karma. "Form is emptiness, emptiness is form." To put it another way, even in having it, it is not; even in not having it, it is. In the "against," there is the "for"; the good contains the bad, and the bad the good. One loves what one detests; one detests what one loves, not that the loved object has changed, but that in step with time, place and circumstances, one sentiment or the other gets the upper hand.

The perfect light of the pearl is a form devoid of form. It has been stated elsewhere that "the entire universe is a precious pearl." If everything our senses grasp is empty and is not, the same goes for the entire universe, which is *a form devoid of form.* This line is an illustration of the phrase in the *Hannya shingyō:* "Form is emptiness, emptiness form." Our passions and our karma distort our vision. What we see is not the truth. What we think is not the truth. We see and think through the smokescreen of our passions.

17

It's through purifying the five visions that one obtains the five powers.
He who has realized awakening knows the inconceivable.

To Dispel the Smokescreen

The five visions[1] are the eye of the Buddha, of the Dharma, of wisdom, of the divine eye and that of the flesh. *It's through purifying the five visions that one obtains the five powers.* "Purifying" signifies acting in such a way that fog does not obscure sight. That is to say, to do zazen and practice the Way, in virtue of which one can acquire the five powers.

There are all sorts of powers: the power of money, of beauty, of tears, of impulses, but in this case it's a question of those conferred by the Buddha Dharma: faith, energy, determination, concentration, and wisdom. We obtain them by purifying our five visions.

He who has realized awakening knows the inconceivable. If a smokescreen obscures your sight, you can discern nothing and it's not words or beautiful speeches that will help you to see more clearly! To purify the five visions is to obtain the five powers and be "he who has realized awakening."

Man understands sexual desire or hunger without needing to have them explained, and once the full maturity of fifty years has arrived, he's perfectly enlightened on these matters. The same goes for zazen. To say that one understands it without experiencing it, or that one has satori without practicing, is completely absurd. In purifying the five visions, one obtains the five powers and the fog lifts of itself. In truth, we are prisoners within the dark clouds of ignorance; we grope our way in the shadows. As soon as the clouds are swept aside, even if only for an instant, we realize awakening.

One day I climbed to the top of Mt. Aso. Its immense crater was covered with clouds. Disappointed, I continued to sit and observe the spot that appeared to me to be the bottom of the crater. Suddenly I heard a rumble mounting from the depths, the mists parted and I saw the bottom, completely clear. I'd barely perceived it when the cloud cover closed again. If we want to know something, we must absolutely establish its truth with our own eyes. Such is the meaning of *he who has realized awakening knows the inconceivable.* To do this, there is no means other than to sit down, body and mind.

18

It is not difficult to see a form in a mirror,
But how can one seize the reflection of the moon in the water?
Going always alone, walking alone, these are
The accomplished ones who together travel the road of nirvana.

The Road of Nirvana

It's not difficult to see a form in a mirror, but how can we seize the reflection of the moon in the water? If we look at the real moon, we will understand that what we see gleaming in the water is only a reflection.[1] At Nansen-ji temple[2] in Kyōto, there is a celebrated painting of a string of monkeys holding each other by the hand, suspended from a branch. They are trying to catch the reflection of the moon in the river. This anecdote is drawn from a sutra. If we also wish to grasp the truth, we must begin by looking at it, and we will perceive that what we see in the water is nothing but a reflection.

In the world of practice, one travels alone. Husband and wife, however intimate they may be, never have identical dreams except in the theater. Their pleasure is also different. The world of practice is not like that of the morning glory vine that needs a supporting wall.

Going always alone, walking alone. Ōbaku Kiun[3] said, "Throughout the twelve hours, lean on nothing." Have no prop. The rich lean on money, others on some person; this is an error. We must be truly ourselves, authentic and autonomous, and walk with an assured step on the highway, without the support of an assistant and without fear. The one who achieves this is the perfect man, without birth and without idea. He is indifferent to the vicissitudes of life and indifferent to the joys and sorrows as he *travels the road of nirvana.* Nirvana is the unproduced, the undestroyed, where there is neither happiness nor unhappiness, neither joy nor suffering.

People always ask me what I like. Since the day I was born I have always eaten whatever is given me without demanding a special dish. I appreciate everything I eat. There's nothing I'm crazy about, nothing that puts me off. I have no more preference about where I reside. As the poet says: "There where I am is my house—the snail." Here or elsewhere, it's all the same to me. Neither happiness nor unhappiness, such is the path of nirvana—and happiness, according to Buddhism.

19

From ancient times, their purity of spirit accords with a natural nobility.
Faces emaciated, bones protruding, they pass unperceived.

The sons of Shākyamuni call themselves poor.
In truth, though poor in body, the way they follow is not.
Wearing coarse clothing, they are poor.
Possessing within themselves an inestimable treasure, they are rich.

They use this treasure without ever exhausting it,
Lavishing it on others, each according to his need.

Rags and a Chipped Bowl, Peace and Tranquility

One distinguishes the traveler who takes the path of nirvana by the restraint and moderation of his bearing, which allows the purity of his mind and heart to show through. Cheeks sunken, cheekbones protruding, he resembles the arhats.[1] No one turns around as he goes by—just a poor man.

Wealth creates problems for the men who possess it, and doesn't create them for those who don't. I hear monks clamoring insistently, "Practice! Practice!" when they should begin by abandoning their own wealth before speaking of practice to others. These same monks feel pity for the poor, but do not make a move to help them. Monks ought to lead a simple life and renounce their fortune, distributing it to the poor. Thus, they would live in communion with them and their practice would be meritorious. Just the opposite, these monks amass money for themselves, feed themselves the finest foods, and hand out a miserable gruel to the poor. I think we ought to reflect deeply on the example of Shākyamuni, who renounced his princely estate.

Long ago, Zōga Sōzu[2] wrote this poem:

> Guardian of the mountains and rice fields, abbot by profession,
> with the first melancholy of autumn he no longer receives visitors.

Zōga was a monk on Mt. Hiei,[3] where he held an elevated rank in the hierarchy and was equally versed in letters. He rejected all concern for reputation and withdrew from the world because, they say, he detested his life as a high dignitary. He was employed as a forester.

Tōsui Oshō left this song:

> Thus goes my life, thus goes my well-being,
> Old clothes and a chipped bowl, peace and tranquility.
> When I'm hungry, I eat.
> When I'm thirsty, I drink.
> It's all that I know.

These men lived poorly but, in truth, their spirit was unacquainted with poverty. Yōka Daishi lays stress upon the poverty of those who follow the path of nirvana. Miserable clothes matter little if their heart shelters a treasure! This treasure is non-born, it neither expands nor diminishes. One can use it indefinitely and it cannot be stolen. This inexhaustible treasure serves to help human beings.

20

The three bodies and four wisdoms are perfected in their body.
The eight liberations and six discernments are engraved in their mind.

Radishes in Brine

These lines describe the contents of the inexhaustible treasure that the accomplished ones use according to everyone's needs, without calculating.

The three bodies[1] are the three bodies of Buddha. Buddhist scholars with fettered minds think it's a matter of three distinct entities. Even if we speak of three bodies, there are not three bodies. If we wish to analyze the concept of Buddha, we are obliged to consider it under its three aspects: Dharma body (Dharmakaya)[2] reward body (Samboghakaya)[3] and the transformation body (Nirmanakaya)[4]. It's solely because we allow ourselves to be trapped by the words that we think of three bodies, when they form a unity. Ask Buddhists which is the principle Buddha of their sect. Some respond, "the Dharma body", others, "the reward body" and still others, "the transformation body." If I were Buddha, I'd say to them: "Your Buddha is pretty shabby!"

We've even seen monks belonging to the same sect, who share the same ideas, organizing debates to determine if the Buddha who is the object of their cult is Dharma, reward, or transformation body! Their debates obviously lead nowhere, since they couldn't lead anywhere. For me, at the beginning the Buddha was the wisdom body and didn't speak to me as Dharma body or one of the others, but when I wished to translate into human terms the non-dual nature of *the inestimable treasure* and *the tranquil man of the Way who has ceased studying and acting*, then I perceived that this nature appeared to me from three different standpoints.

On this subject, the sixth patriarch, Enō Zenshi[5] wrote:"The body of the pure Dharma is your nature, the body of perfect reward, your wisdom, the body of infinite transformation, your practice." Thus, what we call Buddha is our nature, our wisdom, and our practice. If one considers the human being in his essence, it's the Dharma body. When his wisdom is cleared of all impurity, it's the body of perfect reward. When this appears in his comportment and manifests in him through the working of all sorts of transformations, it is the body of infinite metamorphoses. In short, it's a precious stone to be regarded from many angles.

For example, let's take a man who may be the head of a family. Viewed from this angle, he is the Dharma body. From his wife's point of view, he is the perfect reward body because he ensures the maintenance of the family. He's a mailman by profession, but to meet his monthly financial needs, he metamorphoses into a maker of bamboo baskets. Looked at from this perspective, he's the body of infinite transformations. All the same, organizing debates about such obvious facts is senseless!

Thus *the three bodies and four wisdoms are perfected in their body.* But we need one body, so what body is it a question of? To access understanding of this body, our view must embrace its three dimensions: Dharma body, wisdom body, transformation body.

In Buddhist terminology, this body is called "thusness,"[6] i.e., true reality. A preceding verse says, *"Suddenly, at the moment when one realizes the zen of the Buddha, the six great virtues and the ten thousand practices are perfectly accomplished within us."* Long ago, Gutei Oshō never answered his disciples when they posed a question on the nature of Buddha. He only lifted his finger, signifying that it's indescribable. When dying, he said to his disciples, "I have used it all my life without ever exhausting it." The three bodies and four wisdoms were fully realized in his body.

Most people don't like the practice body, but they like the profit they can draw from it. Thus, in Pure Land Buddhism the body is the recitation of the formula namu Amida butsu. It's not that one is crazy about reciting it, but one wishes to go to paradise! Let's say that paradise is the bait that leads one to take the hook.

When I was a child, I disliked chanting the name of Amida Buddha, which used six characters,[7] and when I asked a Pure Land priest if Amida Buddha saved only those who chanted his name, the priest responded that no, he saved even those who didn't chant. So I told the priest that if I'd be saved even if I didn't chant, it would be more convenient not to chant. I often had such conversations with Pure Land priests.

The problem is the same with zazen. Can we have satori without doing zazen? During the Meiji era, a medical doctor said, "I've heard that someone experienced satori while stretched out on his bed with his arms crossed, staring at a crack in the ceiling. This sounds nice and easy so I've decided to do it."

As far as satori is concerned, we commit the error of separating the body of practice from its utilization. We think it's an efficacious product and wish to profit from it: "If I do zazen, what do I get out of it?" To ask this question is to be duped by satori.

Numerous folk say they've obtained satori without practicing zazen. In reality, they imagine they've had satori. It's exactly as if you gave the name takuan to some radishes you'd merely sprinkled with rice bran, salt, and flavor extract. To make real takuan, you must choose daikon radishes and let them dry lightly in the sun. Align them carefully in a tub and sprinkle them with a correctly measured mixture of salt and rice bran. Weight the cover with a stone, pressing down hard. The flavors of the radish, salt and bran mix harmoniously and impregnate the flesh to its core. It goes without saying that their delicious taste depends upon the preparation. The practice of *zen* is exactly like pickling a radish. Let's say that the taste is the radish's satori and that zazen is the pickling brine. The taste is the result of good brine. So, you ask, "What does the radish get out of being pickled?" Well, they're pickled radishes.

From our earliest days, we monks lead a life of "clouds and water" and, just as in preparing radishes in brine, many things can happen. If the radish is submitted to too heavy a pressure, it loses its juice and its flesh is hard. If the rice bran is insufficient, it's too salty, and if there's excess it becomes too sweet. Dried too long, it takes on an ugly appearance. Each phase of preparation must be exact: proper drying, proper salting, proper pressure.

The body of zazen is the accurate balance of the pickling brine. Those who wish to make others eat takuan would do well to pickle some radishes so that they will realize that the body of the pickling brine is the result of an accurate measure of salt, bran and pressure, and that it's from the proper balance of this body that the takuan derives its savor. A successful takuan is not too sweet, too salty, nor too dry. It conserves its nutritive elements, it's pleasing to look at, and its taste is exactly what it should be. A dish is successful when it adheres to fundamental culinary criteria: it contains nutritious elements, it's beautiful to look at, and it tastes good. These three principles must be in balance, for if one is out of proportion, the dish isn't perfect. When these three principles are in harmony in a dish, we can say that it's perfected in its body. Sekitō[8] Daishi expressed it in poetic terms in Sōan, where he compares the body to a hermitage: "Even if the hermitage is small, it contains the world of the Dharma."

A groping life

An analysis of the wisdom of Shākyamuni reveals four aspects: the knowledge of marvelous observation, the knowledge of equality, the knowledge of achieving the task, and the knowledge of the great round mirror.

The first is immediate and intuitive understanding. We know instantly that we perceive the truth. Fundamentally, men blinded by their illusions grope their way forward unable to distinguish good from evil.

Menzan Oshō[9] said in a poem, "After so many years in a pitch black room, a light has sprung forth." Suddenly, you've lighted a match, or rather, lighted an oil lamp since matches didn't exist in the Tokugawa era. In a flash, you understand.

When I served at the front during the Russo-Japanese War, I went out on patrol on a totally black night. There wasn't even a star to orient me. I got lost and wandered and turned in a circle on that infinite plain we call Manchuria. Then, suddenly, right nearby I heard someone spit. Instantly, I knew it wasn't a Russian. The Japanese and the Russians don't spit in the same way; it was a Japanese sound. Reassured, I immediately signaled my presence. It was a sentinel from the neighboring company. In such circumstances, without even a star to guide you, any sort of sign can save your life. Intuition grasps reality.

Next comes the knowledge of equality. You see it as normal when a mosquito bites your neighbor, but when he bites you, you find it intolerable to be "devoured" by mosquitos. This is how men are. When you chance to learn that your old neighbor has pneumonia you put on a concerned face, perhaps you even go so far as to be sorry about it, but the day that you catch a cold or have a little stomach ache, what a tragedy!

It's said that man has four characteristics: he's stupid, biased, proud and vain. He's stupid because he doesn't know himself. Biased, by his arbitrary judgments. Proud, because he always measures himself against others to prove his superiority. Vain, because he's self-satisfied and however ugly he may be, delights in himself and is content with himself.

All man's actions, both now and from the very beginning, are only vanity and partiality. If a glimmer of the wisdom that allows one to see the equality of self and others should appear in the eyes of a man, he no longer sees where his field ends and his neighbor's begins. It would be enough for him to have an instant of light to make the stupidity, pride, partiality and vanity, sources of all his misery, disappear. The one who has seen this light, even for a moment, may perhaps appear eccentric, but that will be proof that he knows.

The development of the knowledge of achieving the tasks corresponds exactly to the process of pickling takuan. It's the realization of wisdom. Some men are remarkable, others less so, and some not at all, but each of them has a body. For this body, there exists only one perfect posture, that which permits entrance into the Buddha Dharma. Up to this point, the knowledges have been purely intellectual, but now, with the knowledge of realization, we become Buddha through our body. To do zazen is to become Buddha.

In Zazengi, Dōgen defines the four aspects of wisdom. Intuitive understanding: "To think from the depths of the mind, without thought."[10] Knowledge of equality: "It matters little if one is intelligent or not. There is no difference between the stupid and the shrewd." The knowledge of the great round mirror: "The Way is fundamentally perfect." On the subject of the knowledge of achieving the task, he has also said: "Once you have seized the heart of zazen, you resemble the dragon when he enters the water and the tiger when he penetrates the mountain."

The four dimensions of the wisdom of Buddha form a single body, that of the Dharma. All these commentaries on the three bodies and four knowledges are boring, but let's remember, *the three bodies and four wisdoms are perfected in their body.* Everything, absolutely everything in the universe, constitutes only a single body.

A unique posture

The eight liberations[11] are also called the eight deliverances from the burden. The figure eight points to the number of stages to pass through to be liberated from all corporeal or incorporeal attachments and attain total abolition of notions and sensations. These stages correspond to the eight spheres of concentration, the first four releasing one from the material world and the final four from the immaterial world: limitless space, limitless knowledge, non-existence of being, and the sphere of "neither viewpoint nor no-viewpoint" which leads to the destruction of notions. Life in the three worlds is nothing but pain and suffering, "a house on fire," as the expression goes. The three worlds are the world of desires, the world of form and the world of no-form. The world of desires is that of the six paths[12] or states of consciousness that impede our progress. At a higher level comes the world of form and higher still, the spiritual world.

You will find a detailed explanation of this terminology in any Buddhist dictionary, but fundamentally Buddhism has no need of words. Each state of consciousness, whether it be belligerent, bestial or something else, is a fact obvious to everyone, and it's the same for the four physical and metaphysical levels. Giving them a name proves they are within the scope of the passions. All names express a passion. For example, he who commits a theft is a thief, he who shoplifts in a department store is a shoplifter. However, if these individuals stop thieving or shoplifting, they are "set free" from theft and shoplifting and can no longer be called thief or shoplifter. Happily, in delivering ourselves from the fetters of the world of desires we enter into the world of form, which is a higher level. Happier still, in liberating ourselves from the material world, we enter into the still higher level of the spiritual world. Thus, in passing through the four physical stages and the four immaterial stages, we realize the eight deliverances.

When we do zazen, our body consists of the legitimate, true Buddha Dharma, and we transcend the eight deliverances and the three worlds. Simply seated in zazen, in the proper state of alertness and the proper posture, the eight deliverances are obtained, *they are engraved in their mind*. We are completely and perfectly liberated from all bonds.

With the four levels of form and no-form, we're concerned with illusions of an elevated dimension. It's as if up to now you've eaten too many sweet potatoes or drunk too much alcohol (although the world of desires doesn't have these sorts of things) and now you yearn passionately for much more refined pleasures, collections of antiques or tea ceremonies, and then you raise yourself yet another notch, interesting yourself in philosophy. And then you rise to still another level and attain the awareness of zanmai,[13] consciousness beyond consciousness. Here you have attained the final level, but you remain still in the domain of the passions. In the zazen of which we are speaking, there is no longer anything. The zazen that we practice transcends all levels of the ladder of the passions.

The six discernments are as follows: the divine eye that allows seeing into all places, the divine hearing that permits limitless hearing, the understanding of limitless space, the understanding of destiny, the understanding of the thoughts of others, and the power of purifying stains. Infinite sight permits seeing clearly and lucidly all things in this world, seeing just as clearly the actions of the hungry ghosts and animal spirits on your back as those of the servant in the kitchen. One sees everything.

I see what my "clouds and water" are up to in my absences and see the wiles of my students when they cheat on an exam. And just as I see all, I hear all. The understanding of infinite space allows me to go wherever I wish while remaining seated where I am. Through the understanding of destiny, I comprehend what I did in a previous world, and by the understanding of others, what others are thinking. Most important is the power to purify stains, since it makes the passions of the body and of the heart disappear completely.

Dōgen says in Zazengi that the eyes must always remain open, but these are eyes that are doing nothing. Even if they are open in a normal fashion, they are without occupation. Eyes eagerly seeking for a flea are the eyes of a killer. Eyes that see a plate of delicious food and look for chopsticks are the eyes of a hungry ghost. The same is true for the ears. The one who stretches his ears to overhear a conversation, wondering if someone is saying something bad about him, has the ears of an easily angered man. Dōgen also says: "The ears must be in the same plane as the shoulders and the nose in line with the navel."

As for the understanding of infinite space: "Worth has nothing to do with an accent or the color of a face." That is to say that one doesn't let oneself be seduced by secondary and insignificant details.

The understanding of destiny means to break with before and after, living in the eternal "now." The past, present and future do not have individual existence. When we isolate a single image from the film of a man's life we arrive at strange deductions. Man is a being who laughs and who cries. Look at this old man pulling a rickshaw. A great smile lights up his face. You say to yourself that this man is happy and you wonder why. Very well, he's happy because the mutual insurance company drew his number. He's forgotten that he'll have to wait ten years to get the money. The money is there before his eyes and the lure of gain leads him forward smiling— in short, a guy who's understood nothing about human destiny. When one breaks with the before and the after and only the eternity of "now" exists, then one truly has an understanding of destiny.

The understanding of others means to not create a difference between self and others and to consider the ordinary man and the saint identical. One is in unison with the Buddha.

The power of purifying stains gives you the awareness that nothing can have a hold on you. Each day is a good day. It is said that at this moment, "The treasure house opens of itself and you utilize it at will."

Speaking of supernatural powers perhaps evokes magic, things like making yourself invisible, or walking on water, in the manner of Tenjiku Tokubei,[14] but that sort of thing has nothing to do with the supernatural powers we're talking about.

To summarize: *this tranquil man of the Way . . . who has ceased studying and acting* is perfectly furnished with the three bodies and four wisdoms, and the eight liberations and six supernatural powers are engraved in his spirit. Such is the treasure held by a man simply seated in zazen with correct posture and in the correct state of awareness.

21

A superior mind cuts through with one blow and attains understanding of all things.
A middling or inferior mind studies much and questions much.

To Live Thoroughly

It is written in the *Shinjinmei:* "The sage ceases acting, the fool binds himself." The sage follows a straight line and immediately *the three bodies and four wisdoms are perfected in his body.* The fool imprisons himself in whys and hows, making long detours without ever arriving. Do intellectuals have superior or inferior spirits? I wouldn't know. The superior spirit leaps straight to the goal, while the inferior spirit is full of all sorts of doubts and considerations. His way of studying is strange; he thinks he can't understand anything without making detours.

Scholars are totally absorbed in merely reading words, and they die before the meanings of the words are realized in their lives. Illusory discriminations exist without number. And we are the same, pursuing roundabout roads before making the definitive decision to practice zazen. On the contrary, if at one go one allows oneself to glide along a straight line by pure intuition, doing zazen, then one cuts short all the equivocations.

When Bashō[1] was at the brink of death and they asked him for a last word, the old poet responded, "All my poems are my last words." How admirable is a spirit of such depth! He wrote as if each poem were his last and plumbed the depths of his self. He lived eternal "nows" with neither yesterday nor tomorrow.

A superior spirit is always profound. He doesn't stop halfway. He does what is necessary, not what is unnecessary. He decides to act or not to act, but in either case he behaves definitely, clearly, without beating around the bush or deluding himself. If he engages in an action, he does his utmost to see it through. If he fails, he recriminates no one, for it can happen that unfortunate criticisms wound a man for life. When we lucidly distinguish what we ought to do from what we ought not to do, passions do not arise. This is the meaning of "A superior spirit cuts through with one blow and attains understanding of all things."

A rich man suddenly ruined suffers great torment unless he fully embraces his new condition. Formerly, they censured the one who thought he was rich. As for men of middling or inferior spirit, they trot around concepts like mice on a wheel without ever arriving at a destination. They are slaves to their intellectual learning. In Kagoshima, the place of their of origin, one hears nothing but talk of Saigō[2] and Togō.[3] It goes without saying that they were remarkable men and all school children learn that they were born in such and such a village, but instead of just being proud of them, wouldn't it be better to be oneself greater than Saigō and Togō? Without needing the arrogance of the local samurai or hoping to receive decorations, it's enough to be authentically oneself. One is in no way inferior. It's the same with Shākymuni and Maitreya.[4] We give way to them in nothing, because we are descendants of one and ancestors of the other. Despite this, because he does not practice, the middling or inferior spirit doubts and hesitates.

Lao-tzu expressed it very simply. When a superior spirit encounters the Way, he embraces it with zeal and practices it. It becomes his daily life. When a middling spirit encounters the Way, he takes it and then lets it go, for fear of suffering or injury or deceiving himself. When an inferior spirit encounters the Way, he bursts out laughing, because for him those who practice the Way are ridiculous eccentrics.

22

Just strip your mind of its dirty clothing,
But don't brag of your progress to others.

A Jewel in the Pocket

This verse alludes to the parable of "the jewel hidden in the clothes" in the Lotus Sutra.

One day two childhood friends who had not seen each other for a long time encountered one another by chance. One had become very rich and the other very poor. The rich man treated his friend to a fine meal. The friend ate and drank to his heart's content and fell asleep. The rich man, in a hurry to get on with his journey, slipped a jewel into his friend's pocket before departing. Upon awakening, unaware that he possessed a treasure, the poor man resumed his miserable life. Years passed until one day they met again: "The last time we were together I put a priceless jewel in your pocket, didn't you find it?" The poor friend put his hand into his pocket and, to his astonishment, the pearl was there.

It's enough to become authentically your self. Sawaki becomes the true Sawaki. Wouldn't he be ridiculous wearing the mask of Shākyamuni? Sawaki is in no way inferior to Shākyamuni or Maitreya. The Sawaki market is not a replica of the Kannon[1] market, or the Shākyamuni market. It imitates no one; it is original and unique. To be real is to be oneself. Doesn't this thing called "self" reside in each one of us? It's sufficient to find it; it forever waits discretely, sheltered from attention. It is clearly our most precious possession. From the moment we are aware of its true nature, it matters little what may happen. "My house is where I am, said the snail." We grasp our true self by stripping it of its filthy clothes.

But don't brag of your progress to others. It's pointless to shout from the rooftops that you've found the true Way, or to take pride in your zeal in practicing it. There's no need to draw glory from it.

23

Accept criticisms and slanders.
Their intent is to inflame the heavens, but it comes to nothing.
I hear them and savor them like sweet nectar.
They melt into me and instantly I enter the inconceivable.

Criticism with the Taste of Nectar

Let them talk; don't worry about criticism. In his time Shākyamuni was also criticized. There is an interesting anecdote on this subject:

One day as he was teaching, a brahmin came to criticize him openly. Shākyamuni listened to him with the greatest attention. His face remained mild, registering not the slightest reaction. When the brahmin finally finished his diatribe, Shākyamuni asked him:

"That's all?"

"—Yes, I've finished."

"—If you had come to offer me a piece of silk and I had refused it, what would you do??

"—I would take it back."

"—Well then, you have just presented me with criticisms that I do not accept. Please take them back."

It's obvious that if your merchandise isn't accepted, the only solution is to take it away. Such is the meaning of this phrase: *Accept criticism and slanders.* Like the sky, let us remain indifferent to both blame and praise. Those who throw up flaming torches, trying to set the sky aflame, will surely wear themselves out. *"Their intent is to enflame the heavens, but it comes to nothing."*

It's even possible to experience great pleasure in allowing oneself to be slandered. It's too bad that men don't appreciate the value of slanders. Sometimes they are unexpected, but it also happens that they whip you full force and the press isn't stingy about publishing them. Slander is a human instinct and, well, this instinct also exists within us. If I do not do that which I am accused of, it's only because I restrain and control myself.

For example, someone says I accepted payment under the table. In fact, I don't do this because it's never entered my head. But, theoretically, this possibility exists within me. The defamer brings to the fore an aspect latent in all individuals, given that each one is a microcosm of society. It's obvious that if someone else does it, I could also. They say that so-and-so keeps a mistress: this possibility exists for me as well! Slanders amuse me and, in truth, *I hear them and savor them like sweet nectar. They melt into me and instantly I enter the inconceivable.* This phrase corresponds to: "The dharma body enters us and we enter the dharma body." It's interesting to note that if one reverses the positions of the subject and the object, the worst slanders become sweet as nectar. The object enters into you and there dissolves completely.

24

Meditate on slanderous words and make them into friends
That will guide you on the way of the good.
If a slander brings up hate in you,
How can you manifest the wisdom and compassion of the non-born?

Friends and Enemies Are Equal

Defamation brings up anger and revolt in you because lying publicity is being inflicted on you. I, however, think that it's a warning from heaven, putting us on guard for the future and drawing our attention to the fact that the possibility exists within us of committing the act with which we are charged. This criticism allows us to thoroughly realize that the friend is an enemy and the enemy a friend.

For example, when enemies surround you and you don't know from which direction to expect the fatal blow, you're on the qui vive, your mind is taut and completely concentrated. In this sense, I think it is a great happiness not to stand in the wings of life. Seeing me constantly disparaged, many people get angry and bemoan my lot, but it's pointless to shed tears on my behalf! In any event, you live your practice strongly when you're encircled by enemies on all points of the compass.

I always intentionally surround myself with lay practitioners, to whose challenges I must respond. When, like the warriors of old, not only do lay practitioners follow you like your shadow, you are also surrounded by spying enemies; you practice from morning to night without relaxing your vigilance for an instant. It's good to be sprinkled with criticisms; it reawakens your ardor. However, although it often happens that I make uncomplimentary remarks to others, they rarely thank me! I don't often get angry, and when I do, it's to put someone back on the right road. In such a case, I would do anything. In exchange, I like it when someone does as much for me, the criticism becoming my friend and guiding me into the good. The people who criticize me are better guides than those who sing my praises.

If slander brings up hate in you, how can you manifest the wisdom and compassion of the non-born? Slander awakens no hatred in the bodhisattvas, whereas in an ordinary man it immediately unleashes anger. The non-born, non-destroyed is the satori of the bodhisattva, the experience of the infinite. On the subject of compassion and patience, I'd like to present you with a page written by Fukakusa no Gensei Jōnin,[1] excerpted from his collection of poems and prose entitled Sōzan-shū:

Seiko, I give you the name of Jinen, compassion and patience, and I want to tell you what it means. When a bodhisattva shows the Way to others, it's compassion. When he practices for himself, it's patience. If you do not possess compassion, you cannot practice patience and the reverse is also true. If you do not possess patience, you cannot practice compassion. If you have compassion, you become patient; if you are patient, you become compassionate. The Four Great Bodhisattva Vows point out the road: The first says, "Beings are numberless, I vow to free them" and the last, "The Buddha Way is unsurpassable, I vow to realize it." To realize the first you must be compassionate and to realize the last you must be patient.

Compassion means we regard all other existences as we regard ourselves, and we regard ourselves as we regard all other existences. The Dharma is a world of equality, where there are neither prejudice nor discrimination, neither feelings of hate nor of love. If someone seeks the Way, you must immediately guide him; if he does not seek the Way, meet him on his own terrain. If he's interested in worldly affairs, speak to him of worldly affairs and by this route lead him toward the Way. Speak of esthetics to the esthete, of magic to the magician, of letters to the lettered. You must grasp him through what holds his attention and lead him toward the Way so that he will enter upon it. It's not because you speak every day of worldly affairs, of arts, of magic or of letters that you are an esthete, a magician or a man of letters. Let's say that what's important every day is to act by practicing non-acting.

Patience doesn't mean to rejoice when everything goes your way, or to be irritated when everything goes badly. Practicing patience means not to be influenced by the appearance of a face or the tone of a voice, a rich dwelling or a title. It's to be in harmony with the place and the time, even if you must live in the depths of a mountain or endure hardships of cold and hunger, clothed in straw and nourished on grasses. Do not let the serpent of torpor approach when you are alone, nor in the obscurity of your room allow the demon of lust to awake. Study despite the cold or the heat, practice zazen day and night.

The important thing is to not bat an eyelash when the winds of the eight directions are unleashed and not be shaken when the three poisons assail your spirit, keeping your gaze fixed on the truth and your mind concentrated on the essence of the Dharma. If, despite your practice, you don't obtain the anticipated results, as long as your faith is profound you will certainly discern the truth. If your power of patience is not strong enough, it's like throwing ice into boiling water. Not only will you not help others, you won't even save yourself. You will be a vanquished and annihilated bodhisattva.

In contrast, if your power of patience is strong when you practice compassion, you liberate yourself from all servitude and no longer will any bonds hinder you from offering aid to all the beings in the universe. Your mission is to relieve men of their suffering and thus to bring them peace and joy. If you doubt this, just look at the plants: they are born in the spring, bloom in the summer, give fruit in the autumn and rebuild their strength during the cold of the winter. Without ever doubting themselves, they accomplish great things. Believe in my words, Seikō. By putting them into practice you will attain perfect understanding and supreme illumination. You will be honored for having aided all men. Seikō, please ardently apply yourself.

25

Penetration of original reality and penetration of the teaching go hand in hand.

When concentration and wisdom are perfectly clear one does not stagnate in the void.

Words Without Words

Essentially, Buddhism is to perfectly penetrate original reality and to expound it perfectly. These two aspects: precise penetation of original reality and precise teaching are extremely important. To penetrate original reality means not being mistaken about true reality. It's to perceive it such as it is. It is something we have to experience for ourselves. To penetrate the teaching is to retain the use of tentative names even while we grasp true reality, for this is necessary to explain and share the Dharma with other people. Buddhism is not a mental construction. Were even a particle fabricated, the truth would disappear. It rests on the principle that all that is produced is destroyed.

Tenkei Oshō[1] stated very accurately: "If you want to have satori, it would be better to free your eyes from their covering." A man's eye is enclosed within the covering of a man; the eye of a woman in a woman's covering; rich and poor each have theirs. Unless we take the covering off our eyes, we cannot see true reality. Among the most difficult coverings to take off are those called "enemy" and "friend."

When we remove all such coverings, true reality is there. The place we are going to is not difficult to reach, that is to say, the place where we remove the coverings from our limited views. When the fog lifts and the horizon appears, we discover the genuine source of the teaching of the Buddha. This original realty may also be called something high and dignified like mountains, something noble and respectable to be venerated, or something central and immovable. The central matter for us is not to have any possessions, to live free from attachments, or to live without narrow preferences. This is the noble way of life. We venerate original reality, hence in our practice original reality is fundamental.

In Shōbōgenzo Hotsu-bodai-shin [Arousing Bodhi Mind] Dōgen said: "Before I myself cross over the river that separates samsara from nirvana, I will strive to help all beings cross over." However, it is not certain that those who have not yet penetrated original reality can help others cross to the other shore. Benefiting others by giving teachings should be done after benefiting oneself by penetrating original reality.

Many errors are committed on this subject. Some say that they don't have time to take care of others and need to concentrate on penetrating original reality themselves. This is also the point of view of Hinayana Buddhism that aims solely at personal deliverance, which comes back to learning to swim oneself, but not going to the aid of others. Of course, when we hear, "Others are to be saved before myself," we may feel it's necessary to sacrifice ourselves for others, a thought unbearable to self-centered people concerned only with their own situation.

If we oppose altruism, to sacrifice all for others, with egoism, to sacrifice all to myself, we end up with aberrant situations. To understand original reality means to refuse extremes and to find the perfect balance between altruism and egoism.

Roughly speaking, original reality is satori, but it would be a great error to so arbitrarily reduce it. So many people delude themselves, saying that they have attained satori. I loathe such half-baked satori. "I have satori . . . I have enlightenment . . ." Truthfully speaking,

The Lifeguard may rescue the drowning child, etc. (one trained in the truth of the water) The ordinary person may attempt it, in which case both may drown.

if they have satori it's because they're fabricating illusions about its content.

In former times, someone said, "If you cannot penetrate original reality, you will not be able to help others." To help others and to penetrate original reality are not two separate things: one cannot dissociate them. Let us call the penetration of original reality "self-interest" and penetration of the teaching "altruism." Thus, self-interest and altruism are one.

When some people are questioned about Dharma, they say "It cannot be expressed in words." This only makes it evident that they themselves do not know. When we want to communicate our experience to others, most things can be expressed, even though we are not eloquent. Thus, if I fall in love, though it may be the secret of my heart and I speak of it to no one, my ears flame and my armpits sweat. A lot of good it does me to keep silent, my feelings manifest by themselves. When one has something to say, one says it. Words are only words, transitory and of no importance. ← Words are both unimportant and important

Tōzan Daishi[2] said, "If you cannot understand my words, you are not my kinfolk." He was speaking of the use of a password on the battlefield; those who know it are friends, those who do not, enemies. I think that those who travel the path with you and share the same thoughts understand exactly what you want to say. Those liberated from the clouds of delusion are able to communicate in words.

Some think that the principle of Buddhism can be understood as a theory for discussion, but it says in *Sandōkai*: "To accord with the principle is not yet awakening." One cannot theorize about love. If a boy likes a girl, he likes her. Other factors can't dissuade him. If a girl does not love a boy, no amount of theoretical discussion will make her do so. Our tendency to depend upon theories leads to delusion. This is why we need both penetration of original reality and penetration of the teaching.

Buddhism is the harmony of two processes: penetrating original reality and penetrating the teachings. One ascends, the other descends. One inspires you toward the heights, the other pulls you toward the bottom. The proper equilibrium is found in the union of the two: you grasp the eternal and don't reject the ephemeral; you grasp the ephemeral and don't reject the eternal. Such is the meaning of this phrase: *penetration of original reality and penetration of the teaching go hand in hand.*

That, It's Thus

The fusion of concentration and wisdom into a limpid whole does not lie within the domain of reason. Zen concentration embraces space and time and all things in the same transparency. Yet this limpid unity of form without form, unchanging and motionless as eternity, also changes and ceaselessly renews itself in infinite diversity. This aspect of ceaseless change is wisdom. Zen wisdom is this eternal changing. Furthermore, concentration and wisdom are not two distinct things; there is not concentration here and wisdom over there. They are one.

Among the writings of Takuan Oshō³ is one that expresses the essence of *zen*: Mysteries of Motionless Wisdom. "Motionless" is concentration. "Wisdom" is the aspect of infinite diversity, always new and changing. And the "mystery" is the total fusion of the immobility of the concentrated mind with the wisdom that constantlhy changes and innovates.

Motionless wisdom is also the spirit of martial arts when they are practiced in the authentic spirit of the Way. If during combat one thinks to repeat a blow that has succeeded previously, it is not true combat, it's staged theater. A given situation never repeats itself. The outcome of a combat depends upon two factors: the first, fixed in advance, is the skill level of the swordsmen, which determines who's strongest. It's certain that I will be beaten if I encounter a fifth dan of kendō. But the second factor is not fixed, and it's finally this that will determine the outcome of the combat.

The same goes for the judo practitioner who will certainly be beaten if he wishes to use the excellent hold he's just learned, and the same is true of the rich man's son who went through his inheritance and is forced to beg. He puts out his pretty hand, but since he relies only on his hand, he's beaten even before he puts it out!

Wisdom is invention, spontaneous creativity. Concentration is the factor fixed in advance, the level. The strongest ought to win, but to win he must be creative, give proof of an inventive spirit. If he's lacking in it, he will always lose to adversaries at a lower level. Victory thus depends upon the fusion of these two factors: it's the mystery of motionless wisdom. We give rise to an eternal truth that is ceaselessly reinvented by wisdom. Since we cannot dissociate zazen from wisdom, they must blend and fuse to be homogeneous. We must lean neither toward zazen nor toward wisdom.

Natsume Sōseki[4] wrote: "Let yourself be guided by learning and you will become dry and rigid; let yourself be guided by feelings and you'll go off the rails. Whatever one does, life is difficult." I would say that if you lean toward zazen, your life will become monotonous, and even if it's a question of the eternal and universal truth, it's not that simple. If you lean toward learning, everything becomes complicated and you'll end up having a nervous depression. For life to be neither monotonous nor complicated, the sole path to follow, if we wish at all cost to give it a name, is satori.

Scholars are like pharmacists who store the licorice in one drawer and the arrowroot in another, or like clerks in a pawnshop who label objects and classify them by their redemption date or their value if they have one. Scholars dissect the complexity of things without ever grasping the thing itself: they lean toward learning without having zen concentration.

Philosophers call pure intuition the faculty that allows us to directly grasp the non-duality of all things, without leaning either toward unchanging nondifferentiation or toward changing complexity. They also use many other terms, but since they think only with words, I can scarcely have confidence in them. However it may be, the important thing is to regard our own reality directly and to perfectly harmonize zen concentration and wisdom, living in neither the monotonous nor the complicated. In Buddhism, this is what we call "true freedom." It's said in the Great Wisdom Sutra,[5] "The bodhisattva who knows true freedom" rests nowhere, neither in form nor in emptiness, in ego or the Dharma. Such is the path we must follow.

Zen monks sketch this path by simply tracing a circle and saying: "What is this?"

If they draw without understanding, the circle is meaningless. But eminent monks demonstrate the path that is neither unchanging nor complicated by using a single undefinable word. One cannot name the truth. No term can express it and yet it exists in the ultimate fusion and perfect unity of concentration and wisdom. But what to call it? It is "thus," pointing to the reality that cannot be named even though it is actually there.

There is an interesting anecdote concerning "someone." One day a visitor came to knock at the gate of a temple:

"—Open up!"

"Who are you?" inquired the little monk on duty at the entry gate.

"It's me. I've come to see the abbot."

It was a warrior of very correct bearing who came often to visit the temple. The young monk ran at top speed to inform the abbot.

"Sir, sir!"

"What is it?"

"U-h-h . . ."

"A visitor?"

"It's someone . . .

"Who Someone? What? Men have names! Idiot, you've already forgotten!"

Before the door opened, the abbot slipped into a thicket from which he could see the entrance and peeked through the branches. He also had completely forgotten the name of the visitor.

"Yes, in truth, it's definitely "someone . . .""

The nature of "someone" or of "what" is truly a complicated matter. It's precisely this that no word can express nor any learning grasp. It's that which one cannot transmit except from "heart to heart" or "mind to mind." *When concentration and wisdom are perfectly clear, one does not stagnate in the void.* For want of a better word, let's call this limpid fusion "thus."

Monotony renders stupid and complication depresses, yet by fusing the two one finds peace and tranquility and is sure of oneself in daily life. In realizing this unity, one becomes "thus"—the one who understands true freedom to act. This is what Shākyamuni taught over the course of forty years and practiced all his life.

The language is clear and simple: I do what ought to be done, I do not do what ought not to be done. Buddhism is perfect harmony without hindrances, like the full moon. At the same time, it is of unfathomable subtlety, as is testified to by the verse:

Penetration of original reality and penetration of the teaching go hand in hand.

When concentration and wisdom are perfectly clear one does not stagnate in the void.

Everything is said in a few words. It is at one and the same time *Sandōkai* (Harmony of Difference and Equality), *Hōkyō Zanmai* (Precious Mirror Samadhi) and *Shōdōka* (The Song of Awakening).

These two phrases of the verse contain the entire wisdom of Buddhism.

26

But I am not alone in understanding this.
All the buddhas, innumerable as the sands of the Ganges, are as I.

The lion roars the fearless doctrine
That shatters the skulls of the beasts that hear it.
Fleeing, the elephant loses his dignity.
Only the dragon, delighted, listens to it in silence.

Fundamentally, There Is Nothing

But I am not alone in understanding this. Only a Buddha recognizes another Buddha, because he has the understanding of the Buddha that can be transmitted only from Buddha to Buddha. He has realized that his true nature fills the universe: *All the buddhas, innumerable as the sands of the Ganges, are as I.*

To practice the Way of the Buddha is neither to be monotonous nor complicated, but to live daily life within the unity of the two. Life becomes the teaching of the Buddha and the teaching of the Buddha becomes life. All buddhas are of the same essence and accomplish the complete fusion of concentration and wisdom. The body of all the buddhas is the truly free life, liberated of all servitude.

This fearless doctrine is equal to the roar of a lion. It is sure of itself, without doubt or hesitation. A person who thinks it's perhaps this or that isn't pointing to the Way of the Buddha. We saw previously that a true monk is revealed through a firm and definite doctrine. Buddhism is to live a life that goes straight toward the clearly defined objective that one has settled upon. When concentration and wisdom are in perfect harmony, we do not stagnate in the void. Such is the path of the sixth patriarch Enō (Hui-neng) when he says: "Fundamentally, there is nothing."[1] Then it's not a question of dawdling over pleasantries like dusting a mirror to prevent dust from accumulating, or asking oneself whether it would be best to not speak about such and such a thing.

The fearless doctrine roared by the lion is the spirit of the eternal solitude of unfathomable depths and infinite, inconceivable space that no borrowed term can express. There are things that exist, yet cannot be put into words, such as the taste of sugar. How to explain it in words? To taste it is the only way. Likewise, for understanding it is necessary to have the experience of "Fundamentally, there is nothing." The one who reveals this truth shatters the skulls of the beasts that hear it.

Today, scholars of Buddhology pass everything through the sieve of history, of archaeology, and of linguistics. But suppose we said to them, "Do not use linguistics, give up English, German, Italian, Sanskrit, and Pali. Use only Japanese. Don't consider the historical dates. And then, please, speak about the true Buddhist teachings." They would have nothing left to talk about. Perhaps even the name of Buddhism would disappear.

Did Shakyamuni leave his family at the age of nineteen? of twenty-five? of twenty-nine? This is a much-debated point. Still, what's the importance whether he lived a hundred or a thousand years? Let them quibble over whether he died two thousand five hundred years ago or two thousand eight hundred years ago. A thousand or ten thousand years, what's the connection with living Buddhism?

This type of dispute that has nothing to do with the living reality of Buddhism falls under the heading of illusions. Moreover, all these studies in German, English, Pali, Sanskrit, etc., stink of boredom. Stop all this uproar! The clear, authentic, pure, unadulterated, unpolluted, unfabricated Buddhism is that there is nothing. This unproduced, unconditioned truth is the fearless doctrine that the lion roars. We can hardly say that the lion Shākymuni didn't know how to make himself heard.

It's a characteristic of scholars to have only numbers and dates in their head. Like the Westerners, our researchers spend their time tapping on their calculators. They have been bewitched by the Western academics. In truth, their studies of Buddhism are weak and of no use to peoples' lives. The Buddhism that they fabricate is poles apart from the true, living Buddhism.

Nevertheless, their studies are extremely useful to me, and I often borrow and make use of their research. Still, whenever possible, I speak ill of them. I am pretty selfish. *Shōdōka says: "The lion's roar shatters the skulls of the beasts that hear it."* Scholastic Buddhism, however, shatters no one's skull.

Fleeing, the elephant loses his dignity. Under the old terminology, the elephant symbolized the Hinayana principle, that is to say the one who holds himself in high esteem and is concerned only with himself. When this naïve soul hears the roaring of the lion, he is stupefied and takes fright. He's made in the image of Sekkō, who had a passion for dragons and collected their representations, but was terror struck when one day a real dragon appeared.

Only the dragon, delighted, listens to it in silence. The dragon symbolizes the great disciple. In that era, it was perhaps Seigen[2] or Nangaku or perhaps Yōka Daishi himself. Certainly it is an allusion to Enō's disciples and, indirectly, to himself, as he experiences an indescribable joy when he hears the lion roar the Dharma.

The fearless doctrine is the authentic Dharma. When you embrace pure and true Buddhism, such bliss is born within you that you want to throw yourself into it. Certain people who listen to me think that I'm poking fun and are disquieted, but I'm only an ordinary man who laughs and cries and if I'm poking fun at anyone, it's only myself.

27

I have crossed rivers and oceans, traversed mountains and waded streams.
In search of the Way, I have questioned masters and practiced zen.
Now that I have found the path of Sōkei
I know that birth and death do not concern me.

To Not Fear Death

It is not so easy to hear the true Dharma and to follow the correct Way. *I have crossed rivers and oceans, traversed mountains and waded streams. In search of the Way, I have questioned masters and practiced zen.*

Daichi Zenji[1] witnesses to this in a poem: "I have traveled through Jiang-Hu, and I have stopped again and again." Jiang is the abbreviation for Jiangsi and Hu for Hunan. These two provinces are situated south of the Yangtze River, which separates Northern and Southern China. In Japanese, the expression Jiang-Hu[2] signifies that a "clouds and water" monk makes a stay of one hundred days to practice zazen in a temple. It was a tradition to travel the country in search of a master.

In our times, even though they detest it, the youngsters take a professor's course in order to pass an exam. The exam is their sole concern, and they are ready to endure anything to get a diploma. Formerly, students were more interesting. They went off on foot in search of a master, passing the night in a temple, eating and attending a lecture by the master, and then, "Sorry, this one doesn't please me." They departed immediately without hesitation, just like we come out of a big store without having purchased anything. They tied on their straw sandals and took to the road again to another temple. When they found a master who suited them, they remained with him for their entire life.

Now that I have found the path of Sōkei. "Sōkei" alludes to the temple of the sixth patriarch, Hui-neng,[3] who taught that "Fundamentally, there is nothing." It's at Sōkei that Yōka Daishi heard the lion's roar, the fearless doctrine, and since then *"I know that birth and death do not concern me,"* because birth and death do not exist. In a country where money does not exist there are no rich or poor, because it is money that creates the rich and the poor. In a country where one is not born, the notions of birth or of death do not arise. Consequently, if one considers the material reality of his physical body to be empty and illusory, there is no longer either birth or death. If we reflect on it well, the physical body does not have real intrinsic existence. It's like a dream. It's sufficient to become aware of this, and then we know that birth and death do not differ.

Kanzan Kokushi,[4] founder of Myōshin-ji temple, kept no record of his teaching, and when Ingen[5] arrived in Japan, he searched for Kanzan's notes and was astonished to find nothing. "How did it happen that his teaching wasn't transcribed?" he asked. "What was his line of thought?" They answered him, "He always said that in us there is neither birth nor death." There's no need to say anything more. If there are neither birth nor death within us, we live in a country with neither rich nor poor, for money also does not exist. There is no satori. There are no illusions. We are not born; we do not die. We are not afraid of birth, we are not afraid of death. We know that birth and death are not our affair.

And you understand that when you have found Sōkei's path.

28

To walk is zen, to sit is zen.
Speaking, remaining silent, moving, being still, the body is at peace.
Facing the blade of the sword, the spirit is tranquil.
Facing poison, it remains calm.

Danger of Death

Zazen doesn't mean solely the seated posture.[1] *Speaking, remaining silent, moving, being still, the body is at peace.* Nevertheless, we must not conclude stupidly that any old thing can be called *zen*: sleeping *zen*, eating *zen*, weeping *zen*!

Even Westerners call their God "source of life." God is the one who regenerates the eternal old things of the past, giving them a new life. Our old and eternal Buddha also is always new. When we know how to distinguish his precise taste, we taste it in each daily activity. When one has transcended birth and death, one knows that birth and death do not differ. One feels reassured and whether the body speaks or keeps silent, whether it moves or remains still, it dwells in peace.

It is not difficult to risk your life. There are even lovers who offer themselves death for their passion. With an arrow driven into his eye, the warrior Kamakura Gongorō Kagemasa still strangled his enemy. His friend tried to pull the arrow out, but was unsuccessful. Then the friend put his foot on Kagemasa's face to gain purchase and extracted the arrow. But Kagemasa attacked him, saying "You insulted this samurai by putting your foot on my face." During that era, death was not a problem. Warriors thought they should die in battle.

This can even happen to people like me. During the Russo-Japanese war I really placed no value on my life. Or at least that's how I felt at the front, but when I'd returned home and practiced zazen, I suddenly realized that I'd comported myself like a vulgar swordsman in the manner of Kunisada Chūji.[3] No more had I been a chivalrous hero passing into posterity like Banzuin Chōbei,[4] only just a Tōken Gonbei, his assistant. In certain circumstances, we always want to push our own limits further. Because men cannot bear to be inferior, they risk their lives in battle. By winning, they distinguish themselves and increase their importance. I think that this was the principle motivation of the warriors of old.

Facing the blade of the sword, the spirit is tranquil. Facing poison, it remains calm. This is how one ought to confront the fatal moment, but for that it's necessary to understand that to be born and to die are not different, and that the wellspring always continues to flow. The mind finds appeasement only when concentration and wisdom blend in a limpid whole. If this condition is not fulfilled, one is quite simply in danger of death.

29

My master had encountered the Buddha Nentō,
He was the ascetic Ninniku during numerous kalpas.

The Experience of "Without Ego"

We always allow ourselves to be fooled by reality. We detest suffering and love pleasure; we detest work and love sleep. We're always engaged in fleeing or pursuing something in a whirlwind of activities. We act contrary to the tranquil man who remains unmoved in the face of the sword or poison.

What do good and bad mean? If you begin a meal with a delectable dish, the following dishes seem flat, yet if the first dish is poor, the one that seemed flat becomes delicious. In truth, in themselves good and bad mean nothing. Yet we always want to have pleasure.

How can we live this reality according to the Buddha Dharma? Man is unhappy when he loses all the good things to which he is habituated, and he is happy when he departs from the misery from which he has suffered cruelly. After suffering comes pleasure; after pleasure comes suffering. Why run in all directions, fleeing one and pursuing the other? It's thus that the average mortal comports himself, when the greatest happiness is precisely not to move. Such is the teaching of the Buddhas of the past.

"My master" here means Shākyamuni. Buddhist sutras report that in an infinitely remote era during a previous incarnation when he was the ascetic Ninniku,[1] Shākyamuni was the disciple of a prior Buddha called Nentō,[2] with whom he practiced patience and endurance.

One day, the king of a country called Kari addressed the ascetic Ninniku:

"You say that you practice patience. Does that mean that you never become angry regardless of what happens to you?"

"—That's it exactly," replied the ascetic. "I have the ability to endure all."

"—We're going to see if you speak the truth."

The king took his saber and cut off Ninniku's hands and feet, then cut him into five pieces and these pieces into little cubes three centimeters square. The texts report that Ninniku remained unmoved. It might be thought that he would have died after they cut his neck, but it's said he had no injury, even reduced to dust. How can such a marvel be explained? Simply by the fact that the ascetic Ninniku was "without ego—without human viewpoint—without ordinary consciousness—without age." That's to say that he was conscious neither of his "self" nor of being a man, and still less an ordinary unenlightened individual. Birth and death did not concern him. Consequently—pssst!!—whatever came along, he recovered his original state.

When man suffers, rejoices, desires, flees, weeps, laughs, etc., his four aspects come into play: the ego, the body, ordinary consciousness, and time. The ascetic Ninniku had abolished these four obstacles that are the cause of all our sufferings, and thus he remained uninjured. His state of concentration is called "diamond concentration"[3] or "without four aspects."

An ogre wants to eat me, the Lord of Death wishes to drag me into his lair, but since I am without ego, without human countenance, since I am enlightened and death is not my problem, no one can catch me. In fact, this is the entertaining side of Buddhism and its mysterious power.

It is said that Shākyamuni drilled himself for a long time, practicing "without four aspects" during numerous kalpas. A kalpa is the time required for a fairy resting upon a cube of stone eighteen kilometers square to wear it away to nothing by brushing it once every hundred years with its train of feathers. In this case, we're speaking of a kalpa of stone, but there's also a kalpa of poppies. This one is an enormous silo eighteen kilometers per side, filled with poppy seeds, and a kalpa is the time it takes to empty the silo by picking out one seed every hundred years.

As for Ninniku, "patience-endurance," it's not a question of the kind of virtue that consists of gritting one's teeth to endure burning moxa. Our own patience is "without ego without human viewpoint, without ordinary consciousness, without age." It is the well-being that we feel when our shoulders are supple and relaxed.

With good humor, Fukakusa no Gensei[4] wrote this poem as he was dying:

> Monk Gensei in Fukakusa has passed away
> Even though he is myself, I would like to express my heartfelt condolences.

This remark would have been impossible without his deep experience of "without-ego."

Similarly, when dying, Ryokan said:

> Showing its back
> And showing its front,
> A falling maple leaf
> (translation by Kaz Tanahashi)

He could not have uttered such a thing, comparing his dying body with the maple leaves falling, unless he had the experience of "without-ego."

Miura Dūsun[5] left this poem before committing hara-kiri: "When the urn breaks, victor or vanquished becomes a clod of dirt." That's as much as saying nothing! Whether the urn breaks or not, one is already a clod of dirt. When one knows this in advance, one doesn't make such a to-do about it!

30

How many times have I been born? How many times have I died?
Birth and death come and go without end.

The Power of Karma and the Power of Vows

They say that at death one enters into the cycle of rebirths. We question ourselves, wondering if we will be reborn as a human being, but no one can answer this question. If I do good actions in this life, will I be rewarded by a good rebirth? It's the ego that poses this question. Does paradise really exist? Here, it's man in his blindness who worries. In this verse, we confront the problem of life and death: *How many times have I been born? How many times have I died?*

In effect, there are two ways of approaching these questions: the first is to cede to the force of karma, and the second is to let oneself be carried by the strength of the bodhisattva's vows. A single misstep, and a person can find himself in the water, about to go under, or another can leap in to help someone by retrieving money accidentally dropped into the water. In both cases, each is in the water, but the first person fell in by mistake, and the second plunged in voluntarily. This makes all the difference.

To be afraid of water is characteristic of the Lesser Vehicle. That is, to be afraid of life and death is a mark of the Lesser Vehicle. It was written long ago: "Life-death is the pleasure garden of the bodhisattva, life-death is also his playing field." Which comes back to saying that one plunges of one's own accord into life and into death. There is an essential difference between the matter of being at the mercy of karma and the matter of acting freely.

The prodigious energy that fills the universe, and that in reality itself is the universe, is comparable to an immense ocean. The water of this immensity, according to the power of karma or that of vows, can become a healing eyewash or a mortal poison, steam or ice, just as the waves are born and die ceaselessly, unique and always different. *How many times have I been born? How many times have I died?* No one can resolve the enigma of death. When a disciple questioned Dōgo Oshō on this subject, he replied, "I won't say, I won't say."

I often say, "Grosso modo, that's it . . ." but here things don't organize themselves "grosso modo." Yesterday comes before today and today comes before tomorrow and tomorrow comes before the day after tomorrow and so on. Each day is unique and different. Certainty doesn't come from a fixed and prettily done up concept. One can't reassure those afraid of death with a phrase. Moreover, it's said, "If a teaching is a fixed object, it is not genuine."

Yesterday I was happy . . . today I am unhappy. Yesterday I wept . . . today I laugh.

Happiness, unhappiness, prosperity, adversity are all as unpredictable as the horse who ruined old master Sai by running away, yet returned months later accompanied by a magnificent thoroughbred. Looking back on my childhood, I think it was pitiable. Not only was I born into poverty, I lost my parents very young and didn't even have adoptive parents to take care of me. I passed my time weeping and sucking my fingers and shut myself in the toilet until my tears dried. Later, in the middle of the winter, I departed for work at the store in a kimono that barely reached my knees. Rising at four o'clock in the morning, the frozen ground crackled beneath my feet and I returned at night by the light of the moon. Thanks to this, I've forged a body that never fails and I never catch a cold. For good health, there's no better education.

When one has been forged by misery, the majority of sufferings are no longer sufferings. One can endure almost anything, and thus one derives benefit from it. A person with rich parents will consecrate his whole life in attempting to preserve his inheritance, and if it diminishes the slightest bit will feel unworthy of his parents. His life will be wasted.

When you are born poor, you also have fewer worries. A scholarship is not available unless one is an orphan, and in my case, I made the request for it myself. I had a regular three-year scholarship and never received assistance from anyone. They didn't give me enough pencils, so I practiced on the ground, which is why I write poorly. I didn't have notebooks with so-called models for writing, because they were of no use. Is this a good thing? Is this a bad thing? Men are mistaken on this subject and parents are idiots. They save up money for their children by depriving themselves, because they fear the children will reproach them for squandering it. But the parents give them money, and what do they do with it? They enjoy the pleasures of life, immediately catch a cold and sniffle. They have passions and want a mistress. These are things we need to think about.

Birth and death come and go without end. Thanks to the power of vows, the bodhisattva lives this continuous process with clarity, putting his extra energy at the service of others. People who are led by karma accumulate debts and interest or are constantly disloyal or unfaithful and cause harm to others. Living to help men or living to harm them are horses of a different color. The one who does nothing but borrow money, enjoy life, ruin his health by eating to excess, drink alcohol and live on credit or by pawning things, is carried away by the current and ends up drowning. He's also the one who cries, "Help! Help!" but the moment the rescue ship has fished him out, grows angry because they didn't arrive quickly enough. No one loves him. On the other hand, helping others, giving them food to eat, teaching them, being of use to them, sharing their load, feeding oneself simply and offering them good things, this is to be reborn indefinitely. Such is the life of the one led by the power of vows.

Birth and death come and go without end, just as clouds float through the sky without wondering what they'll become or even reminding themselves that they can do nothing about it. They pass, pursuing nothing, fleeing nothing. This is not what the run of the mill mortals do, but it's the practice of the bodhisattva's vows.

How many times have I been born? How many times have I died? Shinran[3] said in a poem: "The ferryman goes ceaselessly from one bank to the other." He crosses and returns. Life and death come and go without end. Nothing ever stagnates or comes to a standstill. Even if one attains the state of consciousness where birth and death do not differ, this doesn't mean that all at once everything stops.

Didn't Kanzan[4] always repeat: "In us, there is neither life nor death"? Which is another way of saying, *Birth and death come and go without end.* Life and death are the "the pleasure garden, the playing field" of the bodhisattva, where he flees nothing because he detests nothing, pursues nothing because he hopes for nothing and because there is nothing. Thus there is nothing to run away from, nothing to hide. Naturally and without constraint, at the pleasure of the waves, he is carried along by the current of life and death.

31

Yet, suddenly, when one understands the non-born
One doesn't rejoice at praise, one is not distressed by blame.

Misfortune Becomes Good Fortune

That which lives must die. If there is birth, there is death. All that is produced, perishes. The non-born or non-produced has been invoked previously: *If a slander raises hate in you, how can you manifest the wisdom and compassion of the non-born?*

It was precisely this problem of life and death that led Yōka Daishi to Sōkei to question the Sixth Patriarch, Hui-neng (Enō):

"Life and death are a great matter. Life is impermanent and passes so quickly," says Yōka.

"Why don't you realize that if there is absence of production in life, there is absence of swiftness?" answers the Sixth Patriarch.

To understand life and death, it is essential to grasp the non-born. In the fascicle in Shōbōgenzō titled "Birth and Death" (Shōji), Dōgen presented a mondō that took place between Kassan[1] and Jōsan:[2]

"If Buddha exists in life and death, then life and death do not exist" says Kassan.

"If Buddha exists neither in life nor in death, the error life-death no longer exists." answers Jōsan.

This exchange of views demonstrates how profound was the experience of the non-born in these two worthy opponents. They are each as good as the other; all that differs is the formulation of their understanding. "If Buddha exists in life and death, then life and death do not exist." That is to say, life is Buddha, death is Buddha. Now, if all is Buddha, then life and death have no existence in and of themselves. Jōsan says the reverse: "If Buddha exists neither in life nor in death, the error life-death no longer exists." That is to say, the universe itself is life and death and Buddha cannot be disassociated from it. In a world where there are only the poor, the duality rich/poor does not exist. There are thus neither rich nor poor. Without riches, no poverty. Without beauty, no ugliness. Without ugliness, no beauty: ugliness enhances the value of beauty and beauty throws into relief ugliness.

Without desires, no repulsions; without repugnance, no preference. Without Buddha, no life, no death: "Life and death no longer leave me perplexed." As someone once said, in reality "it's this rascal of a Shākyamuni who one fine day came into the world and threw delusion into the mind of men." In effect, he's the one who made men become conscious of their error. The entire sky, the entire earth, is life-death, the entire universe is life-death.

During a conference on the Heart Sutra, a leading French scholar of Buddhism, commenting on the phrase "form is empty" regrettably gave the word shiki the sense of "color." Now, shiki[3] includes the whole physical world, all matter that has a form, and in the non-born it's a matter of all phenomena and not solely of color. In consequence, "form is empty" signifies that limited and finite reality is at the same time infinite and unlimited. Good fortune is also bad fortune and poverty, riches. The macrocosm does not differ from the microcosm. The good is an evil and the evil is a good. The sky is the earth and the earth, sky. There are not good things on one side and bad on the other. In fact, this point of view that takes in the totality is very subtle. It is extremely interesting to contemplate the world in light of the non-born.

It is essential to understand the non-born well. If there is non-born, there is non-differentiation. If there is non-differentiation, there is no longer good fortune nor bad fortune, neither pleasure nor suffering, neither love nor hate, neither good nor evil, neither birth nor death.

From the moment that one understands the non-born, *one doesn't rejoice at praise, one is not distressed by blame.* Honors mean glory and prosperity; disgrace is shame and humiliation. All that is relative. Men always want to know their destiny because they think there is good fortune on one side and bad on the other. Kaga no Chiyo[4] wrote this poem right before getting married: "I pick the first persimmon of the year, although I do not know if it is bitter or not. " She seemed to think marriage was a risky prospect, wondering if married life would be bitter or sweet. Marrying a woman with such an attitude, the bridegroom may not have been completely happy.

Good fortune is born from bad fortune, and from happiness, unhappiness. If you sweat from an overheated room, you catch a cold when you go out into the cold, but if, like me, you live without heat, you're unacquainted with colds. Good luck? Bad luck? I don't know. There are even folks who catch a cold from sleeping late. If they rose courageously at three a.m. every morning, they'd toughen up and never be sick. So perhaps it's good luck to not be able to linger in bed. You can't arbitrarily judge good fortune or bad fortune. If there were no joy, there would be no sorrow. Let's comport ourselves rightly, act rightly and it's all right if this or that arrives. When you understand the non-produced, you are indifferent to slanders and praises. You seek nothing; you flee nothing.

32

Entering the deep mountains, I live in a hermitage
Under a great pine on a steep peak overhanging the abyss.
I sit tranquilly and without care in my humble abode.
Silent retreat, serene simplicity.

Far from the World

It's a mistake to think that the mountain is an ideal place to find calm. I knew an abbot who'd made this choice. He yawned constantly: "Oh! How long the days are! If only a visitor would think to bring me some sushi[1]!" It might be a good idea to live deep in the mountains if they weren't infested with demons ceaselessly prowling in the vicinity. They quickly visit, and the solitude doesn't last long. The hermitage we're talking about here is in a place so isolated that you don't even hear the lowing of a cow, and where there is no human trace. Dōgen Zenji said: "The dusts of the world do not reach it." In this place, the snow falls in silence; man is motionless.

What world is this? It's a world of man alone with himself, within his deep mountain where he withdraws far from the noise and activities of life. A world where he sees no one. When they speak of an isolated place, I always think of the toilet. There also it's the deep mountain. No one. No link with anything. Alone with yourself. Such is the Way of authentic religion. When we're face to face with someone, we go on stage and play a role. The majority of things we do under the eyes of others, but the place where no one sees you, where you come to grips with yourself—this is your deep mountain.

There's no longer any reason to lie to your parents, to your children, to your wife. At the moment when one can no longer lie to others, then one is oneself. You are in the deep mountain when you can no longer lie to yourself and this "self" can no longer deceive you. Daichi Zenji[2] said, "Wherever you may be, when it's no-thought, that's the mountain. No matter where this blue mountain may be, you are at home." This is precisely the sense of the phrase, *"Entering the deep mountain."* This place does not need to be isolated or out of the range of noise. Right in the middle of the Ginza, on the bus, on the train, what does it matter? One comes to grips with oneself and doesn't let go!

Thus, at the University I don't even know the students' names. It matters little to me that the supposed response they give to me may be coming from their substitute. I let it happen. I don't worry about the truth of the signature on the attendance list. They're free to make noise. In fact, though they may fool their professor, they can't fool their classmates. If somebody wants to attract attention, he doesn't deceive his buddies, who will despise him. Just as on the stock exchange, his stock will never be snatched up. On the other hand, someone admired by his peers will take on worth, and this will be increased that much more as the practice of zazen brings him calm and equilibrium.

We should be able to enter the deep mountain no matter where we are, even on a train. The toilet's not the only place we can find isolation and be completely our self. The mountain is everywhere. When one is without birth and without thought, one seeks nothing. There is no longer either joy or sorrow, neither attraction nor repulsion. If things still divide into those that one loves and those that one does not love, it's a village, not the deep mountain.

Under a great pine on a steep peak overhanging the abyss. The image of the cliff evokes height and that of the abyss, depth. Men need both height and depth. So and so is a good speaker, but not deep, while someone else is recognized for his deep views. The bottom of the profound depths shouldn't be visible. Such is the Way of the Buddha, of an infinite height and a depth beyond sounding. It's a magnificent sight to contemplate. It could be the subject of a painting in which to suggest a very high mountain you wreath its summit with light clouds, and to paint a deep valley you fill it with mist. Between the two, you paint a great pine with a master seated at its foot. *Under a great pine on a steep peak overhanging the abyss, I sit tranquilly and without care in my humble abode.* Someone once told me that he had this experience and that he caught a cold. Well, if you go into the mountains like that, it's not so surprising that you come home weeping with an empty stomach. Wherever you are, you should be "under the pines on a steep peak, sitting in tranquility." Such is the dignity that lies beyond description.

A Sole Mission

No noise reaches the person seated in the correct posture where the knees push the floor: *silent retreat, serene simplicity.* Men are always doing something. They behave as if firecrackers were going off on all sides and they don't know where to put themselves. "I don't have the time . . . I'm busy . . . I'm overwhelmed . . ." Their head is full of contradictions and they never take the time to put it in order. Well, the more the world becomes complicated, the more necessary it is to simplify it, to unify it and to rediscover the fundamental unity.

If you ask yourself why you eat or why you drink alcohol, your response is, "Because I want to, that's all." The majority of people don't even know why they act; for this reason their life is incoherent. It's exactly like a lunatic who laughs and cries without knowing why. "I did it because I wanted to . . . I went over there because I wanted to . . ." It's the behavior of a child.

I sit tranquilly and without care in my humble abode, silent retreat, serene simplicity.

Sawaki eats in order to do zazen, shaves his head and wears the okesa to give more strength to zazen. That's all. He practices zazen and makes others practice it. He only possesses simple, indispensable things. All the rest is merely chatter, even if one talks about it for a year or for a century.

Studying texts, some people fall into a depression: "This character signifies this . . . and that one that . . . therefore, this phrase means that . . ." They then speak about wonderful matters which neither I, nor anyone else, understand. They work so much there's no time to do zazen. They no longer eat, filling their stomachs with their studies. They say, "It's not easy to explain *zen*, so it's necessary for us to translate difficult texts." Red-faced with excitement, they pass the night in studying and the day in discussing. All that is useless. There is only one thing to bear in mind: in silence, avoiding all agitation, we must carry out our own unique and simple mission. *I sit tranquilly and without care in my humble abode, silent retreat, serene simplicity.*

After having avenged his lord for an insult, Oishi Yoshi[3] withdrew to Senkakuji temple and declared: "Whatever may be, never a shadow of doubt clouded my purity of intention." The situation required no other outcome but death. Knowing that he must die, he did what he ought to do, in full awareness and singleness of mind, without weighing the risks that he ran or envisaging escaping from them. Those whose mind is full of contradictions live in anguish. Conversely, where thought is unified, everything becomes simple: I have some money? Fine! I have something to eat? Fine! They offer me trophies and medals? Fine! The speeches that accompany them? Fine! Let's accept all this bric-a-brac for what it is.

But, in contrast, there is one thing that is most important, even if everything else in life should disappear, something to which all attention must be given: "peaceful and happy, the monk resides in the silence and serenity of his hermitage". Those who do not find this unity are always unhappy. No one knows why we were born human beings. Parents bring us into the world, we can do nothing about it, and here we are. Just as with the birds, the male gathers food and the female sits on the egg. When the warmth has produced its effect—cheep! cheep!—the little ones fly away. Animals are not completely different from us, we are only a little bit more elaborate. Man is the animal that smokes, nothing more. He would no longer live in anguish if he had a single place to reside in silence and serenity. Let us say that this is the one great cause for which we are born and live.

It's not that Kusunoki Masashige[4] wanted to die when he committed suicide on the field of battle, but in losing the fight he had failed in his obligation to Emperor Go-Daigo. Loyal and upright man, in perfect unity with himself, the only possible avenue was to take his own life. It was exemplary. Masashige will live eternally in the Japanese soul.

33

When we awaken, we understand that merits do not exist.
Everything is different from the conditioned world.

Everyone in the First Row

We have already encountered this meaning at the beginning of the poem: *When we awaken to the Dharma-body, there is nothing.* To awake is to become aware of one's self, of one's true reality. Our supreme mission is to know ourselves. Our objective is to be a true person: *This tranquil man of the Way, who has attained awakening and ceased studying and acting.* This true man, free and independent, walks with an assured step, following the universal order. He knows that seeking to acquire merits represents sterile and useless efforts. His personal mission is not included within the ephemeral nature of conditioned phenomena.

Conditioned reality governs our acts: an action presupposes a profit and a profit supposes an action, just as the place of honor goes to those superior in the hierarchy. Thus we live gambling upon illusory values.

Does sitting in the seat of honor imply that one is more remarkable than someone seated in the last row? We don't know what history will remember in ten thousand years. They also didn't know three hundred years ago. When the warrior Teraoka Heizaemon said: "I earn only one go, but I am a warrior;" this was a true man who didn't seek merits and whose mind was at peace. Had he desired but one more go, he would have made entry into the system of the conditioned. Not being satisfied with one's lot is to run a marathon every day. When one lives peacefully seated and happy, *without care in my humble abode,* one doesn't think So-and-So is outstanding because he gets a high salary or that someone else is a washout because he gets nothing. All men, without exception, sit in the front row: every man is Buddha.

34

A gift motivated by the desire to be reborn in heaven
Is an arrow shot into the empty sky.

To Solely Seek the Way

The preceding verses indicated clearly the conditions of the law of non-acting: *When we awaken, we understand that merits do not exist.* This phrase is absolutely unambiguous: there is no need to seek merit. Hoping to obtain something—gain, profit or advantage—you submit yourself to the law of acting: you love, you don't love, you flee, you pursue. You run after a girl and flee her mother. When you are truly yourself, you will not find yourself in such awkward situations! To be just as one is, this is the law of non-acting. It's certainly not to chant "namu amida butsu . . . namu amida butsu," so as not to fall into hell while gobbling up the neighbor's eggplants. To be just as one is, this is to act without the mind of profit or obtaining, without the ulterior motive of gain, just as the nose is the nose, the eyes are the eyes, the mouth is the mouth, the navel the navel.

The "motivated gift" in the verse is a simplification due to the poetic form of the text, and requires some clarification. Actually, here it concerns the six perfections or virtues embodied by the bodhisattva: giving, precepts, patience, energy, concentration, and wisdom. Since they are inseparable, Yōka Daishi cites only the first, but any perfection carried out with any sort of motive falls into the domain of the law of acting.

"Why do you observe the precepts?"

"Because I don't want to go to hell."

We don't know what will happen after death, but if we must go to hell, once there, we'll be fine. No bad place exists for a mind at peace. It's because we're afraid of hell that we wish to go to paradise. But what do we know about heaven and hell? They are both man's creations, fabrications of his thought that have no absolute value. Man exists within the hazard of circumstances, without knowing where he's going. Such is the human condition.

If, in the name of the Buddha Dharma, someone proposes to take you somewhere for ten thousand yen, you can be sure they're more interested in money than in the Buddha Dharma. Giving that is practiced in the spirit of obtaining something indicates that an action, a practice, or a morality must prove to be useful and efficacious. One keeps accounts. One evaluates the giving, precepts, patience, energy, concentration and wisdom, and then one calculates their profitability. What's more effective? My answer would be to not seek profit. All the sutras ceaselessly repeat this. At the beginning, Shākyamuni himself ran into this difficulty when he practiced asceticism in order to obtain virtue. His efforts failed because he sought a profit. This is why the Scriptures place so much emphasis on this danger.

It's not the Buddha Dharma to break one's back in order to seduce one's beloved or to climb higher in society. If one has the slightest ulterior motive for profit, that's not the Buddha Dharma. Every action, however laughable it may be, becomes great action if it is true, accomplished without the mind of gaining, without thinking of oneself, casting off one's ego. However, most of the time men act only for themselves, in their own interest.

We others, we don't act for money, even if we have nothing to eat. (Perhaps if they offered something else . . .) We will not lose our footing even if dying from hunger, because we are attached neither to money, nor to life nor to death. This does not mean that we renounce life, but that we act disregarding our ego. It's interesting if we focus the eyes of the mountain upon ourselves and our thoughts. The mountain doesn't say to me, "Hey, you down there, Sawaki! You're terrific!" It neither admires nor criticizes me. Dōgen Zenji also said: "The disciple of the Buddha Dharma must work hard at not practicing for himself." He added, "One must not practice the Buddha Dharma with the goal of obtaining advantages from it."

What good is zazen? To this eternal question, I always respond: "Zazen is good for nothing." Of course, those asking that question don't return to do zazen, but it's of no importance, for they will always be good-for-nothings. Dōgen also said, "You must not practice the Buddha Dharma to obtain a miracle." Though we make fun of this sort of thing, since childhood we've been accustomed to reading stories of marvels and we begin to dream: "Wouldn't it be marvelous to return upon this earth completely new?"

The Jataka Tales have transmitted extraordinary parables from Shākyamuni's past lives on the subject of giving. Prince Satta offered his body to feed a hungry tigress and her children. Sessan Doji heard the first half of the verse on impermanence and to learn the other half, he offered his body to feed a monster so that it would be able to recite the verse. The verse is:

> All conditioned things are impermanent.
> These are the dharma of arising and perishing.
> When both arising and perishing perish,
> That tranquil extinction is called nirvana.

Aren't these marvelous stories? These persons seek the Way so ardently that they abandon their own bodies, not clinging to life, seeking nothing other than the Way.

When Prince Fuse entered the mountain, he had abandoned everything: wife, children, treasures, and his elevated rank. He renounced all, not because he wished to obtain something, but because he had quite simply become aware of his true nature. Unless it is unattached to material gain, the practice cannot be called Buddha Dharma.

The Circle of the Six Paths

We reject barbarity, desiring to raise ourselves toward culture and civilization. To work for progress is a motivated gift. The six paths, or six destinies, are the six degrees of the progression of the human condition, namely, hell, greed, animality, the state of anger, the human state, and temporary bliss. Below, there exists a gross and rough magma and above, a domain of pure clarity, but these two extremes are outside the norm and do not belong to the world in which the wheel of life turns.

The lower level is, for example, that of the young child who paddles barefoot in the mud without thinking of harm, or walks on the tatami with his shoes covered with dirt. In this, he's close to the cat, but as he grows up such behavior is no longer permitted and he is scolded. We always have a desire to educate, to police manners. We always want to improve our window-dressing, because we believe in the principle of civilization.

When we give, it's not without ulterior motive. It's said that one seed multiplies itself by ten thousand so that a millet seed yields many hundreds of seeds and thus to give yourself pain now will later be rewarded a hundredfold. This is to give with an ulterior motive. In repressing barbarism and progressing toward a more civilized world, one raises oneself to a superior level. We wish to flee the suffering of the hell state, with its insatiable desires and bestiality and to live in an ideal world, magnificently pure. We say to the poor: "Work! Work!

You'll get to be someone, you'll know pleasure, and eat well." So he works and breaks his back to build savings. The community grows richer and no one's left to pull the weeds that invade the fields and rice paddies. What to do?

Just as the eyes are the eyes, the mouth is the mouth and the navel the navel, so must a farmer be a true farmer and the accountant a true accountant, the municipal collection agent handle the receipts and expenses and the secretary take care of correspondence.

Civilization goes round in a circle and leads to dead ends, just like a poor man who wants to enjoy the hot springs every year. He amasses a bit of money, penny by penny, with cracks gashed in his hands by his work. He goes off to the waters, but however great his pleasure may be, it doesn't last and the money runs out. He must go home and pick up his work again, and once more he breaks his back in order to go again the following year.

This is the problem with self-interested giving. We accept giving ourselves some trouble on the condition that we'll be recompensed for our efforts. We estimate that observing the precepts is well rewarded. Patience and zazen also give good results. We evaluate the best return for gaining paradise and endure what's painful in order to obtain our objective. But in time the money runs out, the vacation is over and we come back home. Exactly like a balloon that, although well filled at take off, doesn't climb into the atmosphere indefinitely. The moment always comes when it softens and falls back down. Or, again, an arrow shot into the sky that mounts to the limit of its momentum and finally falls back to earth. *A gift motivated by the desire to be reborn in heaven is an arrow shot into the empty sky.* The gift given conditionally is an investment in a future happiness, but like the arrow, it falls back to the ground.

35

Its force spent, it falls back to earth,
At risk of provoking an undesirable rebirth.

The Merit of the Gift

Many people confuse the Buddha Dharma with moral teachings. The
Buddha Dharma and its practice are unlimited. By wishing to obtain
a benefit from our practice, we assign a limit to it and therefore it's
no longer the Buddha Dharma. They say that men are eager to climb
and reluctant to descend. They love that which is high, they do not
love that which is low. Yet even when you recite namu amida butsu
you must do it without a goal, without desiring a superior rebirth,
without fearing an inferior rebirth, just as it is illusory to practice
zazen with the goal of obtaining something or avoiding something.

The merit of the gift is illustrated by an interesting parable in
the *Maka Kashōdo hinnyo-gyō.* The venerable Kāshyapa [1] had come
to teach the Buddha Dharma before a gathering of the poor. He
explained to them the principle of poverty thus: "You are poor because you were miserly in a previous life, and your poverty is all the
more great because you felt envy." The venerable Ananda taught the
Dharma to the rich and explained to them that their wealth was the
fruit of a virtuous previous life and in order not to lose it they ought
to practice charity.

Kāshyapa scanned the assembly and directed himself toward the
poorest to beg. When one has business with the poor and is oneself in
a more elevated position, the alms don't amount to much. He looked
to the right, to the left, searching for the poorest among the poor. The
poor, nothing but the poor, they were all so poor! Finally, he spied a
wrinkled, half-dead old woman. She was covered with filth, without

a scrap of cloth on her body. The old woman's naked body wasn't beautiful to look at and her heart barely beat.

Kāshyapa stopped before the old woman. "Divine master . . ." she said to him. Never in a hundred million kalpas had she felt such emotion, and the thought came to her that had she been a concubine or something of that sort, she would have loved to make him an offering. Kāshyapa, who possessed supernatural powers, understood this woman's feeling exactly. He decided to activate his magic powers: he stepped on the gas and whup! he was right next to her. The old woman was transported with joy. Once again he stepped on the gas and suddenly melted into the air. He somersaulted like a leaf, doing loop the loops. Flames and water spurted from his body, a very sophisticated technique called "fire-above-water-below." He plunged toward the earth and landed right in front of the old woman.

Before this unimaginable spectacle, she was in ecstasy as though touched by grace. Plunged into bliss, she was overwhelmed with gratitude. At this moment, Kāshyapa again stepped on the gas and asked her, "Well, grandma, aren't you going to make me an offering?" The old woman was so moved it took her breath away. "I'd like very much to make you an offering, but as you can see, I've not even a scrap of cloth to cover myself, nor a grain of rice to eat." Beside her in a chipped bowl was a rice gruel that stank of sourness and in which insects floated. Seeing the bowl, Kāshyapa said to her: "Why don't you offer me this bowl of soup?" "You would accept such miserable food?" "Of course I accept it," he answered.

With trembling hands she presented her bowl to him. The Venerable One received the offering, asking himself what he ought to do. "If I take it away with me, she'll think that I've thrown it away along the roadside and will feel humiliated. Very well then, bottoms up!"

And before the old woman's eyes he drank it off at one go. "I'm infinitely grateful to you," he said to her, and at that instant she rendered up her life.

At exactly the same instant, a princess was born in the Kingdom of the Skies. In the celestial world, birth happens without pain. One is born like an apparition. Suddenly, a supernatural form glowed in a ray of light and scented the air with fine perfumes. The vassals who saw it queried one another about her lineage: "I wonder who her parents are?" "She is certainly of high birth." They directed their second sight toward the heights, but saw nothing. "Then she must be run of the mill." They lowered their glance toward the horizon line, with no more success. "Perhaps she might be an aristocrat from the world of men?" So they plunged into the world of men and turned up nothing. "Might she be a commoner?" Still nothing. "How! Could she issue from the lowest strata of society?" Exactly so. They discovered that she was born of an old woman who had only filth for covering. Then the celestial vassals escorted the princess to earth and brought her to follow the teachings of Shākyamuni.

Only the disinterested offering has merit. One has the impression that the spirit of profit is more developed in China than in Japan. For example, in Japan they inscribe only the sum of money among the records of subscription at a temple, whereas in China the name of the head of State, the sum of money, and the name of the subscriber are indicated. Let's say that's a gift that calls for remuneration. The merit of the Buddha Dharma is to practice without goal, without a gaining mind. One is truly disinterested.

A monk said to Sōchō[2]: "The clear and serene moon shines so high in the sky!" Sōchō responded: "Because you are very far below her." The monk said, "I beg you, help me raise myself toward her."

"Why do you wish to attain her? Doesn't she come to you?" To make efforts in a spirit of gain, no matter how intense they may be, is like wishing to climb to the moon by scrambling up a rope. It's essential to understand that one must accept oneself, here and now, just as one is, without seeking anything. If you don't grasp this in your guts, you don't enter into the Buddha Dharma. In consequence, as the poem says, "He who flees the "here" to find the "elsewhere" brews tomorrows without repose." Elsewhere does not exist.

36

How can this compare with the gate of unconditioned reality
That one clears at a leap, entering the land of the Buddha?

The Measure of a Man

The unconditioned is that which is not born and does not perish. The conditioned is the perishable, the ephemeral world of phenomena.

I remember a snatch of a story about a beggar that I read as a child: "I cried to him, 'Go away! Go away!' But the more I drove him away, the more he harried me. I turned around ready to give in to him, and I discovered that he had disappeared." There is a beggar within us when during zazen we think:" Satori . . . satori . . . for pity's sake . . . satori . . ." Or when we stick our hands out right and left: "Paradise . . . namu amida butsu . . . give me paradise . . . namu amida butsu . . ." We know in our depths that it's wrong, but the more we drive away the thought, the more it obsesses us. The beggar lies in wait, crouched in the shadows before the gate of the unconditioned.

This is also expressed by the poem Iroha[1]: "Once past the high mountain of this ephemeral world, there are no longer intoxicating dreams." Or, again, Dōgen in Fukanzazengi: "Stop all movements of the conscious mind, cease the functioning of your intelligence, abandon the idea of becoming Buddha."

From the moment when mental activity ceases, one enters at a leap into the world of the Buddha. Zen monks boast of their method, thinking it to be of unparalleled efficacy: "With us, you enter into the world of the Buddha with a single leap." But this manner of thinking in terms of profit is totally ineffectual.

The expression "the world of the Buddha" is difficult to understand, but if one replaces the word "Buddha" with "thief," everything becomes clear. For example, let's suppose Sawaki wants to become a thief. He can put years into preparing himself or realize his objective in an instant. He goes to the supermarket and with a swipe of his sleeve filches an object that disappears into his pocket. A clerk sees him, challenges him, and telephones the manager. A frightened little old man appears and orders him to follow him to the office. He empties his pockets, and in a tick of the second hand it's done. They take him to the jail and boom! the door closes on him. Sawaki has become a thief: in an instant he entered the world of thieves.

There's no need to break your bones to become a thief, and still less so to become Buddha. It's not useful to progressively pass through the fifty-two stages of the bodhisattva path. It's not a question of time or effort. If at a precise moment one does something in unity with Buddha, then one is Buddha. Dōgen said it clearly in the Zanmai o zanmai chapter of Shōbōgenzō: "Zazen instantly transcends this world, making us penetrate into the secret of the patriarchs and become Buddha. In transcending the erroneous and heretical practices, we enter into the dwelling place of the Buddha. Zazen alone permits us to attain the perfect enlightenment of the Buddha, without doing anything else. We must be very aware of the fact that there is a great difference between zazen and other practices, and understand well that it is by the proper practice of zazen that Buddha entered nirvana."

The man who gets drunk and the man who does zazen belong to two different worlds. When one enters at a bound into the world of true reality, one becomes the true man of non-acting. If I reference again the mental picture of Sawaki and the thief, we notice that it's one and same man in question: he is Sawaki, then he is the thief. The ordinary man and Buddha are not two entities separated by a space. They make one and are of the same dimension. This dimension is that of man, of infinite space, and of eternity. I would estimate mine to be, in terms of time, three hundred great kalpas, and in distance, a thousand billion kilometers, but this remains very approximate.

Tettsu Zenji[2] wrote this poem about his portrait: "Each one is born with a different karma, but I've never doubted that I was Buddha. Up until this day, we've lived together without knowing our mutual face and today I no longer know which is the one and which is the other."

"Each one is born with a different karma" signifies that each human creature is a being differing in his face, his character, his destiny and even his longevity. From every point of view, each one of us is different. We are the fruits of a long succession of antecedents: food, climate, mode of life, over-nourishment, under-nourishment. Some exercise and are careful about their health, others neglect it. All these factors differentiate individuals.

Someone said to me, "You're busy, aren't you, now that you've come to Tokyo from the countryside?" Actually, sometimes I'm so busy I don't have time to use the toilet or cut my nails, a condition that sometimes continues for a few days. I go through such a situation using my entire brain, mouth and hands, enduring it only because I built up my physique when young. All these things also make the difference among individuals. No man is identical to another and cannot be imitated. If each being is unique, each being must grasp itself firmly and not let go.

"I have never doubted that I was Buddha." To put it another way: we cohabit with ourselves: the ordinary man Sawaki cohabits with the Buddha Sawaki. "Today I no longer know which is the one and which is the other." This is to say that together we make no more than "one." Such is the practice of the Way of the Buddha: today it is I whom I encounter.

37

Seize the root, don't worry about the branches,
Just like the transparent jewel swallowed up by the light of the moon.

The Mind of the Way

This is the most important verse in *Shōdōka*. An old adage says: " In the age of the last Dharma, people do not seek true reality, but desire the divine powers." True reality is the essence and the original source, while divine powers are merits. We like the merits and dislike the essence. We love to receive a salary, we don't love work; we love the reward, we don't love the effort. Nevertheless, the main thing is true reality. The divine powers are only appendages. *Seize the root, don't worry about the branches.* We must seek the truth without worrying about divine powers. Let us seize the essence of things; the rest is secondary and unimportant. When we have an accurate and panoramic view of our nature, what does it matter whether others criticize or admire us? Still, the majority of people seek only praise.

It is written in Dōgen's Gakudōyōjinshū: "They throw out the root and run after the leaves . . . When something enjoys people's favor they practice it, even while knowing that it is contrary to the

Way. They abstain from practicing what is neither praised nor renowned, when they know it is the true Way. What sadness!" Later on, he explains the reason for this: "Some are taught to seek awakening outside of the mind, others to be reborn in another land. Such doctrines are sources of error and confusion, they are responsible for wrong thoughts. Suppose that someone gives you a good medicine and doesn't show you how to use it, the illness that you contract will be worse than if you had taken poison. In our country, it seems that since ancient times there haven't been good doctors capable of giving good medicines nor anyone to verify their effects. It is already so difficult to eliminate the sufferings and diseases of life, and we would wish to escape from the pains of old age and death! All that is the fault of the masters and not that of the disciples."

Only the mind of the Way is important. Whether or not the theoretical doctrine is of great depth doesn't enter into consideration! *Seize the root, don't worry about the branches.* Go directly to the mind of the Way. The rest is secondary. Without dwelling upon appearances or seeking profit, question yourself about the rightness of your own practice, and if it's perfectly correct, the fact that others criticize you or heap you with praise is without importance. This verse contains the essence of *Shōdōka*.

A Total View of the Pure Truth

Just like the transparent jewel swallows the light of the moon. This image symbolizes the one who seizes the root without worrying about the branches. Traveling back upstream within the poem, we reach the passage: *the gate of unconditioned reality that one clears at a leap, entering the land of the Buddha . . . the three bodies and four wisdoms are perfected in their body . . .* and we arrive at the source: *This tranquil man of the Way, who has attained awakening and ceased studying and acting.*

What then is this transparent jewel whose breadth, height, and depth are without limit, within which the past, the present and the future transpire? The *zen* of the Buddha, of course. This pure jewel is our original body, our essence, the target of our quest.

For the Zen disciple, Ko and Kan[1] are six of one and half a dozen of the other. When Ko-the-barbarian arrives, it's Ko. When Kan-the-civilized arrives, it's Kan. The disciple welcomes beauty just like ugliness, just as a mirror reflects the object before it with no intervening value judgment. For the mirror, beauty is not beauty, ugliness is not ugliness. "There are dwellings the ray of the moon does not reach, but it illumines the heart of the man who receives it," says the poem. It is man's discriminations that stain the jewel. If we reflect for a moment on all our prejudices and value judgments about good and evil, our preferences and aversions, we perceive that fundamentally they have no intrinsic existence and are illusions.

In the *Daijō kishin-ron*[2] the pure jewel signifies the essence of mind, the true reality. Each individual sees reality differently, according to his abilities and his disposition. Ask people about the apparent diameter of the sun and one will respond: "About five hands' breadth," and the other, "let's say a foot." According to his imagination, he will see a kilometer as easily as a league. He could also very well answer, "No, since it enters my eye, it equals a millimeter." Because of our senses we have an erroneous view of reality. The sutra tells us: "The original body of the true Dharma is neither produced nor destroyed. It manifests itself thanks to the power of the vows of great compassion. In our original mind there is neither coming nor going, whereas in our illusory body all is production and destruction."

Just like the transparent jewel swallows the light of the moon. We understand this phrase with our intellect, but not in the depths of our heart. Mental constructions cloud the transparence of the crystal, just as tinted glasses intercept the rays of the sun. The goal of our practice is to clean the jewel, to restore its original purity and transparency so that its tone, colorless and transparent, when placed on a green cloth radiates green, on a red cloth red, and on a white cloth white. In truth, this crystal, though colorless and without stain, always appears different.

Shigetsu Zenji[3] wrote: "When the sea is agitated it's difficult to recover a gem from the depths of the water." If our mind is disturbed by the waves of illusion, we will not recover true reality. It is the role of religion to show us the existence of this eternal transparency.

A poem says: "When my mind is at peace, everything around is tranquil. The day stretches out with the innocence of a little child. The calm of the mountain resembles the ancient days." To stretch the day gives a sense to life and makes us happy. The length of the day is of variable dimension. There are men of short days and men of long days. Some, although on a tight schedule all year long, realize a balance sheet of very positive activity. Others have no time for leisure and complain that the days are too short, yet when one looks at what they garnered over the preceding year, there's nothing there.

In April of 1937, the aviator Iinuma took four days and four nights to reach London at the controls of his airplane, Kamikaze, and he notes in his memoirs that these four days and nights seemed to him longer than the twenty or so years since his birth. His impressions are very interesting and there's no doubt that, despite the ordeal, each moment was rich with substance.

To stretch out time is happiness, and time is extraordinarily long when one does zazen, while an hour, two hours, or even the entire night passed in chatting and drinking with friends are nothing. When the day stretches out like a little child, it's because it's filled with very rich content.

They say that during zazen illusions abound in the consciousness, but, in fact, these are not illusions. It's our mind's contents that are manifesting, and we have every reason to be astonished. "That's me! How insignificant!" There are all sorts of things within us, the devil and Buddha, lust and bestiality; in truth our substance is very rich. There's no notion of time and space. There is paradise and hell. Just as the light of the moon penetrates the transparent jewel, we are perfectly reflected in the mirror of our mind. Our mind contains billions of thoughts and not merely three thousand as the texts say. Like a kaleidoscope, the mind produces infinite combinations of images. In the peace of zazen, one realizes that all the Buddhist philosophies, whether Tendai[4] with its three thousand thoughts or Kusha[5] with its seventy-five categories, are incapable of drawing up a list of the contents of the mind. The psychic phenomena are infinite.

To Embrace Contradictions

Man attaches too much importance to intelligence. He thinks it's essential to know why fire is hot. It's trivial and pointless to talk about it. What's important is to understand how one makes use of it. For example, if you say, "Give me a light!" because you want to smoke a cigarette, and somebody hands you a torch, it would be inappropriate. On the other hand, if you are an arsonist it would be completely welcome. If it's cold and you say, "Give me some fire!", you wait for someone to bring you a kotatsu[6] full of hot charcoal, but if they give you a torch when you'd greatly prefer charcoal in the kotatsu, you'd be very annoyed. Thus, a single expression assumes all sorts of meanings according to the context, and the manner in which one uses fire is always different. Everything is always new. The *zen* of Buddha is to look at the world with completely new eyes, with the innocence and amazement of a child.

Seated in zazen posture, we exhibit the calm of the mountain in ancient days. Zazen is the fundamental and eternal posture that, without discontinuity, traverses past, present, and future. It has not changed since Shākyamuni. The day stretching out like a little child is eternally new, and in the peace of the mountain you become the eternal figure of the past. Seated simply, you become a Buddha living just as *the transparent jewel swallows the light of the moon.* This single phrase contains the essence of Buddhism.

The dualism of the eternally new and the eternally ancient does not lead to an impasse. In the pure jewel there is not on one side the infinitely large and on the other the infinitely small. The jewel embraces all without distinction, both macrocosm and microcosm, just like a tiny drop of dew reflects the moon. It has been said previously that when one awakens to the *zen* of the Buddha "the three bodies and four knowledges" are realized and harmonize fully within the body. Thanks to them, beliefs in the fall of man into hell or in the Buddha coming to save all men are no longer contradictions. Whatever one does, one cannot cut off illusions. If you wished to eliminate them you wouldn't be able to do it, you would remain hemmed in by an impasse. That is to say, one cannot limit that which is without limit. Since the transparent jewel takes in everything, within it there is no longer the slightest contradiction.

There is an enormous contradiction between the law of impermanence that rules the ephemeral world of phenomena and the law of causality that links things in the long term. But *the tranquil man who has attained awakening and ceased studying and acting* embraces this contradiction in the spirit of zazen, which transcends the rational, just like the *transparent jewel swallows the light of the moon.*

The ephemeral world of phenomena is a process of production and destruction. What was there before is no longer there now, and what is there now is not what will be there. That which was yesterday is no longer that which is today. The dinner you ate yesterday is today's bowel movement. The Zen master Nishiari Bokusan Zenji said one day to Professor Murakami Senjō[7]: "Your urine stinks." It appears that the latter took this badly. It's the law of causality within time that the smell of urine varies according to the food you eat. It is inescapable that if you stuff yourself with beef and onions, even in secret, that your urine will smell bad the next day. As a result, today is the continuation of yesterday and tomorrow the continuation of today. This year is the continuation of last year and next year will be the continuation of this year. And yet, according to the law of impermanence, everything is eternally new. When one embraces these contradictions smoothly, one passes through the gate of the unconditioned and enters at a leap into the world of the Buddha.

38

I know now that this wish-fulfilling jewel
Is an inexhaustible treasure for myself and for others.

The moon shines on the river, the wind plays in the pines.
Pure twilight of a long night, why all this?

The Riposte of Egoism

I know now that this wish-fulfilling jewel . . . he's not understood with his intelligence, he's awakened to the true reality that does not lead to an impasse. He has become "the bodhisattva who knows true freedom" as it says in the *Hannya shingyō.*[1]

We corner ourselves in blind alleys at every turn. The rich enclose themselves in the cul-de-sac of money, and the poor in that of frustration. We stuff ourselves with a delicacy until we make ourselves sick, and complain if it's a bit tasteless. Man is the prisoner of his karma. It's the nature of the human condition. In liberating ourselves from what binds us, we discover an open and unlimited space. It is written: " The sage has no ego. For him, everything is ego." Having no ego, he is the sky and the earth, the entire universe. There's not him and others: he is the others and the others are he. You are me and I am you.

Musō Kokushi[2] wrote this poem: " Throw away this tiny little thing called 'me.' Then the three thousand worlds are your self." When you use the toilet, you place yourself in the position of the person whose job it is to clean it, or in the bath in the position of the person who will come after you. When you take in a friend for the night, you feel what you'd feel if you were the one being received, and if someone offers you a meal you put yourself in the place of your host.

If you apply this principle to commerce, you necessarily attract clients and business prospers. The buyer identifies with the seller and the seller with the buyer. It's disgraceful for a client to be welcomed with a hostile look when he comes into a store and also unacceptable that the client carelessly rummage through things and soil them to the point of rendering them unsalable under the pretext that they're not what he wants.

In actuality, today the seller doesn't identify with the client or the client with the seller, which is why we live in a paradise of tricksters. They fix up goods of no worth so that they appear worth something, such as suspending crackers on the second level of the box so it appears full. You're touched by the generosity of someone who gives you an enormous box of cakes, but when you open it—oh deception!—it's full of emptiness.

Let us offer by putting ourselves in the position of the person who receives, and receive with the sentiment of the person who offers. Then we will live in a world that lights up in all directions. When we identify with others, we discover that our ego is everywhere, that it fills the universe. The husband is in total union with his wife and the wife with her husband, parents with their children, and friends and neighbors interpenetrate reciprocally, and on and on. When you are at the bedside of your feverish child, placing a packet of ice on her forehead, your neighbor across the way refrains from playing the trumpet. Likewise, you don't turn your radio up loud at the hour when your neighbor goes to bed. When you put yourself in the place of another, your light shines throughout the universe, illuminates the entire past, and is resplendent in the present moment.

Our behavior in daily life, in each moment of the day, reflects upon our antecedents. If we tarnish the present moment, darkening it, we tarnish all those who up to the present moment have given to us, nourished and educated us. On the other hand, if our attitude today is true and worthy, all those who have contributed to making us what we are also are true and worthy. Our light illuminates both past and present. Though it seems strange, in truth the ego carried to its zenith becomes universal. All, absolutely everything in the universe, becomes oneself.

At the end of the Meiji era there was a popular expression: "science overcomes nature." Some decades later we no longer speak of anything except "nature's counterattack." If you consider civilization to be a means of subduing nature, you've got to expect a riposte on the part of nature. Numerous examples also prove that when one acts thinking solely of self, there is a return shock whose injuries we suffer, and we do wrong to our self.

If our "me" is not to receive a riposte, it must live in symbiosis with the sky and the earth. If you think that money makes happiness and in consequence spend your life economizing for your children, you will make prodigal sons of them, and the repercussion will come when they have to go to work. I think it's not necessary to stockpile either money or belongings for our children.

I have long reflected on the problem of poverty. If parents leave their children without money, they will have to endure a terrible ordeal, yet there is no better school for forming courageous and independent men. I have a small head but strong legs—I could be a mailman; all that I possess is my voice—why shouldn't I be a street hawker?

The Other Is Oneself

To reach this furthest extent of "oneself" that is "the other," it's sufficient to not think of self and to live solely for others. An egoistic act sets in motion a reaction, but so does a generous act.

In the village of Takegahana in the province of Mino, there was a tradesman named Hotoke[3] no Sakichi. He believed in the principle of the reciprocity of actions. The practice of Mr. Hotoke (Buddha) was to buy high and sell cheap, but the same principle applied to his clientele, who had to buy at the highest price. This is the reason that in that area he was nicknamed Mr. Buddha. He didn't use a scale to weigh things. He had never even owned instruments for measuring. It was thus that he made his business prosper, even as he sheltered his clients from punishment.

One day his mother told him that she'd like to sell some rice cakes that she'd made. Sakichi responded that their business brought in enough to live on, but if she simply wished the pleasure of selling them, she should come herself to the shop to sell them. He said to himself that the profit wouldn't be very much and so the price to pay in return wouldn't amount to much. In order not to infringe on the business of the rice cake seller at the corner of the street, his mother saw to it that her rice cakes were unsalable. They were plain and unappetizing and, on top of that, expensive. All conditions were fulfilled so that they wouldn't sell. It was a success. Sakichi decided to set up a rice cake counter in his store. It was the tiniest counter imaginable, the cakes were worthless, they were expensive, and he didn't try to sell them.

The seller at the corner sold less and less and Sakichi's mother more and more. Sakichi calculated that the rice cake counter brought in too much and that he had no reason to make so much profit. He took the money, went to his neighbor, apologized and explained that he'd set the money aside to compensate his neighbor for the damage he'd caused.

The rice cake seller emphatically did not put himself in Sakichi's place. He was so outraged that he told Sakichi he was nothing but a Buddha turd who'd made him lose all his clients. And now he was bankrupt, even though his cakes were large, delicious and inexpensive, while Sakichi's were worthless and expensive. It was unfair, since he was his family's sole support.

Sakichi answered: "You're right. That's why I've come to compensate you. I thought about it every day and wondered: should I go today? Or tomorrow morning ? I truly apologize." The merchant, who was brandishing his fist to punch Sakichi, suddenly discouraged, let it drop and said: "No, that doesn't settle it . . . " "But yes, yes, I beg you to take this money, " insisted Sakichi. The merchant was ashamed and rushed off, with Sakichi, money in hand, in hot pursuit.

Sakichi always comported himself in this fashion even when faced with a thief. One year, it being New Year's eve, he had just collected a debt, and as he passed the frontier of Hida Province, a highwayman leapt upon him, shouting:" Your purse or your life!" Sakichi answered, "Here, take it. Even though it's the last day of the year and I don't carry back much money to the house, I have enough to live on. Well? Take it . . . go ahead. And, you know, your clothes look very thin to me. Take this as well, " he said, taking off his fur-lined kimono. The thunder-struck thief looked more closely at him. "You remind me of someone. You wouldn't by any chance be the Buddha of Takegahana? They say that if you steal from the Buddha you get yourself brought down by his allies. I give it all back," and, so saying, he fled. Sakichi pursued him, shouting, "No, no, since I'm giving them to you . . . ," but the ruffian ran so fast that Sakichi couldn't catch him.

Sakichi didn't do things by halves. He broke all records when he built a chapel in honor of the five hundred disciples of the Buddha and put in seven hundred disciples. The village also became celebrated for a bridge that he had constructed without even putting his name on it. So that he could care for his mother he never married. His sister did the same. Both remained celibate to eliminate obstacles to the practice of filial piety. On his eightieth birthday, he received a commendation from the lord of the province, and on this occasion he wrote a poem: "I had the good fortune to come into this ephemeral world, I have lived without ever experiencing the slightest dissatisfaction." He didn't have an education and lived solely for others for more than eighty years. He was easy to approach, always happy. He didn't live on the defensive, showing his teeth with sword in hand ready to massacre the one who approached him. In fact, one felt him to be relaxed and at ease. It was in spending thirty, fifty years of his life utilizing the *"inexhaustible treasure for myself and for others"* that he experienced this feeling of serenity, of calm, and of peace. The highest degree of our self is the other, and the highest degree of the other is our self. It's truly a strange mystery. They call it *the wish-fulfilling jewel* or *the precious pearl.*

This *inexhaustible treasure for myself and for others,* magic pearl, precious stone or transparent jewel, is also expressed in the exquisitely beautiful phrase: *The moon shines on the river, the wind plays in the pines, pure twilight of a long night, why all this?* The moon shines in the clear sky, the cool wind sings a strange song in the pines. I feel sorry for those people who think that our world is hard and without pity and that we must choose the lesser of two evils. They distrust everyone and lived obsessed with the fear that someone will steal their purse.

39

Buddha nature, jewel of the precepts, is inscribed in the depths
    of our being.
Drizzles and dew, mists and clouds, clothe our body.

The Triple Training: Precepts, Concentration and Wisdom

Buddha nature, like a pure crystal without obstruction, becomes ours when it is inscribed in the depths of our being.

But what does this "jewel of the precepts" mean? We find this term in the phrase "to take refuge," i.e., take the precepts, where it is a synonym for ordination. The precepts[1] are the form under which Buddhism manifests itself, the correct form taken by buddha nature, the form of the pure Dharma that has been neither deformed nor altered.

Concentration is the peaceful place where one lives without effort in true reality. True reality is not confined in a box and is not a fabricated object. Just as the nose resides below the eyes and the mouth below the nose, true reality is things' mode of being, just as they are.

Wisdom is the lucidity that permits the true to be distinguished from the false. Precepts, concentration, and wisdom constitute the "triple training." Buddhism is the usual path for practicing them. This triple training allows us to see the Buddha in his three dimensions. A man appears extremely different depending on the angle from which you observe him.

Take myself as an example. Perhaps I wouldn't go so far as to say that I seem to be a pink confection in my parents' eyes, but nevertheless I am completely adorable. If I had children, they'd see me as a father; and grandchildren a grandfather, all the while being a father-in-law to my son-in-law. If I intoned pleas like a beggar, no doubt I'd be seen as a beggar. The same person appears under different aspects. To see the buddha nature from all its angles is to see a single, same thing from diverse angles.

What do the precepts consist of? It's really difficult to make a rigorous analysis of them and, frankly, it annoys me to appear a tiresome scholar, since that's not my style. So I'm going to try to simplify things by dividing them into two groups: the basic precepts and the particular precepts.

The basic precepts are received by all groups of people: lay/monks, men/women, young/old. In addition to these, the particular precepts are restricted to certain groups, such as only lay people, only novices, or only male or female home-leavers.

The five basic precepts[2]
1. Not killing
2. Not stealing
3. Not having illicit sexual relations
4. Not lying
5. Not drinking alcohol

The eight precepts leading to purification[3]

The five fundamental precepts above, plus:

> 6. Not using elevated seats
> 7. Not adorning oneself with flowers, hair ornaments, necklaces
> 8. Abstaining from songs, dances, spectacles, music

The ten precepts (novices)

The eight precepts above, plus:

> 9. Not receiving money or objects of value
> 10. Abstaining from taking food outside of the prescribed hours.

The full Vinaya precepts are the precepts for bhiksu and bhiksuni. There are 250 precepts for the bhiksu and 348 precepts for the bhiksuni. The rules are identical, though the number differs according to sex, because physiologically women have more constraints than men. For example, they can't urinate standing up, and they have babies whereas men do not. In our times, there are also men who wear makeup, but they are less careful about it than women. On the whole, the life of a woman is more complicated than that of a man. It's because she is a precision instrument whose handling requires more care that it's necessary for her to observe a hundred more rules than men.

Given that a man's a man and a woman's a woman, each has his/her rules. These bhiksu and bhiksuni precepts in the Vinaya are examples of particular precepts, while the ten precepts received by all, regardless of gender, are basic precepts.

Next come the three treasures[4] (or three refuges)

> I take refuge in the Buddha
> I take refuge in the Law (Dharma)
> I take refuge in the Community (Sangha)

The three pure precepts[5]

To not violate the precepts

To do good

To save all living beings.

The ten Bodhisattva precepts[6]

Four basic precepts, plus:

5. Not selling alcohol

6. Not to speak ill of others

7. Not to praise one's own merits or denigrate others

8. Not to be greedy or dishonest

9. Not to allow oneself to be angry

10. Not to speak ill of the Three Treasures

Concerning the basic rules, the sixth patriarch of the Tendai School remarked: "There are no small or great precepts, their usage depends upon the person who receives them." In our current mode of speaking we'd say that they are a function of the competence of their user.

In very ancient times, there was a very rich man named Hōgen. One day the Buddha said to him, "You ought not to take what does not belong to you." The phrase was engraved on his mind and he couldn't stop thinking about it: "I ought not to take what does not belong to me, but what belongs to me? I don't know!" He reflected at length on the question: "Is my purse mine? Is it the money that's mine? If they belonged to me, they would be fixed in nature and no change would occur. But the purse that was full yesterday is empty today, so there has been displacement and movement. Formerly, I was rich. I had a residence, granaries, goods. Today I am a monk. I no longer have anything. I conclude from this that nothing is mine by nature. Before, I had wife, children, parents, servants, and now that

I've entered into religion I no longer do. Thus they don't belong to me. " He asked himself if his three kesa and bowl were really his.

There are three kinds of kesa, the five-row kesa, the seven-row and the great kesa. The kesa serves as both ceremonial vestment and work garment. It is sufficient unto itself. The bowl is a begging bowl, though it also has other uses. It is called ho in Sanskrit, and is made of iron or pottery. One uses it for door-to-door begging for food. The kesa is also called funzō-e, "gathered from refuse." It is made from pieces of cloth thrown on the trash heap as unusable due to mildew, having been chewed by mice, burned or other similar reasons. These rags are gathered and the useful scraps sewn together. This is how one makes a true kesa. But this absolutely does not mean that it was soiled by the refuse. One simply utilizes what has been thrown in the trash. I always repeat that to create a kesa from rags is to actualize the true buddha nature of the cloth, because one really brings a dead fabric back to life.

The kesa is made from rags like an apron made from sacking, but you don't wear it like an apron. Become the kesa, it's a symbol and no longer a mere assemblage of pieces of cloth. If you want to wear fancy silk, you'll just have to give up the idea, otherwise your garment will look like it's been hung up for display. The same goes for food. You can't say, "Today I want this or that." You must eat what's been placed in your bowl. Someone said, "A monk's mouth is like an oven." An oven doesn't know what will be put into it. We think that the kesa and bowl are ours, yet they belong to us no more than the things we eat or wear.

Admitting that the kesa and bowl don't belong to us, we could still think that our naked body is the sole thing remaining ours. However, the naked body is not ours either. Man is like a film that unspools, a sequence of uninterrupted images. He's a baby and, suddenly, there he is with the emaciated visage of an old saint of antiquity. His skin is wrinkled and he can't even iron it; he wears dentures, his hands and feet are dead branches, his head crowned with snow. This naked body does not belong to us.

A beautiful woman? What's a beautiful woman? One's never seen a beautiful woman of eighty years! All girls are beautiful at eighteen, for the space of an instant. Even if at twenty or thirty they can still create the illusion, when they reach seventy or eighty nothing remains of the beauty of years gone by. A sumo wrestler also flourishes for the space of an instant, but arrived at seventy or eighty, where's his strength? Paralyzed or diabetic, he flaps his wings. And yet a person who has bad circulation thinks his blood belongs to him.

Nothing belongs to us. We are part of a chain of conditioned production. We flow like the water of a river. A succession of "I" flows by at the whim of the current. Nothing belongs to us in and of itself. The milieu, the environment, the climate, the customs and all sorts of factors create a situation within which we are perpetually in motion.

Conditioned Production

Once, when I was thirty, someone asked me if I was approaching seventy. At the time, I ate badly, I studied like a madman, I lacked sleep, I was neurasthenic, and my face was creased by the wrinkles of malnutrition. No wonder I resembled a septuagenarian. Comparatively speaking, I must therefore now be about a hundred to a hundred fifty, though no one has yet interrogated me on the matter. We are a conditioned product, which is why we change in step with our nourishment. Someone who resembled a dried up turnip would recover his sparkle if he filled his stomach with good portions of rice and roasted barley. He would rejuvenate. Thus, I who at thirty appeared to be seventy, now that I'm sixty-six don't appear to be a day over seventy.

If the body changes, ages, or rejuvenates as a result of nourishment, it's because we are the product of conditioning, and it's proof that our body is dependent and not something we possess in and of itself.

Hōgen then asked himself if the sole thing he possessed was spiritual. Does this spiritual "thing" exist forever? Absolutely not. If we had an immutable "I" that transcended all changes, education would be useless. It's precisely because the "I" is changeable that a bad boy can improve or that a good boy deprived of education may turn out badly. Little by little, our "I" is transformed by the milieu, education, culture, and all sorts of factors.

We always speak of man's innate nature, but what is this "innate"?

There is an enormous difference between a baby uttering his first cries and the shameless guy he becomes. Little by little, he's lost his artlessness. In the beginning he was innocent and without shame when they laughed at him. He peed anywhere and cried "Wah! Wah!" But as he grew he began to perceive that they were making fun of him and he was ashamed. Becoming aware that it was idiotic to behave thus, little by little his innocence disappeared. He put in place a whole system of fortifications so that they'd no longer make fun of him, and so that they'd admire him, he equipped himself with machine guns and antiaircraft guns. He has even gone so far as to invent rays that permit him to read inside men's stomachs. He's become totally brazen.

But now this shameless guy whom we could imagine continuing indefinitely on this road has suddenly weakened like the flame of a burned down candle, no longer resembling anything but a glimmer that barely lights up the toilet. Thus it is that body and mind change due to the milieu, education, and all sorts of factors. Neither the one nor the other is fixed and unchanging.

Although in the old days there were sleeping cars on the train to Shinano, I couldn't get a reservation and sat up all night. The train swayed and jolted along all night, making it impossible to close an eye for a moment. Disembarking on the platform deep in the mountains, you thought only of going to bed and sleeping all day. However, this didn't take into account what made Shinano so famous. Suddenly, becoming conscious of the clarity and luminosity of the air, you lost all desire to sleep. I'd say that it's the nature of Shinano that doesn't want to sleep. Even the sun shines in fullest brilliancy, unlike being veiled in haze in Tokyo. The poet Kobayashi Issa[7] wrote: "In Shinano, the moon, Buddha and I are right next to one another." Because the air is transparent, the moon is more beautiful, and the pickled radishes look better than elsewhere. The men are more handsome, too. Perhaps due to the climate? Or the quality of the air? To the environment? Everything, absolutely everything, is different. It's strange.

Men are also transformed by methods of education. This is why a Chinese is a Chinese and a Japanese, a Japanese. Their sensibility is different. The heart is also the result of conditioned production. Nothing belongs to us by nature. Nothing is fixed and invariable. Everything is dependent and provisional. There's no innate self-nature.

From the precept, "Not to take what does not belong to you", Hōgen understood that he ought not to claim for himself that which was not his, which is to say: his dwelling, his treasures, his properties, his wife, his children, his family, his servants, his *kesa*, his bowl, his body, his heart. He suddenly realized that he had nothing: everything was empty of self-nature. He had understood his non-birth and no longer had to fear death. It's sufficient to dwell in the place where one has no knowledge of birth; if there is no birth there can be no death. They say that he had satori at that moment.

The One-Mind Precepts According to Bodhidharma

A text by Bodhidharma[8] is titled: "One-mind precepts." He employs the expression "one-mind" to express what we today call "buddha nature." In the introduction, he says: "To receive, is to transmit. To transmit, is to awake. To awake to the Buddha-mind is to truly receive the precepts"

For example, when we receive the precept of not killing, the preceptor asks us, "From now on until you attain buddha-body, will you continuously observe it? Then we answer, "Yes, I will." This statement of "Yes, I will" is what is meant by "receiving" the precepts. "To receive" means "to transmit" and "to transmit" means "to awaken to." Therefore the true meaning of receiving the precepts is to awaken to the buddha-mind. It is meaningless to insincerely repeat, "Yes, I will." Receiving the precepts means to receive the buddha-mind as your own mind.

When you have realized the mind of Buddha, it's enough to ask: "Does the Buddha lie? Does he get drunk? Does he covet something?" The answers are obvious. Of course, you'll say to me, "I know that's one of the precepts, but just for now can't I eat fish? Can't I get married?" I'd answer these questions by saying that they didn't pose a problem in the era when the Buddha Dharma was transmitted. Comprehending the essence of the mind of the Buddha does not mean being a fragment imbedded in the universe. It's to be the universe itself.

A chapter of the "One-mind precepts" begins with this phrase: "Self-nature is wondrous and imperceptible." This means that the whole universe is your realm and that I am included therein. In consequence, to kill a being is to carry out an attack on oneself. Therefore, it's not because killing is forbidden that one does not kill, but because one cannot take life from a part of oneself. For the same reason, one does not steal, one does not envy others, and one does not allow oneself to become angry. There is no barrier between self and others. We are of a single piece, without joint or seam. To understand the precept of the buddha nature is to realize that our nature is infinite.

The precepts have been the object of deep studies that approached them from all angles: the substance, the aspect, the practice and the Dharma. According to the specialists, the analysis of the substance of the precepts is very difficult. They say that when Hōnen Jōnin[9] was a young monk, he questioned his master about this problem and that the master didn't know what to say and apologized.

The substance of the precepts arises from seeds enclosed in the alaya[10] consciousness from which all psychic phenomena develop. It's very difficult to understand. From the point of view of *zen*, it is faith that produces the substance of the precepts. As for the aspect, they present themselves under numerous forms, but thanks to concentration and wisdom, we have a great margin of freedom. For the novice, let's say that it's to find one's true face. The practice of the precepts rests upon zazen and upon wisdom. In the Teaching system the categories of precepts are the 5-8-10 precepts and the Full Vinaya precepts. In the Sōtō tradition, we have only one kind, the Sixteen Precepts (3 Refuges, 3 Pure Precepts, 10 Prohibitory Precepts.)

In the Shōbōgenzō chapter titled "Receiving the Precepts," Dōgen wrote: "In India and in China, all the buddhas and patriarchs who have transmitted the Dharma have always affirmed that receiving the precepts is a prerequisite for entry into the Dharma. One cannot be considered to be a disciple, an heir of the patriarchs, if one does not receive the precepts. The observation of the precepts is necessary to practice zazen and follow the Way because they further the prevention of evil, moving one away from it, and transcending it. To receive the precepts is already to become The Treasury of the Eye of the True Dharma. There is no doubt that all the buddhas and patriarchs who have preserved and transmitted the true Dharma have received and observed the precepts. Consequently, all those who follow the teaching of the Buddha must not violate them."

The Precept of the Whole Universe

Let's return to the emergence of the body of the precepts. Imagine that a seed buried in the consciousness takes life and breathes out seeds that in their turn produce new seeds and that this goes on indefinitely throughout life.

The substance of the precepts has different origins that can be classified into different categories. The first is called the "The Well-Come." According to the sutras, Shākyamuni touched the heads of his disciples and said, "The Well-Come has arrived." In an instant, their hair fell off like great drops of water and a kesa clothed their body. It was enough for Shākyamuni to approach and touch you for the substance of the precepts to be revealed to you. This type of genesis existed only during Shākyamuni's lifetime. After his disappearance, the "personal vow" appeared, in which you value the images and external forms of the religion and you practice while waiting for Buddha to come touch you. The third category is that of "the three refuges." The precepts manifest themselves thanks to "the three treasures," the Buddha, Dharma, and Sangha. The fourth is that of the sudden vision: for a second you catch a glimpse of the truth and the substance of the precepts is produced. This is what they call "a second's satori." The fifth is "the escorted by zazen." When you enter into the state of consciousness of the *zen* of the Buddha, you cannot break the precepts. Moreover, there are also the three masters and seven witnesses. These are the masters of precepts, studies, and practice and their seven assistants. Under their direction, and following their example, you are led to accept the precepts.

The first ordinations in Japan go back to the Nara period. The Chinese monk, Ganjin[12] Oshō, was invited to Japan to reform monastic discipline, and had the first ordination platform erected near the Great Buddha at Tōdaiji in Nara. It took Ganjin fifteen years to reach Japan. He made five unhappy attempts that ended in shipwrecks, false departures, and mishaps. Only on the sixth attempt did he succeed in making the crossing and setting foot on Japanese soil. He arrived blind and weakened. Welcomed by Emperor Shōmu, he conferred the precepts on him as well as on the Empress Kōmyō and all the civil and military dignitaries at court. After that the government thought that one ordination platform in the capital was not enough and two more should be built: in the east at Yakushiji in Shimonotsuke province and in the west at Kanzeonji in Chikuzen. When the monk Dōkyō[13] was banished from court he became head of Yakushiji and later Sugawara no Michizane,[14] condemned to exile, resided at Kanzeonji.

The fundamental precept upon which our religion rests is the infinity of our own nature. We don't attain the Mahayana by getting rid of the Hinayana, or satori by eliminating illusions, or good by suppressing evil, but by grasping our limitless nature that fills the sky, the earth, and the whole universe. One does not comprehend through reasoning, but by practice, by turning back upon oneself and practicing with one's body. *Buddha nature, jewel of the precepts, is inscribed in the foundation of our mind.*

The entire universe, all beings and all things are our own infinite nature. The *Shinjinmei*[15] says: "Without seeking the truth, only cease having preferences." A poem also expresses this: " The clouds dissipate, the moon I thought vanished shines in the lightening sky of dawn." We do not need to call on reason to realize that our own nature is limitless and that it has never ceased to shine like the pale moon of early morning. When we become aware that the Buddha and we are only one, we realize the futility of the men who struggle for nothing in their prison. We become *the tranquil man of the Way, who has attained awakening and ceased studying and acting.* This man is very close to us, since *"Buddha nature, jewel of the precepts, is inscribed in the foundation of our mind."*

Buddha nature is also explained in the *Bonmō-kyō*:[16] " This precept-light is neither mind nor material. It is neither being nor non-being, is limited in neither cause nor effect. This precept-light is precisely the original source of all buddhas and the root of all bodhisattvas. It is also the root of all the children of the Buddha in this Great Assembly." Which comes down to saying that our buddha nature is inscribed in us: Buddha and I are but one. Such is the precept of buddha nature.

The Body Clothed by "The Rice-field of Happiness."

Drizzles and dews, mists and clouds clothe our body. The kesa is this vestment. We've come from seeing buddha nature from the point of view of the precepts, and here we're going to observe it from another angle: that of the kesa.

One day a "clouds and water"[17] asked me what the kesa signifies. I answered him, "The kesa is something unclear." He stared at me with surprise and shock, with an air of thinking that I was saying just any old thing that came to mind. In truth, the kesa is indefinable, as much by its "worn out" color, the color of ruin or rags, as by its dimensions, that do not respond to any precise rule. It's not limited by any definite form. It is for this reason that it has been called "of happiness." They say that Shākyamuni measured six foot one inch and that Miroku (Maitreya)[18] will measure a thousand feet. But the kesa that Shākyamuni transmits to Miroku is neither large nor small. It's a formless robe and "a rice-field of happiness." In actuality, it's something inconceivable.

The kesa, vestment of "drizzles and dew, mists and clouds, " is the symbol of the substance of the Buddha Dharma. The sky, the earth, the entire universe are this one and same kesa. Nothing exists outside of it. One doesn't ascend to paradise, nor descend to hell. One goes nowhere, one arrives nowhere. There is only one kesa and man owes it to himself to wear it.

Prince Shōtōku,[19] who introduced Buddhism to Japan, wore the kesa to administer affairs of state and when commenting on the three Mahayana sutras.[20] Emperor Shōmu[21] also wore it to govern, and many generations of emperors had faith in the kesa. In the world of warriors, Kikuchi Taketoke,[22] Takeda Shingen,[23] and Uesugi Kenshin[24] benefited from its infinite virtues. To wear the kesa and to transmit it is man's supreme happiness. The one who thinks it's just cloth representing narrowly restrictive formalism is the toy of his bad karma, but the one who rejoices in wearing it has his good portion of happiness.

It's Daichi Zenji who best expressed the great happiness secured by the kesa of the entire universe:

Clothed with the rice-field of happiness, my body is glad.
Tranquil man, I have gained the universe.
I abandon myself to it, going or staying at its will,
The fresh breeze accompanies the white clouds.

40

The bowl has subdued the dragons, the staff has separated the tigers.
Its suspended metal rings sound loud and clear,
We do not carry these emblems in vain.
We intimately follow the imprints of the Buddha's staff.

In the Footprints of the Buddha

After the kesa, it's customary to speak of the bowl[1] and the staff, a monk's equipment. *The bowl has subdued the dragons* refers to a story from ancient China. It took place in the far distant past in the land of Shin, where a terrible drought raged in the region of Tch'ang-gnan, because the dragons were withholding the rain. In order to make the dragons come, the hermit seer Shōkō used his magic powers to accomplish the rite of the king dragon of the sea to make the dragons come. He enclosed them in his bowl, and at once the rains fell abundantly. This anecdote is the origin of the symbolism of the bowl that signifies that we hold the whole universe in our hands. It confers upon us the prodigious power to make the world move.

As for the anecdote about the staff,[2] it's about the monk Chū Zenji of Shantong, who interposed his staff between two tigers who were fighting. They showed their teeth, growled and fled. The metal rings rattle at the top to signal the presence of the monk. Both bowl and staff have symbolic value. They signify that we live in the image of the Buddha, whose footprints we follow. *Buddha nature, jewel of the precepts, is inscribed in the foundation of our mind.* The kesa, mists and clouds, drizzles and dew, clothes our body. The bowl has subdued the dragon and the staff pacified the tigers. All these traditions are inherited from Shākyamuni.

41

Do not search for truth, do not cut off illusion.
Understand that both are empty and devoid of character.

The Treasure Is Right Here

This phrase was already encountered in the first stanza of *Shōdōka*. The tranquil man who has attained awakening *doesn't set aside illusions and no longer seeks the truth*. Most men seek truth and flee illusions. They are in a hole, turning in a circle to find a good spot and run away from a bad one. The one is worth no more than the other, but they continue revolving in the same hole.

Everyone would like to have a good memory for remembering what others have said and done, but in merely memorizing what's been said, we live on imported goods and reduce our individuality and originality to nothing. On the other hand, it's very annoying to forget everything. So, is it better to have a good or a bad memory? Is it preferable to forget what's been said? Is it preferable to remember it? Where's the truth? I don't know.

Shākyamuni said, "You must not pass your life in wandering. You look for a house when you already have one. Do not construct another." Men pass their time in moving out. Belittling what they have, they run after something else. You can understand this if you watch a child. He has a doll, but if another child has a caramel, he wants a caramel; if he has a caramel and he sees a whistle, he wants the whistle. Then it's a top, and it never ends. The moment he sees something else, what he has no longer interests him. This is what Shākyamuni means by "wandering." We look for what pleases us, but our point of view changes constantly.

Shākyamuni admonishes us, "You already have a house. Do not

construct another." Aren't we each born with a countenance, a brain, a body? Well then, repose in peace within your dwelling without going to look elsewhere. Even so, we folks undervalue what we are, the moment in which we live, and the place where we live, and we go off in search of something else.

It is written in the Lotus Sutra: "The treasure is very near you." The ultimate place of peace is here, not at the ends of the earth. It's also said, "Although it's right here, you don't see it!" The truth is so near and you don't see it! The treasure is so near and you don't see it! The Buddha is so near and you don't see him! You travel far, very far, to look for the Buddha or for satori, and you fall into hell. You hurry in confusion and violent haste and when you arrive, there is nothing. The fog suddenly lifts and it was only a mirage. You want to return to the country you came from, but you perceive only that you are encircled by mountains sharp as swords and that there is no going back. It's the hell of the man dying of thirst in the desert.

We wish to escape from a world we judge detestable, but after having left it, we miss it like a lost paradise. Men always want to leave for somewhere else and upon arriving at the destination they feel like a rat in a sewer. The country from which they've come appears once again wonderful.

The more we search, the more we get stuck in the mire. The more we sink in, the more we suffer. I read this phrase in the biography of the painter and poet Buson[1]: "He was of a playful and carefree nature, his peaceful soul didn't seek new horizons."

When one seeks nothing, even satori, one has no tensions and is at ease. It's very important to experience this well being. If one has need neither of money, nor renown, nor societal status, nor satori, nor even of life, one experiences a sense of well-being without equal.

On the other hand, there are people who desire to simultaneously have satori, sleep late and eat well, or who wish to not have desires but love money and pleasures. There are also the lazy ones who dream of being a marvel at work. This endless chain of "I want this, I want that" leads inexorably to suffering. As the proverb says, you want to eat fugu and live to a ripe old age. In short, you wish to win on all fronts.

The Spark between Two Flints

Do not search for truth, do not cut off illusion. We must see the world as it is. I knew a philosophy professor suffering from tuberculosis who passed his time in reading books of philosophy. He told me that he was battling with the truth. Actually, he died suddenly of a pulmonary hemorrhage, spitting blood on his journal. Perhaps he died on the field of battle, but he was fighting with his chimeras, not with the truth.

Truth is not a rigid and fixed concept. You cannot make a list of it and put it away in a box. You can't say that it's here or there. Truth is that which is, things' manner of being, however imperfect they may be. The truth is there without searching for it or fleeing from it. Truth? Illusion? These are just two fleeting words, expedients of circumstance by which we let ourselves be fleeced. More than by the reality of facts, men allow themselves to be had by the terminology of our civilization.

The Chinese poet Hakurakuten[2] wrote an interesting poem on this subject:

> Why battle with the horns of a snail?
> I am a spark between two flints.
> I accept good fortune, I accept bad fortune; more than that, I rejoice in it.
> I remain like an imbecile, mouth open without laughing.

A blow to the right, it disappears; a blow to the left, it disappears. How can you battle with the horns of the snail that retract as soon as you touch them? Truth and illusion are words, as fleeting as the horns of a snail. Truth is not found in the fixed vocabulary you learn from a philosophy textbook. That truth is merely a pile of knowledge that serves for passing exams.

"I am a spark between two flints." As if it suddenly leapt from its lodging, fire springs up when you strike two stones sharply together. Good luck? Bad luck? Happiness? Unhappiness? We always worry about what will come later, but what's the good in that? Since our life is as brief as a spark?

"I accept good fortune, I accept bad fortune; more than that, I rejoice in it." I am content to be rich, I am content to be poor, for my baggage will be that much lighter. I always say that when one has no belongings, one has no fear of being stripped of them. When you don't have a yen, no one comes to solicit you. Besides, nothing makes you stronger than lack of money. I also think money is useful, though I'm not talking about laughable little sums of two or three yen, but of millions, billions of yen that one could make good use of.

"I remain like an imbecile, mouth open without laughing." He remains imperturbable before both good and bad fortune. He doesn't laugh, but no more does he weep. He has the look of an idiot. He's a man who has understood the truth.

Examples of Ordinary Men

Understand that both are empty and devoid of character. Duality is truth/illusion, happiness/unhappiness, wealth/poverty, health/sickness, love/hate, good/evil. When you eat refined dishes daily, little by little the extent of the delicious savor shrinks, you grow weary, and what at the start seemed delicious ends up no longer being so at all. In the same way, if you eat tasteless nourishment every day, the extent of the tastelessness shrinks and the impression of tastelessness fades away. Both tasty and tasteless are conditioned and dependent productions. All conditioned production is empty. Good/bad, big/small, pleasant/unpleasant, light/dark, I like/I don't like: these have neither fixed character nor self-existence. In no matter what domain, all that is produced and fabricated is devoid of character. Although all phenomena are empty in themselves and there is nothing, we remain attached to something. Something holds us prisoner, as if we were caught in a net, and for this reason we laugh and cry, we grow angry and we speak ill of others. All these phenomena have no self-existence. To convince ourselves of this, let's think of our own life twenty, thirty or forty years ago. What remains of this past that seems to step out of a dream? At bottom, memories are all relative and without importance. Only the certainty of death is not a dream. The only important thing about which we cannot deceive ourselves is that one day we will enter our coffins.

Nevertheless, we do not know where we come from or where we go, and the date of our death is not fixed. As a result, the only thing that matters is to accept ourselves just as we are, in our present reality. Let's take ourselves in hand, hold firm and not let go. When we grip ourselves firmly, we can neither chase something nor flee.

When not seeking the truth and not cutting off illusions, one preserves an imperturbable calm. Seated with dignity, the legs well pressed into the ground, the back steady and the stomach relaxed, the body remains calm and the mind is tranquil. Yesterday was a good day, today is, too; tomorrow will be a good day and the day after as well. If I get a raise, so much the better! If I don't, too bad!

One day someone told me his story on this subject. This person began teaching at the same time as one of his comrades. When the first raise in salary came, his friend got a raise but he did not. It was the same with the second, and then the third, and on the fourth occasion, when his friend again got a raise but he did not, he felt bitterness. However, there was no need to feel bitterness. In my case, until I became fifty-six and got the job as a professor at Komazawa University, no one came to hire me, and I had no desire to be hired. Although I worked hard and kept busy traveling and teaching in many places, I did not seek anything. I lived a peaceful and agreeable life.

Because a millionaire's money extends well beyond his gate, no true human personality is revealed. He wears a mask of money. Our biggest task in life is to live at peace with our self, without fraud and fabrication, no matter what our work in life. We must give ourselves completely to the present, with no drifting backward, anchored firmly in the here and now.

When you wish to become this or that, you get nowhere; it's only agitation. There are monks who return to lay life, come back, and depart again. Nishiari Zenji called them "tororo " (a Japanese potato, yamaimo) because just like we grind tororo, add some soy sauce flavored broth, grind the tororo again, add broth again etc. etc., these monks shave their heads, return to lay life, let their hair grow, shave their heads again, return to lay life, etc. etc. They haven't understood that because dualisms are empty, truth and illusion are not different, so they veer from one side to the other without finding repose.

42

The absence of character is neither emptiness nor non-emptiness.
It is the true reality of the Buddha.

The luminous mirror of the mind illuminates without obstruction.
Its immense radiance penetrates innumerable worlds.

The Image in the Mirror

The absence of character is neither emptiness nor non-emptiness. Absence of character implies characteristics, just as multiplicity implies unity. The one includes the other, cohabiting without difficulty. The same goes for loving and not loving, macrocosm and microcosm, good and evil. When we ask ourselves, "Where is the good? Where is the evil?" we can say to ourselves that they are not far, one from the other, since they are indissociable. They are our manner of being, our human condition. When we no longer consider them as opposing entities, we grasp the body of the Buddha in its essence. *"It is the true reality of the Buddha."* It is the satori of the Buddha.

Dōgen Zenji wrote this poem:

Flowers, crimson leaves
Winter's white snow.
Reflecting, I regret seeing
And admiring them only as form.

In the countryside he sees simultaneously the colors of illusion and those of satori, admiring them all the more in that they are fundamentally empty and without character. When one sees the beauties of nature and all things in their double aspect, one doesn't lose oneself in a dream.

The luminous mirror of the mind illuminates without obstruction. The mirror of our mind does not discriminate. It neither loves nor detests this or that. For it, all is luminous, encountering no obstacle as far as the deepest ocean depths. Formerly, there was a monk in China named Gensha no Shibi.[1] One day as he was departing to make a visit to a master, he stubbed his foot against a stone, lacerating it. He felt an intense pain and thought, "Where does this pain come from, since my body is without substance?" At that instant he had the satori of the

Buddha. He understood that the absence of character is neither empty nor non-empty. It is the true face of Buddha. He turned around on the spot and re-entered his monastery. Seeing him return, his master Seppō was astonished, asking, "Why aren't you making your visits?" (During this era, travel from monastery to monastery to visit masters was the practice.) Gensha's response was very surprising: "Bodhidharma[2] didn't come to China, the second patriarch Eka[3] did not go to India." Said Seppō, " Speak! Explain yourself!" Gensha answered, "The world of the ten directions is a pure and single jewel." He meant that the entire universe was a single transparent jewel, the jewel symbolizing unity. In consequence, it was useless to go anywhere—there was nothing to seek or anything to flee.

It is written in the *Kegon-kyō*[4]: " All phenomena, like the different waves of the sea, emanate from the same principle and are one with the mind of the Buddha." Also: "The single is identical to the multiple, the multiple is identical to the single." *Hōkyō Zammaï*[5] expresses the same thing with more subtlety through poetry, "When you look in a mirror, it produces a reflection that looks at you. It is exactly like you. It is not you, and yet, it is just like you." Happiness is unhappiness, wealth is poverty, you are me and I am you. Thus, the two cohabit without trouble in the one. As in the mirror, you are my reflection.

Speaking of the mirror, I remember this poem from ancient times: "The image that the mirror silently returns to me sulks when I sulk and becomes angry when I become angry." It is not only the mirror that reflects our image, men do so as well. When I become angry, the face of my partner in conversation changes and his expression becomes nasty. When I smile, I receive a smile in response, as if an electric current passes between us. Those who don't understand this

principle have too narrow a life. In contrast, others acquire the mysterious power to divine what their partner in conversation is thinking.
The world becomes transparent like a crystal box. *The luminous mir-*
ror of the mind illuminates without obstruction. Its immense radiance
penetrates innumerable worlds.

43

It is here that the innumerable phenomena reflect.
It is a jewel of perfect light, with neither inside nor outside.

Suddenly revealed, emptiness eliminates the chains of cause and effect
Which provoke confusion and disorders that attract misfortune.
Yet, to reject the existing and attach yourself to emptiness is also a disease,
Like throwing yourself into the fire to avoid drowning.

Abandoning illusion to seek the truth
Reveals a mind of preference that leads to fallacious choices.
The student who practices in this spirit suffers from a lack of discernment
That allows him to truly mistake a thief for his son.

To Throw Oneself into the Fire to Avoid Drowning

It is here that the innumerable phenomena reflect. Shadows are no exception, because the precious mirror, pure and transparent, reflects all
things clearly and neutrally. The beauty of a long face or the ugliness
of a short face doesn't appear in the mirror. A long face is a long face,
a shadow is a shadow, nothing else. "Beautiful, ugly, good, evil" are
relative, conditioned products of the mind.

It is a jewel of perfect light, with neither inside nor outside. Our
mind has the same root as the sky and the earth where all things are
only a single entity. It has neither exterior nor interior, its clarity
contains the entire universe. There is nothing to exclude and noth-

ing to seek. But here a difficulty arises that makes us risk falling into a trap.

Indeed, it would be a mistake to believe that the principle of causality no longer exists. Yet, if one says that there is neither happiness nor unhappiness, neither good nor evil, neither cause nor effect, neither paradise nor hell, it may become tempting to think that acting evilly is without importance. It would be a poor interpretation of the meaning of emptiness if one believed that one could do evil without falling into hell and that there is no point in acting for the good. All the same, given the fact that there is nothing and all is empty, why should I sow seeds of good if I don't harvest any merit? And what about the future? It's enough to leave it to chance, it's just a matter of luck! This is how one falls into heresy, by suppressing the principle of causality.

Nevertheless, undeniable proof exists of the relationship between cause and effect. Steal and you will see whether cause and effect don't exist! Borrow money and don't pay it back and when the bailiff comes to your door you'll understand what causality is, discovering hell when you find yourself naked in the street.

Suddenly revealed emptiness eliminates the chains of cause and effect that provoke confusion and disorders that attract misfortune. Yet, to reject the existing and attach yourself to emptiness is also a disease, like throwing yourself into the fire to avoid drowning. Torments, sufferings, calamities, and disasters spring up tall and strong on this compost heap. The vegetation there is luxuriant and produced in abundance. Disburdening yourself of causality attracts misfortune. Getting rid of everything and denying everything because nothing exists also leads to chaos. If you plunge into the flames in order to escape the water that terrifies you, you will not die of drowning, but you will burn to death.

Abandoning illusion to seize the truth reveals a mind of preference that leads to fallacious choices. The student who practices in this spirit suffers from a lack of discernment that allows him to truly mistake a thief for his son. To summarize in Buddhist terms, let's say that to pass through the gate of the Buddha there is only one rule: reject nothing. One sets nothing aside, seizes nothing, flees nothing, pursues nothing. Selecting by throwing away one side and holding on to the other leads to arbitrary classifications. All discrimination is artificial and false.

He who hopes to find the truth by picking it up from one side and rejecting it from the other, deceives himself and practices without having understood the essence of the Way. *The student who practices in this spirit suffers from a lack of discernment that allows him to truly mistake a thief for his son.*

44

We squander the riches of the Dharma and destroy its merits
By relying on discriminating thought.
This is why the zen disciple rejects this,
To enter immediately into the non-born through the power of direct
recognition.

The Power That Resides in Zazen

We squander the riches of the Dharma and destroy its merits as the inevitable consequence of our mental activity, creator of illusions. This is the fabricator of happiness and unhappiness. It is an argument *a postiori* to think that to be born poor is a misfortune. Being born, the baby doesn't say to himself, "What a pity to be born poor!" He experiences no frustration. It's only much later that this thought will appear. Nothing of all that exists for him, because he has no awareness of being born.

Later on, he will believe or not believe in God, in ghosts, and in paradise. These are illusions, some of which even end up undermining the foundations of the Buddha Dharma.

This is why the zen disciple rejects this. Illusions are synonymous with mental activity. For a man, water is water, for a fish, his dwelling. The appearance of things is a function of karma. When one is dying of thirst, there's nothing more delightful than to drink one's fill of tea; the pleasure is much less if one has a headache. Our mental activity has the ability to put all sorts of faces on one and the same thing. It even succeeds in hiding it altogether. When the intellect ceases acting and reasoning, truth appears openly in all its splendor, sparkling with light, but for it to manifest we must stop our cerebral machinery, putting it out of service.

Daichi Zenji[1] wrote: "The actualization of ultimate truth in practice transcends rational and analytical reasoning." The actualization of reality is beyond words and formulations. In neither increases nor decreases. It is unique.

During zazen, we set aside analytical and conceptual thought, producer of illusions solidified by our karma. We clean house, sweeping away concepts. By getting rid of all these specks of dust, we simultaneously do away with the ordinary man's state of consciousness. Thereafter, there is nothing to do. The moon is the moon, the mountain is the mountain, the sea is the sea and not something else. The sky and the earth have the same root, all things are only a single body, and this body is absolutely not conditioned by anything else. It is true reality. Through the power of knowing and seeing, *zen* permits immediate entry into the non-born.

That which is not produced cannot be destroyed, and the non-born cannot die. To put it another way, it is awakening to the unproduced. If the illusions of the ordinary man are not dispelled, one cannot discover the Buddha. In the Buddha Dharma, it is extremely important to have access to the essence of Buddha. Thus the first thing is to eliminate illusions and to do this there is no other method than to pass through via the gate of *zen*. That is to say, to identify with zazen.

When we identify with zazen, nothing any longer exists. Sawaki and zazen are one. Outside of zazen, no Sawaki. If there is no longer Sawaki, there is no longer intellect to fabricate illusions. With illusions eliminated, nothing but zazen remains. During zazen, one is in harmony with Shākyamuni, Bodhidharma, and all the patriarchs and ancestors. One becomes the entire universe. Thanks to the power of the Buddha, we enter into the non-born. This power resides in zazen. Through it, illusions disappear and suddenly one is the non-born. Keizan said at the beginning of Zazen Yōjin-ki:

> Zazen immediately opens the mind of man and permits him
> to find peace in the essential. Thus, the true face of the mind
> appears and releases its fundamental clarity. He who wishes
> to open his mind must abandon all learning and reasoning,
> divest himself of the law of men and of the Buddha Dharma,
> detach himself from all illusions. When he arrives at the heart
> of the unique truth, the dark clouds of the phantasms will
> disappear and the mind will become shining and luminous
> like a ray of moonlight. Zazen rends the darkness, and in
> the state of "just-as-we-are," we become Buddha. We don't
> discover the Buddha through the power of reasoning, but
> through the power of zazen.

45

The great man seizes the sword of wisdom,
With its adamantine flame and point of prajna.

The Energy of the True Man

With our sudden entry into the non-born in the preceding verse, the first part of *Shōdōka* has been completed. We are also in the middle of the poem. It began softly with *this tranquil man of the Way who has attained awakening and ceased studying and acting,* and the tone has remained the same throughout this first stage. From now on, everything changes. The tone rises and the words become astonishingly strong: *The great man*[1] *seizes the sword of wisdom.*

Our hero is a man like any other and does not become a combative brute just because he wears a sword. The great man is he who knows buddha nature. Put otherwise, he is the contrary of the one who debases his own person. The true man comports himself with moderation and does not put his life in peril. He takes himself solidly in hand, without harming himself. It's the greatest and most precious satori. In any case, he doesn't allow illusions to steer the wheel of his life into disorder and agitation. Our hero is each man or woman who is simply true.

He doesn't scurry about in every direction like a newborn mouse. He doesn't exert himself to put on airs, he is neither conceited nor pretentious. He is the opposite of an arrogant man full of himself.

The first lines of the *Hannya Shingyō* are: "Avalokiteshvara Bodhisattva, when deeply practicing *prajna paramita*, clearly saw that all five aggregates[2] are empty and thus relieved all suffering." This also refers to "the great man seizes the sword of wisdom."

Yamanake Shikanosuke[3] made use of bad luck all his life. They even say that he dedicated a cult to the new moon. I like this warrior very much because he didn't care about serving Toyotomi Hideyo-shi, the all-powerful master of the time. Rather than becoming the rich lord of a fief with revenues of thirty or forty thousand koku,[4] he chose not to be acquainted with the display of power. To love life is to seize the sword of wisdom. I don't use the word "life" in the sense of physiological longevity, for to pass "life" in the chaos of illusions, with nothing in sight but the ups and downs of fortune, is not to live. The true man lives otherwise.

In his Treatise on the Five Rings, Miyamoto Musashi[5] wrote a chapter titled "Empty," in which he says, "The body relies on the errors of the mind and the eyes upon the distortion of vision." It's not only the eyes that deform things. The same goes for the nose and the mouth. Let off a fart under a dog's nose and he'll find the smell delightful, asking for more, while a man will say to himself, "That guy's disgusting!" Where does the distortion lie, with the man or with the dog? In the Buddha's teaching, this distortion is called "karma." Karma is at the origin of our distortions, and when they occur the true man cuts them off with his sword of wisdom.

Without the sword of wisdom, the present is empty of substance. The young say, "You'll see, someday I'll succeed." They dream of the future: honors, glory, and fortune. Though they don't know what they'll do, they want celebrity. On the other hand, the old, with no more aspirations toward the future, turn to the past: "Ah! In my day, it didn't happen like that . . . one was like this . . . one did thus . . ." When you ask them about the present, they answer that these days everything goes badly. This is truly talking nonsense! To refuse present reality is completely contrary to the attitude of the true man. The Way must be lived in the present, just as it is. Life must sparkle with all its fires, here and now.

This reminds me of a portrait of Miyamoto Musashi. He had large eyes, a bald cranium and wore two wooden sabers. He had a robust face with a formidable glance. When I read the phrase, *the great man seizes the sword of wisdom,* the image always comes to mind of Musashi wielding his great sword in an attack on his adversary. I think that when one is courageous and authentic, one carries the sword of wisdom. To handle this sword, everything must be in itself authentic, otherwise you don't have the strength to wield it. Authenticity and soundness of judgment permit one to remain indifferent to criticism or praise. If one considers an action to be just and true, blame or praises bring neither special pain nor special joy.

As they say, "The moon high in the sky is untroubled by the winds from the eight directions." This refers to the eight elements that fan one's love and hate—and hence are called "wind." They are: profit, sorrow, slander, fame, praise, censure, pain, and pleasure. Praise or criticism, happiness or misfortune, you give or you receive, you feel at ease in all circumstances of life and, no matter what happens, always retain your composure. When you seize the sword of wisdom you don't lose your head or fall to pieces. You live life to the full.

Yoshida Shōin[6] was put to death for opposing the opening of the country. His last words were, " I knew it would end thus, but I was compelled by the spirit of Yamato." It can't be said that he abandoned his cause in the middle of the road. It was the same with Sakuro Sōguro[7], crucified in 1655 for presenting a complaint to the shogun concerning the great misery of the peasants. To achieve something fully does not mean saying that nothing can be done, nor is it to take one's personal interest into account and do nothing. The true man doesn't tell himself fairy tales and goes all the way to the goal he has targeted.

A text from the Unkō school of the Way of the Warrior[9] says, "The secret of the Unkō art rests entirely on these principles: to not reflect, to not seek, to not hope, to not hoard, to not take, to not reject. In grasping the true substance of the united mind, one creates the breath, the eternal breath." It concludes by saying, "The essential thing is to achieve oneself, without appealing to the outside." That is to say that the objective is our own essential nature. Rich or poor, man or woman, the mind is untroubled and the sword of wisdom continues to gleam, striking cut and thrust upon everything that can darken the mind. Such a man is impressive, walking with head held high along the road of the Way. An old one has said, "Before subduing the demons, you must subdue yourself." When one gives rise to the mind of the Way, the demons exit the audience chamber.

Zazen Fills Space

To do zazen is to carry the sword of wisdom. The zazen posture inspires fear. I recall that one evening when I remained alone in the dōjō, sitting zazen for an hour or an hour and a half, my posture drew the attention of people passing in the corridor. Seeing me, they remained rooted to the spot, speechless, and then felt themselves drawn irresistibly into the room. Apparently what they saw was not merely their kind priest. Rather, it appears that when I am doing zazen I am a completely different man.

Another time when I was doing zazen at a friend's home, he opened the door to say, "Dinner is served!" Seeing me, he was struck dumb and left the room quietly. Afterward, he said to me, "We're old friends and I'm not shy with you, but when I opened the door zazen filled the room and I fell to the floor in a prostration." It's not only my zazen that fills space, it's the same for everyone. The sword of wisdom is the symbol of zazen; whoever does zazen seizes the sword.

When I was a young worker at Eiheiji, they'd sent me to look for some sugar, and I was running with a bowl in my hand when I became aware of four or five silhouettes solidly established in zazen behind a screen. My heart gave a leap and my legs stopped dead. I finished my errand on tiptoe. Zazen inspires the same terror as a warrior with muscles taut, ready to strike with his three-foot polished blade. Among all the positions of the human body, the zazen posture is the most dignified and carries the greatest force of authority. At the very beginning of *Shōdōka* we encountered the pleasant gentleness of *the tranquil man of the Way who has ceased studying and acting.* Now we discover the severe gravity of *the great man who seizes the sword of wisdom.*

Viewed from the inside, zazen is clarity and transparence. When one does zazen, one doesn't have too high an opinion of oneself, which would only hinder one from straightening the head. To speak truthfully, zazen is not a propitious moment for clarifying what's not going well with you. When we struggle in the midst of a household quarrel or celebrate with geishas, we aren't aware of the comings and goings of a flea. But when we're doing zazen and a flea tries at all cost to get into our shorts, we can't help feeling it and can't stand to sit motionless. In zazen we are transparent, feeling even the smallest stimulation. A guy in the midst of a brawl doesn't feel the nail that tears his foot, and someone else in a state of drunkenness scrapes his knee, rolls on the ground, and wallows in the mud without noticing it. During zazen, illusions appear, but it's nothing. One knows that things are what they are.

In our zazen, we can clearly see the distance between the Buddha and the ordinary man sitting inside the Buddha. A plaque on the wall of many dōjōs reads: "The vantage point from which one embraces the universe at a glance." Thanks to this panoramic vision, the contents of zazen are of an unheard of richness. One is in harmony with the Buddha and, at the same time, one shoulders all the business of the ordinary man; one is made up of all the contradictions. They say that religions don't fear contradictions, but none equals zazen in this capacity for embracing everything.

The ordinary man carries within himself a quantity of matters, but during zazen he doesn't ask himself if it's good or bad. He takes everything just as it comes . . . clouds pass . . . is that a demon emerging? Or is it a snake? They depart without leaving traces. A beautiful girl arrives and fades away like a mirage. During ten years, twenty years, no matter!

Good Use of Faculties

Further along in the poem we will find this phrase: *Heretics have intelligence but they do not have wisdom.* Buddhism is the religion of wisdom. The true man carries the sword of wisdom. Wisdom is our sole aspiration. Our supreme ideal is becoming a true man. In our world, they say, "No remedy for stupidity." The Buddha also said, "You ought not to make friends with a fool."

Here's the story of an imbecile son who was very devoted to his father and practiced filial piety with fervor. His father was bald as an egg. One day the flies proved particularly aggressive while he was taking a siesta. They didn't stop coming and going on his hairless head (certain texts even speak of mosquitoes.) The devoted son chased them away with ardor, but to no effect. They immediately returned. He was exasperated and finally became angry. Grabbing a stick of wood, he brandished it high over his head and brought it down with a thwack on the flies. The flies fled and the skull flew into splinters. At that instant, the god of the trees intoned this refrain: "Better to have a wise man as an enemy than a cretin for an ally." When the enemy is wise, you're enriched by divining his intentions. (Of course, we're not speaking here about false sages.)

Even if it's done out of compassion, to display the nature of a true man, when you make friends with a fool you must expect some cruel disappointments.

It is of vital importance to seize the sword of wisdom, an essential factor in the chain of causality. It must be the unique aspiration of each human being, even without money or rank, to make the sword of wisdom gleam without the slightest particle of falsehood or error tarnishing it.

The human race is distinguished by its intelligence and its manual dexterity, thanks to which man constructs all sorts of machines. He also has a propensity to quarrel, and uses language with dexterity. In short, man is endowed with all sorts of talents. Unhappily, it turns out that an individual who makes good use of his faculties is rare among humans. The moral of the story is that he shouldn't make poor use of his gifts, and, for my part, I'd say that he must do his utmost to deploy his talents for the best. A crook makes poor use of his gifts. So do a usurer and a person with three secondary residences who supports many mistresses. Each in his way is an example of talent badly employed. To start with myself, when I look closely at myself, I see only that I am a wretched utilizer. Paths without error are extremely rare.

To make the most of one's abilities is to identify with the Buddha or with God. I would say that we must know ourselves to the bottom, then deploy our best efforts to cut off the passions that induce us to make bad use of ourselves. In this way, we stand upon our own summit, a peak dazzling with light that contains the entire universe, and we brandish the keen blade of wisdom. To express it differently, to seize the sword of wisdom is to raise human capacities to their optimum level.

The man who attains this ultimate state of being, where the sky and the earth have the same root, where he is one with all things and the entire universe, this man has the capacity to come to the aid of others. Even though he's not officially patented, for all that he is no less a Buddha: "Beings animate and inanimate become the Way; grasses, trees, lands and worlds, all without exception become Buddha."

I have lingered for a long time on this single phrase, *the great man seizes the sword of wisdom*, because it is fundamental. As for the sword *with its adamantine flame and point of prajna,* it has the hardness and brilliance of a diamond, the symbol of indestructibility. Let us then be reassured. The sword of wisdom is solid. Its point does not bend nor does its flame go out. Its sharpened point is the man who, having risen to his highest degree, utilizes his capacities to the utmost. At that moment, he has in hand a diamond flame. It's a shame that people spend their lives sewing clothes for dead children, fabricating mortuary masks or constructing tombs like secondary residences, when life wriggles before you! We must seize the sword of wisdom with its adamantine flame, wielding it vigorously for work that is true, immediate, and fresh: truly authentic.

46

He not only shatters the heretical mind,
He reduces to nothing the boldness of Mara.

Beating the drum, he activates the thunder of the Dharma,
He spreads a cloud of compassion and rains a torrent of ambrosia.
Dragons and elephants frolic and trumpet his infinite blessings,
Awakening all beings of the three vehicles and the five families.
Unadulterated, the hini grass of the snowy mountains
Yields the pure clarified butter that alone nourishes me.

Human Dignity According to the Dharma

This passage illustrates the line in the *Hannya shingyō* (Heart Sutra): "Far beyond all inverted views, one realizes nirvana."

He not only shatters the heretical mind, he reduces to nothing the boldness of Mara.

By heresy is meant beliefs outside the teachings of the Buddha, all that which assigns limits to the unlimited and leads to an impasse. True reality is without characteristics. Well then, if we enclose it in a fixed concept, we create an obstruction, and end up believing that we'll find happiness in paradise. When these false views appear, outside the Way, the true man *seizes his sword of wisdom with its adamantine flame and point of prajna* and cleanly cuts them off. He attacks not only heretical beliefs, he *reduces to nothing the boldness of Mara.*[2] Whatever we may call them: Māra, Tenma, Akuma or something else, demons are of all kinds. It is they who give rise to dualistic thoughts within us and have the power to make us see a dualistic reality in which happiness is separated from unhappiness and illness from health. There is also, of course, the demon of the five aggregates. All these demons inhabit our own consciousness. The sword of wisdom puts them to rout.

Beating the drum, he activates the thunder of the Dharma. He spreads a cloud of compassion and rains a torrent of ambrosia. The true man seizes his sword of wisdom and teaches the Buddha Dharma. The growl of thunder, the roll of the drum, the rain of ambrosia are metaphors used to express the Mahayana. They don't evoke a swindler's little conjuring tricks, but rather the majesty of the doctrine that teaches human dignity.

Like the man who has seized the sword of wisdom, the *dragons and elephants frolic and trumpet his infinite blessings.* Dragons and elephants symbolize an assembly of persons who practice zazen. They frolic because this is their manner of being and expressing themselves, while the true man is economical with his gestures. Without moving an inch and without the slightest effort, he unleashes a power of teaching without limits.

One day long ago, someone noticed Shariputra[4] when he was answering a call of nature in a field. This man felt such deep gratitude at it that he joined his hands and prostrated. The story recounts that at that instant he had a revelation of the true buddha nature. It seems that seeing Shariputra in the posture of answering his call was something that inspired a profound effect. Something within Shariputra compelled respect. Doing zazen or reading the sutras, we must give rise to this respect, as well as in all our daily activities like eating or going to the toilet, things to which in general we grant little respect. Thus, infinite blessings spring up in each moment of life, like the dragons and elephants that frolic in it, without any necessity to explain the Dharma.

Men who have been forged thus in the Way of the Buddha have attained awakening, *awakening all beings of the three vehicles and five families*. According to Buddhist tradition, the three vehicles are the shōmon, engaku and bodhisattva,[5] who have already entered the Way. The five families are the five "natures"[6] or categories of human beings. The three first are those destined to achieve awakening. The fourth is that of the undetermined, which does not pose problems since each of us is of an undetermined nature at our origin. In the final category are those whose nature cannot comprehend the Way.[7] Nevertheless, here we are told that even this group will have revelation of the buddha nature if they encounter a true man who carries the sword of wisdom.

These days everyone gives precedence to rational understanding. Yet here reason is worthless. With only pictures as explanation, you'll never shoot an arrow into the target. We don't learn and feel a posture from a book. The same is true for zazen. You won't understand it without seeing it done and doing it yourself. Today, quantities of books are written on *zen* by people who don't even practice. One day long ago, when Rishōkoku was visiting Yakusen Igen Zenji[8], he paid him a compliment: "You've trained your body so well that you resemble a crane." Truly, it's to this that we aspire.

Unadulterated, the hini grass of the snowy mountains yields the pure clarified butter that alone nourishes me. The white cows that solely crop this herb give sweet and creamy milk, comparable to no other. The "snowy mountain" is the Himalaya, which symbolizes Shākyamuni. It is in this region that he taught the doctrine of the gate of the Dharma. He preached only a single doctrine, pure and unadulterated. He certainly did not envisage two, much less three, vehicles.

The teaching of the Buddha is to become Buddha. Every man who seizes the sword of wisdom becomes Buddha. Or, if you prefer, every man who eats the pure grass of the Himalaya becomes Buddha. You as well as me. Thanks to the teaching of the Buddha, our body, just as it is, expresses the best of itself. By actualizing our buddha nature in our daily life we optimize our faculties as a human being. Thanks to this, we can lead a life worth living.

47

One nature perfectly penetrates all natures.
One phenomenon contains all phenomena.
A single moon appears in all waters,
Its myriad reflections emanating from a single moon.

One Thing, Ten Thousand Things

One nature perfectly penetrates all natures. One phenomenon contains all phenomena. The *Shinjinmei* says the same thing: "One is all; all is one." One, all, little, much: we must revise all these concepts that we formulate about things. Men nearly always reason in terms of quantity. Well, if we consider things from the standpoint of their intrinsic substance, each one is unique. There's only one fact. Whatever quantity might be mentioned, mud will always remain mud and gold will remain gold. As poor as you may be, if you are awakened to the Buddha, you are Buddha. As rich as you may be, if you are prisoner of your illusions, you remain an ordinary man. *One nature perfectly penetrates all natures. One phenomenon contains all phenomena.*

Menzan Oshō tells this anecdote in Kenmonhōeki: One day old Sonnō said to an adept of the Pure Land school who'd come to visit him: "They tell me that in your tradition when a practitioner of namu amida butsu dies, Buddha comes to his aid. Is this true?" "Yes, it's the truth. Buddha manifests at the moment of the practitioner's death." Then old Sonnō said to him: "I wonder if Mister Amida uses his supernatural powers to fly in the air? Because in this world there aren't merely one or two who die at the same time. The world is so vast that they die here and they die way over there. There are hundreds of men dying everywhere. Zip! he comes here. Zip! he goes over there. Obviously, we're speaking of Amida Buddha, but even so it's a task to break your bones!" The worthy man, no longer really understanding at all, kept quiet, merely responding, "Ha!"

Then old Sonnō explained to him: "Amida doesn't save men by flying to their aid. He is Amida Buddha, treasure body of the Dharma world. Like the moon which, although unique, is reflected in all waters and is seen everywhere, he assists all beings while remaining motionless. He doesn't give himself the trouble of going to the rescue of each man here and there." The moon is reflected in the Yang-tze and the Sumida rivers, in a mosquito-infested swamp of stagnant water, a puddle of urine, a drop of dew suspended from a blade of grass, and in a pot of water.

Banzan Zenji wrote this poem: "The mind, solitary moon, contains all things in its light." It's thus that our mind functions. Or to put it another way, *"One nature perfectly penetrates all natures, one phenomenon contains all phenomena."*

Let us consider sleeping and eating. If a thief goes out in the evening without eating, he has an empty stomach and can't accomplish his task, nor run fast enough to get away. Similarly, he ought to think about taking a nap and putting on clothes suitable for passing unnoticed. A good plate of grilled sausage with rice gives him the necessary energy to take off at full speed. The policeman who will eventually have to chase a thief also takes a nap and he eats, since if his stomach cries famine he'll be unable to catch the bad guys and wrestle with them. He also changes clothes to put on the uniform suited to his function. Thus, one eats and sleeps to steal but one also eats and sleeps to catch a thief.

If an ordinary man studies, it's to better fabricate illusions. He attends the university, and the more he progresses in the sciences, the more he fabricates. Be that as it may, it's also necessary to eat, sleep, and change clothes in order to fabricate illusions. The Buddha also eats, but why does he do so? He eats to work for the benefit of all beings. He gets up early for others, he sleeps at night for others. Whether he laughs or he weeps, whatever he does, he does it to serve all beings.

Buddha and ordinary man, thief and police officer, all make the same daily gestures, even though in a totally different spirit. That's why it's said: *"One nature perfectly penetrates all natures. One phenomenon contains all phenomena. A single moon appears in all waters, its myriad reflections emanating from a single moon.* It's also written in the *Kegon-kyō*: "Single and multiple coexist without any difficulty." One is all; all is one.

In the first volume of the Wanshi kōroku, Wanshi Zenji[2] remarks, "Once the high walls that surround us are brought down, existence appears in all its splendor and the ten directions perfectly make response." In our daily life, existence becomes truly marvelous when the barriers that impede our liberty are destroyed. In contrast, if one carries in his heart bad intentions, resentment or bitterness, existence becomes narrow and rigid. In the Bendōwa chapter of Shōbōgenzō, Dōgen also says: "When you let go, the Dharma fills your hands." Nothing remains in the hand, but this nothing brings out the all. It's the principle of the Way, when you strip yourself of all, the infinitely subtle appears.

"The ten directions perfectly make response." The echo answers you, and you respond in echo. Liberty is total in the ten directions and the four quadrants. Yamabiko, god of the mountain, calls, "Hello!" and he is answered, "Hello!" Exactly as a mirror reflects a face, no matter what the face may be.

The mirror is innocent, nothing hinders it, and thus it sends back images exactly.

It is illusions that impede man's vision. *The tranquil man who has attained awakening and ceased studying and acting* is innocent like the mirror. No matter what turbulence and vicissitudes loom before him like immense cliffs, given the fact that he's not bound by false concepts, the ten directions respond to him perfectly. He is obstructed nowhere, neither in the vertical nor the horizontal.

48

The Dharma body of all the buddhas penetrates my nature,
My nature and Buddha forming one nature.
When one stage is passed through, all are.
There is neither form, nor mind, nor karmic act.

Cease Fire!

When I practice the Way of the Buddha, *the dharma body of all the buddhas penetrates my nature.* Buddha resides in my body. That he should live in me is nothing extraordinary. When you're under the influence of alcohol, drunkenness lives in you. When you furtively sneak into a house to pinch something, a thief lives in you. If you smash your fist into someone's head, you're inhabited by an angry demon, and by a starving demon when you secretly go to the kitchen to eat. There's an animal in you when you complain and groan like a beast. When you practice the Way of the Buddha, Buddha resides in you. The essence of all the buddhas penetrates your nature. You are in symbiosis with the Way and a mutual exchange takes place. The distance that separates you from the Buddha disappears. You can't place your palms in gasshō and simultaneously quarrel with your wife.

As often as not, man conducts himself so as to demean himself. Man has the capacity to raise himself to a superior level, but not only doesn't he try to attain the average level, he seems intent on descending to the lowest level. A horse doesn't act below the average level for a horse. A dog doesn't comport himself below his level as a dog. Only man commits acts below his level as man. When in lust or brutality he falls into hell, he debases his quality as a human being, and it's only when he has exhausted his error that he becomes a man again. He may experience a temporary joy, but once the reward is used up, he falls again to the average level of the ordinary man. Men who attain the superior level are very rare. The majority of men remain below the average, because their training and education pull them toward the bottom.

Good training is that which permits the Dharma body of all the buddhas to penetrate my nature.

They say that man is egoistic in his family relationships and that this is the reason for domestic dramas. Let's suppose that a husband and wife are in the throes of a quarrel when someone rings the doorbell. The husband slips into the toilet and shuts the door. The wife runs to the kitchen, where she opens the faucet full blast, creating a noise that will allow her to pretend that they didn't hear the doorbell. With just enough time to allow the fever to cool, she combs her hair and touches up her makeup. The husband coughs in the john, another stratagem to show he is occupied. Noise of water. He washes his hands, runs a comb through his hair, comes out, and goes to open the door. "I'm sorry . . . please . . . come in." The wife arrives: "We're happy to see you . . . come on in. . ." They act as though they've forgotten their quarrel. How many people live in this way! I say to them: "Cease fire!" You absolutely must stop shooting at life.

My Nature and Buddha Forming One Nature

My nature and Buddha forming one nature. When the body of all the buddhas penetrates my nature there is interpenetration and fusion. My nature dissolves into the Buddha and he into me. That's to say we're not merely stitched together like two pieces of cloth. Even if my face remains that of an ordinary man, on the inside I have become Buddha. For instance, there's a saying about greetings: "The one who prostrates and the one who receives the prostration each has a nature empty and without characteristic." To put it another way, a single body plus the body of another make only one.

In Buddhist rituals, there are many salutations. We often bow in gasshō, but that also forms part of the practice of the one who's greeted. You don't cease saluting the master teacher and the master of discipline, but when you ascend to the high teaching chair, you feel no embarrassment at being honored and absolutely do not have the feeling of being venerated like a god. From the instant that two persons engage in a reciprocal bow, there is a fusion between the two, since the nature of the one as of the other is "empty and without characteristic." A perfect salutation is truly not a stupid formality. When each one disregards his self, the two egos disappear.

Dōgen Zenji wrote in the collection of poems, *Songs on the Way of the Sheltering Pine*,[2] "Snow covers the winter grasses, the white egret hides itself in its whiteness." As taught by the Buddha, the true sense of the salutation is to make the ego disappear. Supposing that a demon wants to trap me, he can't get his hands on me while I salute the Buddha because I no longer have ego. I cannot be seized because the nature of all the buddhas penetrates my nature and my nature has dissolved into that of the Buddha. The Way of the Buddha is practiced in the midst of the ordinary man's illusions. You don't practice because you've had satori. You practice because you have sexual, nutritional, and other needs that in no way differ from those of an ordinary man. You don't practice to become a sort of mummy. One is similar to an ordinary person even while being one with the Buddha. The awakening to the Buddha and patriarchs, this merging of ordinary man and Buddha, is of great subtlety.

A master asked a devout person who was praying for happiness in a future life: "You don't think then that you'll go to paradise?" "No, I'm an ordinary man. I will certainly go to hell!" "Then what does the Buddha do?" "The Buddha helps me, but . . ." "If you fall even though the Buddha comes to your aid, mustn't there be a gap somewhere?" The worthy man answered, "Yes," but did not understand. When the nature of all the buddhas penetrates my nature and my nature dissolves into the Buddha, there is no gap. Concerning the man who falls and the Buddha who helps, the *Hōkyō Zanmai*[3] has this phrase:

"When there is fusion, there is happiness." This fusion takes place during zazen: *When one stage is passed through, all are.*"

There is neither form, nor mind, nor karmic act. It's written in the *Bonmō-kyō*[4]: "Without karma, without mind, without thusness, without cause, without effect." I will add: "Without ego, without beauty, without ugliness." All these things are illusions, conditioned production. One cannot understand the teaching of the Buddha unless one gets rid of the tutelage of phenomena, of mind and of action.

49

A snap of the fingers and the eighty thousand teachings are accomplished,
And in an instant the three great kalpas are destroyed.

Like a Screw

From the moment one gets rid of the tutelage of phenomena, of mind and of action and seizes the nature of reality, one experiences the Way of the Buddha. As the *Kegōn-kyō* states: "As soon as awakening takes place, one becomes completely buddha." When the nature of all the buddhas penetrates my nature, I awaken and my nature unites with that of the Buddha. What differentiates the ordinary man from Buddha is the way in which each utilizes his own body. One puts it at the service of illusions and the other at the service of the Way.

When I look back on my life, I could have been something completely other than a monk. As a child, I imagined myself practicing all sorts of professions. Is it a stroke of chance that I became a monk and dedicated all my strength to it? For example, I could have become a road worker on the railroad. I would have swung my pickaxe, digging up the dirt during the day and in the evening returned home to drink great cups of saké. I would have loved this life because it would have been mine. Or maybe a narrator of rakugo,[1] though I don't know if I would have been up to snuff. Or yet again, a teller of popular stories. I would have loved to sing naniwa[2] or recite gidayu,[3] accompanying myself on the shamisen.[4] I could truly have become anything, a good guy or a bad guy. Life is like a screw; it can be screwed in here or there, and fulfill multiple purposes. It's the same for illusions and satori.

The present moment traps eternity, the present moment saves life. Dōgen has written on this subject: " Even if a person lives a slave to appearances and in agitation for a hundred years, if for a single day he commits himself to an active practice, not only his life benefits from it, but also that of all beings for eternity. That day your life will have been worthy of respect, the same as your body. When your practice is sustained, you love your life, your heart, your person, and you respect yourself. It's by active practice that all the buddhas are actualized in daily life and that one attains the great way of the buddhas." In living the present moment to its fullest, one saves eternity. If the present moment is not completely lived, one debases eternity.

A snap of the fingers and the eighty thousand teachings are accomplished and in an instant the three great kalpas are destroyed. However brief it may be, the fully realized moment is eternal. All errors are annihilated and one becomes Buddha.

50

Numbers and words are neither numbers nor words,
What do they have to do with my wonderful awakening?

Neither laudable nor subject to blame,
Like space without limits, its body is empty.

Paradise, Hell: Words

The Buddhist point of view on numbers is very interesting, and not only on numbers, but also on time, degree, and direction. What all these notions have in common is being without substance. Can we observe a number under the microscope? Use the four directions to make up a potion? Take the measure of society's levels with a yardstick? Thus, a long time and a short time, numerous and rare, high and low classes, large and small, good and evil, all these notions are without substance. The texts say: "To live in the illusory is to shut oneself into the fortress of the three worlds[1]; to comprehend the true nature of reality is to open the ten directions. Fundamentally, east and west do not exist. Do you not find north, south, east, and west wherever you may be?" This is the meaning of *numbers and words are neither numbers nor words.* You could also say that there is no direction in directions, or time in time, or degree in degrees. Time itself does not exist and the same is true for all measurements. That which we estimate to be remarkable or banal is neither fixed nor constant. When I was a young monk, I told myself that at sixty I would be a remarkable old monk. Now I'm sixty, and perceive that there's nothing remarkable about me. There is no number in numbers. All value is relative and exists only hand in hand with something else. Paradise and hell are merely different words.

In the same way, light is not light, existing only in relation to darkness. I'm writing by the light of an electric lamp, and if at this moment a blackout occurs, I am in darkness. When I was a child seated on the tatami by the light of an oil lamp, I nevertheless succeeded in learning my lesson: "Thorough study is the work of Confucius and his disciples. It is like the door that opens onto the Way of virtue . . ." When the oil ran out, I lighted two big sticks of incense that allowed me to continue to read. Light is not light, darkness is not darkness.

What do they have to do with my wonderful awakening? Uninterrupted buddha nature is within us. Bodhidharma talked of "the marvel of our own nature," and Sōzan Daishi[2] of "the perfect light of our awakened nature." These expressions convey the identity of our nature and buddha nature. We experience our true nature in zazen when we are hishiryō, beyond rational thought. Perfect concentration is the awakening to our true nature, which the *Daihatsunehan-kyō*[3] calls "buddha nature" and the Lotus Sutra "the true character of all the buddhas." The *Hannya shingyō* (Heart Sutra) tirelessly repeats: "all phenomena are empty." In consequence, *numbers and words are neither numbers nor words*. All phenomena, good/bad, happiness/unhappiness, fortune/misfortune, have no connection with our true nature.

Neither laudable nor subject to blame. Judging the value of things via good or bad is without foundation: this being, that is; that being, this is. There's nothing to add. A horse's head is long, that's the way it is. There's no intrinsic validity to the idea that a light complexion is more prestigious than a dark complexion. A bird is a bird, an egret is an egret. One day a guy told me that I was ugly (which was very discourteous), but Sawaki is Sawaki. Does he have a dark complexion? A beat up face? A flat nose? All these physical characteristics are relative, there's no need to praise or to censure them. Truly, there's deep insight in that statement.

If we look around ourselves, we realize that there's nothing to flee or to pursue in this world: *Like space without limits, its body is empty.* Nothing is fixed or constant. The universe is without limits. One can't say that it's good or bad, bright or gloomy, that one loves or doesn't love. There's nothing to say.

51

It is always right here, clear and tranquil.
But, friend, if you seek for it you will not see it.

It can be neither seized nor rejected.
It may be grasped only within the heart of the ungraspable.

When speech is silence and silence is speech,
The door of the great gift opens of itself, without obstruction.

The Dharma Fills the Sky and the Earth.

It is always right here, clear and tranquil. It is omnipresent where I stand, feet solidly planted on the ground, right here, in this moment, just as I am. One must not escape either from the place where one is, or from the present moment, or from oneself. However, though we should seize life in its fullness, here and now, we always think of "later" and "elsewhere." By disregarding the present, we always seek to run away. By neglecting the present, we empty it of its substance. We get bored where we are and want to go see what's going on elsewhere, and yet again elsewhere. The quest continues without end and we never find peace. In Gakudōyōjinshū, Dōgen says on this subject, denouncing false masters: "They search in the branches without paying attention to the roots." Truth is everywhere, in the tea as in the rice. It fills the mountain as it fills the river. It is there where we are, in the tearoom, in the fields, in the toilet, in the dining hall, in the bath. Every place, whatever it may be, is filled with the Way. In consequence, *friend, if you seek for it, you will not see it.* It is useless to depart to seek the Way; you will not find it elsewhere than here. In *Hōkyō zanmai*[1] there is also this phrase: "Turning away and touching are both wrong."

The Way is to take things just as they are: *It may be grasped only within the heart of the ungraspable.* The strange taste of the word "ungraspable" disappears if I simply say that one cannot lay hands on the Way, since in truth it fills the sky and the earth. It cannot be seized because it is everywhere.

When speech is silence and silence is speech, the Dharma fills the universe. One teaches it as much through silence as through eloquence. Everything speaks of the Dharma. It expresses itself equally well through the hand, the foot, or the navel. In action or immobile, without the slightest effort, the body seated, standing or lying down speaks of the Dharma. *The door of the great gift opens of itself, without obstruction.* We are free and can go toward others to help them.

52

If someone asks me upon what principle I stand,
I answer: "The power of the great wisdom."

The Power of the Great Wisdom

Following the thread of the poem, we have progressed step by step on the Way, and in the previous verse the door has opened wide. From now on, we no longer face obstacles. We are completely free to go meet others. Questioned on the principle that guides him, Yōka Daishi answers. *"The power of the great wisdom."*

An eternal question to which we must so often respond! Most people think that a religion is a social group's adherence to a system of beliefs. In reality, each individual has his own religion. Religion is the tranquility of mind felt when one is truly oneself. It structures our daily life, yet we can't explain it or show it to anyone. I think that religion is this security hidden in the depths of the self, different for each person, which permits staying on the road without anyone's help.

Shigetsu responded to this question: "It's the essence of ourselves that dwells in us." I also think that religion is the true reality that lives within us. Fundamentally without illusions, without satori, universal, of the same root as the sky and the earth, it fills the universe. Such must be our religion.

It is obvious that if our own essence is religion, the quarrels that agitate adherents of the Jōdō and Zen branches of Buddhism appear completely ridiculous, just as it is useless to ape Shākyamuni or Master so-and-so. Other times, other customs. The essential thing is for each of us to seize our own tranquility of mind, here and now. Put another way, "The power of the great wisdom."

Maka hannya,[1] the great wisdom, is composed of the term maka (Sk. maha), which signifies great, manifold, profound, weighty. The substance of this word is so rich that it is untranslatable. Hannya (Sk. prajna) is wisdom. Maka hannya thus signifies the supreme wisdom, great, rich and profound, so profound that it is unfathomable, absolute wisdom.

There are all kinds of power: a child's tears, a woman's anger, the power of the scholar, the tradesman, the sumō wrestler. Here, it's a matter of the power of maka hannya. Wisdom is a force that never leads to an impasse. It's the power of true liberation. The bodhisattva of true liberation[2] holds this power.

How has he attained it? He has clearly seen that the five aggregates are empty[3] and "relieved all suffering."[4] He's obtained it after having abandoned his self. Those who remain walled in by their self do not have wisdom, which manifests only when one has genuinely cast off the self. We see clearly the nature of the self only when we look at it objectively.

We can use a mirror to see our face and body, but how can we see the ego? It's enough to do zazen. Nothing compares with zazen for exhibiting one's ego. All our ugliness appears during zazen. The more pure the zazen, the more clearly we see into ourselves, and the more clearly we see, the more the ego appears dirty. To truly know yourself, you must do zazen. Dōgen wrote in the Genjōkōan fascicle of Shōbōgenzō: "To study the Buddha Way is to study the self. To study the self is to forget the self." To do zazen is to know oneself. It's the power of maka hannya.

The lives of the old ones show that they all had the power of maka hannya. For example, take the great scholar of wisdom, Kanadaiba.[5] He didn't give lectures or commentaries on the texts; he deepened his wisdom by living it in daily life. One day a heretic mortally wounded him, and as he was on the point of death his disciples asked him for the name of his attacker. He answered, "If I give you his name, he will become your enemy and you will kill him." He died saying nothing.

All phenomena are conditioned productions. To hate one's enemy or love one's friend are mental constructions. When one holds the power of maka hannya, the enemy obliges you to make an effort and thus becomes your teacher. Likewise, if you have an overly attentive mother too loving in your regard, you'll rest snuggled into her down robe and become weak and without defense. In the old days, they said, "Travel shapes youth." By being abandoned to one's own efforts, one acquires true force of character and a spirit of independence.

To various degrees, all my life I have been the target of criticisms, slanders and persecutions. Things are what they are, but these attacks have had an extremely salutary effect on me. Without them, I could have fallen very low. Whether they criticize or praise you, arrange your enemies and your friends in your medicine chest and use them like remedies for the welfare of the Way. It's an example of the efficacy of maka hannya. By regarding yourself objectively and understanding that the five aggregates are empty, you come to the aid of all those who suffer. Wherever you may be, you are no longer unhappy. Everything becomes the Way and true happiness.

53

What are good and evil? No one knows.
Progress or regression? Even heaven cannot measure.

To Die to Live

When absolutely everything in the universe is the Way, what do good or evil, progress or regression, truth or error mean? All day long we make use of ready made formulas that mean nothing, saying, "I'm fine, thanks!" when everything is going badly. These are words that reflect only themselves. Perhaps it's a peculiarity of the ordinary man to reflect only himself. Shākyamuni said, "Gold is a venomous serpent." And Confucius, "Good food is an evil." Thus one speaks badly of something that is good. What is good? What is evil? One no longer knows.

It's written in *Hōkyō zanmai*,[1] "In darkest night it is perfectly clear; in the light of dawn it is hidden." And in *Sandōkai*, "In the light there is darkness, but don't take it as darkness. In the dark there is light, but don't take it as light." This is exactly what is meant by *What are good and evil? No one knows.*

Progress or regression? Even heaven cannot measure. Who can know whether something's proceeding in the correct direction, or in the opposite? What's good or bad for the health? A remedy becomes a poison, and a poison a remedy.

In the Gion quarter of Kyōto, there was an oiran (high status courtesan) named Jigoku Dayū who became a disciple of Ikkyū Osho. Someone said about her, "When I come to visit her she is not Jigoku (hell), but a Buddha." It is said that young people who came to play with her received teachings from her and left better people.

Thus, things in this world are not what they appear. As Hakuin

Zenji[5] says, "When 'there is' appears, so also does 'there is not.' Moon reflected in the water."

The power of maka hannya is not dependent on criteria founded upon reason, good sense, or imagination. We find two examples in Kabuki plays: Benkei beat his master Yoshitsune to keep his identity secret, and Oishi Yuranoske ate fish rather than a vegetarian meal on the anniversary of his lord's hara-kiri, to hide his intention of avenging his lord. When one steps back to judge human actions, one no longer knows where the good and where the evil. But thanks to the power of maka hannya, one knows that no matter where, or whatever the difficulties one may encounter, the good exists within the evil.

54

My practice began very early and extended through numerous kalpas.
I am not some joker who speaks lightly.

To raise the banner of the Dharma, establishing the teaching of our school,
The clear-sighted Buddha designated the monk of Sōkei.
Kāshyapa, the first, transmitted the lamp.
His line numbers twenty-eight generations in India.

Now, crossing rivers and seas, it has entered our land.
Bodhidharma was our first patriarch.
We know that six generations have transmitted the robe.
Innumerable are their successors who have attained awakening.

Serious Topic

My practice began early and extended through numerous kalpas. Here Yōka Daishi makes his own declaration of faith. The object of his faith is time eternal, without limits, and his practice is the teaching of the Buddha that allows the infinite to be grasped. This truth is the nature of the timeless Buddha, the true reality that knows neither boundaries nor measures.

I am not some joker who speaks lightly. Within this doctrine there is neither mystification nor falsehoods. Eternity is abolished in an instant when one experiences the non-born and the without-character. Dōgen wrote: "If you practice actively for a single day, it's as if you had practiced or helped others for a hundred years." Eternity is now.

To raise the banner of the Dharma, establishing the teaching of our school. In our time, too, a flag marks every gathering for zazen or each master who transmits the Dharma. Formerly in India they raised a banner and still today in certain regions you can see pennants of all colors floating in the wind, vestiges of former times. In our times, "to raise the banner of the Dharma, establishing the teaching of our school" means, in modern terms, relating one's own experience of awakening. Those who talk of the Dharma without personally having experienced it are parrots. Like dictionaries, they quote what belongs to others. To teach the Dharma is to recount what one has personally experienced.

The clear-sighted Buddha designated the monk of Sōkei. This is a reference to the sixth patriarch Hui-neng (Jp. Enō) who was the most extraordinary representative of the Buddha in the land of China.

Kāshyapa[1] was the first to transmit the lamp. *Zen is not book learning, but is instead an intuitive comprehension transmitted directly from master to student. Today, even if we detest the professor we must attend lectures in order to sit for an exam. Formerly, Zen monks had neither the time nor the patience to listen to masters who didn't suit them. They spent a night in a temple listening to the master and asking him questions; if they weren't satisfied they continued on their way to the next temple. One day they found a master and stayed with him. This is what they called "wandering."[2]

Rationally, transmission of the dharma is an inconceivable process. It's not an intellectual understanding resulting from an oral teaching or reading matter. It's the fusion of two beings. I always liken it to being tuned to the same wavelength. For example, it was sufficient for Kāshyapa to meet Shākyamuni for all his problems to be resolved. Their nature corresponded, which is why Shākyamuni had him sit beside him on a day when he had assembled all his disciples, an action that blew an ill wind through the gathering. They shared the same seat. Transmission is a direct and intimate connection, from person to person.

A current saying is: "My body is here, but my mind is at Zenkoji in Shinano."[3]

Or again, in this poem: "Though your body is no longer in this world, morning and evening, how could I forget your heart?"

To transmit the lamp is to transmit the flame. Shākyamuni passed it to Kāshyapa, who passed it to Ananda. It then passed from mind to mind from Shanavasa to Uptagupta to Dhītaka, arriving finally at Bodhidharma, the twenty-eighth patriarch.

The relationship that developed between Shimokōbe Chōryū[4] and his disciple, Keichū Ajari,[5] illustrates the intimate understanding that takes place between two persons. Keichū wrote: "It is only you who know me, and I think they are rare who know you as well as I." People tuned to the same wavelength are in fact very rare. Tokugawa Mitsukuni[6] had commissioned Shimokōbe Choryū, a scholar of ancient philology, to write a book of commentaries on the Man'yōshū, but illness prevented him and it was his disciple, Keishū, who finished the work, which is titled, "Commentary on the Man'yōshū, completed by Keishū, substituting for his master." Keichū's remarkable labors marked an epoch in the history of the study of ancient texts. I would call this kind of exchange a reciprocal exchange of personality. It is thus that the transmission of the Dharma takes place and that it is inscribed in the traditional lineage. Dōgen thoroughly investigated this question in many chapters of the Shōbōgenzō: "Prediction,"[8] "Face to Face Transmission,"[9] "Transmission Document"[10] and "Transmission of the Robe."

Now, crossing rivers and seas, it has entered our land. It was Bodhidharma, the 28th Indian patriarch, who introduced Zen Dharma into China. His interview with Emperor Wu of the Liang dynasty is reported in the Hekigan-roku. Emperor Wu asked Bodhidharma:

—What is the essential principle of the awakening of the sage?

—To be vast and empty, no sage existing.

—Who, then, faces me?

—I don't know.

Bodhidharma is the first Zen voice heard in China. The text adds: "Not being in accord with the emperor, Bodhidharma crossed the river and withdrew to the land of Wei." He didn't profit from the opportunity that had been offered, but rather passed to the other shore of the Yang-tze River and retired into the Shaolin monastery on Mt. Song, where he practiced zazen for nine years "facing a wall." And the text concludes, "They made Bodhidharma the first patriarch."

His disciple Eka became the second patriarch. One day he arrived at Bodhidharma's dwelling place and asked to be enlightened about the Way, but received no response. Standing in the snow, he waited for Bodhidharma to pay attention to him. He was finally buried in snow up to his waist, and they say that to prove his sincerity he cut off his arm at the elbow. The master at last gave in and accepted him as his disciple. It is to Eka that he will later say, "You have grasped my marrow." Sōzan,[12] author of the *Shinjinmei*, is the third patriarch, the fourth is Dōshin,[13] and the fifth, Kōnin,[14] who lived on Mt. Obai, north of the Yang-tze River. It was here that he discovered one day the qualities of a young kitchen employee pounding rice. He was called Enō (Hui-neng) and became the Sixth Ancestor.

We know that six generations have transmitted the robe. Enō gathered and sold firewood for a living. One day while he was making a delivery he heard someone reciting a sutra: "You must bring forth the mind that lives nowhere." He was overwhelmed by this phrase from the *Kongyō-kyō* (Diamond Sutra) and decided to present himself at the monastery on Mt. Obai. They took him on in the kitchen to pound rice.

One day, the fifth patriarch said to his disciples, "I wish to transmit the Dharma to one of you, so I would like each of you to compose a poem expressing your understanding. If it is in accord with the Way, the author will become my successor." Jinshū,[17] the most brilliant of his disciples, composed the following poem:

> The body is the tree of awakening
> The mind is like a clear mirror on its stand.
> It must be polished ceaselessly
> To wipe away the dust.[18]

He hesitated to deliver it to his master. Three times he directed his footsteps to the stairs leading to Kōnin's room, but in the end gave up. He hung the poem on a wall where everyone would see it. In passing, the fifth patriarch read it and observed, "If one practices the Way in this spirit, one should not be mistaken." All the students learned it by heart, the monastery hummed like a beehive. The future sixth patriarch, who was pounding rice, asked his comrades, "Hey, fellows, what are you mumbling?" "It's Jinshū's poem. Everyone knows it by heart." So he decided to also compose a poem. "Listen to me, " he said to them, "Listen to my poem!" No one wanted to listen to him: "Shut up, imbecile, don't talk nonsense!" So he asked a young monk to find a candle and take him to the place where Jinshū's poem had been posted. Beside it, he had the monk write his poem:

> There is no tree of awakening
> There is neither clear mirror nor stand
> There has never been anything
> Where then could the dust gather? [19]

The disciples were all astounded and so, apparently, was the fifth patriarch, who said, "There's nothing more inopportune or more stupid!" rubbing it out with his sandal. The matter rested there.

That night, the patriarch descended to the kitchen, where he found Enō pounding rice. "Is the white rice finished?" he asked. The future sixth patriarch immediately responded, "It's ready, but it's not yet sifted." He struck the mortar three times. It was at midnight that the fifth patriarch recognized Enō as his successor in the Dharma. The master gave him orders to flee. Enō leaped into a boat, Kōnin handed him a pole and he disappeared. Swarming in every direction, the disciples threw themselves into pursuit.

Enō lived for fifteen years in the mountains like a recluse, and then one day made his entrance into the world. He was ordained a monk, received the precepts and planted the banner of the Dharma at Hōrin-ji temple[20] on Mt. Sōkei. It's there that Yōka Daishi and a great number of disciples experienced profound illumination through contact with him. With Hui-neng (Eno) and his eminent successors such as Seigan[21] and Nangaku Ejō,[22] *zen* took on prodigious scope.

Innumerable are their successors who have attained awakening. Dōgen wrote in Gakudōyōjin-shū: "When the robe [23] arrived at

Mt. Sōkei, the Dharma spread throughout the universe." And in the chapter titled "Transmission of the Robe":[24] "All the buddhas have perfectly transmitted the Dharma of the robe, the transmission has been very correct in China and has remained so later on." It's in this way that the gate of the Dharma has been bequeathed to us.

55

Truth is without foundation and illusion is empty from the outset.
If we simultaneously dismiss both existing and non-existing, emptiness is
*   also non-emptiness.*

Truth and Illusion

Truth is without foundation and illusion is empty from the outset. What is truth? What is illusion? Ask an owl what night is and it will tell you that it's day. Likewise, water is the friend of the fish and the enemy of the drowning man. Truth or illusion? Man decides it in his own way, but in true reality neither truth nor illusions exist. It is written in the *Shinjinmei:* "Do not seek truth, be content to not judge." Considered carefully, truth and illusion are points of view. Well now, a point of view is a perspective, an aspect under which a thing presents itself. You have your point of view and I have mine. Our points of view on the same object can be totally different. Dōgen wrote in Gakudōyōjinshū: "The sixty-two opinions have their origin in the self." For some, gold is a treasure, for others, an enemy. There are those whom gold makes swell with pride and those whom it diminishes. One day, a fellow came to say to me: "These days I am finally beginning to understand that when I have no possessions my world becomes larger." Indeed, the more we human beings possess, the more difficutlt our lives become. Others, who have nothing, celebrate every sort of windfall, such as being offered a free train ticket in response to an invitation to the other end of the country, lacking which, they'd have had to scrape the bottom of the drawer. Truth and illusion are defined by man and have no existence in themselves. As it's said these days, they are concepts, fabrications of the mind. One cannot say that this is the truth and that is an illusion. This being, this is; that being, that is.

Many young girls learn the art of the tea ceremony[1] without understanding its profound meaning. They merely repeat, like parrots, "It's a tableau of extreme beauty," and they bow like monkeys. It's not a matter of beauty. I love fakes. It can seem curious to love fakes, but in our times photography and printing have made such progress that they achieve counterfeits that have the taste of the authentic thing. Since the savor is the same, what does it matter to me! A fake is a fake, I take it as such, and that's fine. Moreover, when an old text is run off on aged paper, you don't really see the difference.

I often hear people say they prefer one sort of yōkan[2] to another. In Tokyo, we have them brought from Kyōto, and in Osaka, from Tokyo. As far as I'm concerned, I'm fully satisfied with bowls of rice and pickled radishes.

A long time ago, on a day when I was traveling by train in the Kansai, I remember that I read in a local newspaper about the considerable quantity of sardines caught in the sea near Ise, and the profit that would be gained from it. A photo showed a beach buried in sardines. The sardine is considered to be an ordinary fish because it's very abundant in our seas. If one fished for it only once a year, no doubt its taste would seem more delicious. Trout is greatly renowned because it's rare. One day I joined a fishing party in the Tamagawa River, but I never saw a trout suspended at the end of the rod. The sardine lives in schools and with one haul of the net you take mountains. It is transported by the truckload, salted, dried, boxed, and the surplus becomes fertilizer. We have little regard for it, and yet it's not bad at all. It would even be superior to trout if it were as rare.

Good and bad are conceptual values that do not exist in themselves. The same goes for truth and illusion. There is no good without evil. It's simply man's karma that produces dualism and determines what's good and what's bad.

Human Rules

Mujū Hōshi[3] wrote in Collection of Sand and Stones, "Tendai Daishi[4] has said: The true person of no-nature does not even do meritorious things, much less harmful things." Said otherwise, happiness is a merit obtained through a virtuous act. So then good would be ambivalent: on the one hand one does good, and on the other one wants to do evil, but one represses the evil to do good! A dangerous model! Thus when someone is watching, you display your lovely actions, but if no one sees you, might as well steal something!

This is the way that cats behave. An old woman who owned a cat always said, "My cat is thoroughly honest. He never takes what I don't give him." It was certainly true. The moment the cat began to stretch out his neck, clack! She gave him a little tap on the muzzle with her long pipe. He didn't have time to even stretch out a paw. It's equally so for men—punishment descends when one is caught in the act.

As for me, I was timid and fearful. Born in poverty, orphaned very young, mistreated by an adoptive mother, I was raised by blows of punishment that rendered me fearful: "You mustn't do that, it's bad!" "You don't do that in front of people, it's bad!" This is how you become a fearful adult. You're afraid, but only when someone's watching you, so it's enough to not seem impudent in front of others. This is how the lazy and the fearful behave. The old woman's cat was prudent and honest because he feared the pipe, but when he could slip into the neighbor's yard, he daringly devoured sardines and fish heads.

We don't act in the name of virtue and we don't do evil when we're perfectly free and the universe penetrates all things. You and I are totally bonded with one another, without the slightest chink separating us, but for offenses to spring up, all it takes is for a partition to rise between us. Heaven and earth have the same root, all things are one, and this is why *truth is without foundation and illusion is empty from the outset.* There is neither truth nor illusion. There is neither good nor evil. There is neither having nor not-having. There is neither large nor small.

Mt. Fuji is regarded as a tall mountain, yet it appears trifling when viewed from the summit of the Himalayas. They say that the Pacific Ocean is immense, yet it's only a portion of the terrestrial globe and when viewed from the standpoint of the universe, it looks like a footbath. We can sound its depths. It's hard to imagine the degree to which man is a minuscule little animal. Seen under a microscope, an amoeba resembles a submarine gliding in the depths of the sea. For it, the small plate where it moves about is as large as the Pacific Ocean. Saying that a thing is large or small is the result of erroneous vision. It's up to us to view our world otherwise.

What is it that delights these little men in their miniscule world? They love to have a good time and to receive gifts. They consider birth a happy event, when it can be a great misery if the baby is disabled, or grows up to be a hoodlum. They also think marriage a matter for congratulations, though we don't know whether the son-in-law may reveal himself to be an inveterate drunkard. Joys and sufferings are completely relative notions, changing and deceptive. Nothing makes it possible for us to declare with certainty that this event is happy and that event unhappy. The good bears within itself the bad, and vice versa.

Therefore, *truth is without foundation and illusion is empty from the outset. If we simultaneously dismiss both existing and non-existing, emptiness is also non-emptiness.* These two verses contain the entire universe: good and evil have no existence in themselves. Given this, the following remark of Shinran's becomes an obvious fact: "There's no need to draw glory from virtue, nor to have fear of evil." All men, without exception, are neither good nor evil.

56

The twenty gates of the void are without foundation.
The nature of Buddha is one; just so his essence.

The Moment Is Eternal

The twenty gates of the void are without foundation. It's thus that one defines the void. The twenty gates are enumerated in the *Hannya shingyo,* the Larger Prajna Paramita Sutra: internal emptiness—external emptiness—internal and external emptiness—emptiness of emptiness—great emptiness—emptiness of supreme truth—emptiness of the conditioned—emptiness of the unconditioned—absolute emptiness—emptiness without end or beginning—emptiness of the non-dispersed—emptiness of the dispersed—emptiness of fundamental nature—emptiness of specific characteristics—emptiness of common characteristics—emptiness of all the Dharmas—emptiness of non-perception—emptiness of non-being—emptiness of own being—emptiness of non-being and own being.

This exhaustive list of the void demonstrates that the void presents no aspect. If it had an aspect, you could measure it—this one is so many millimeters and that one so many grams. In the void there is neither duration, nor good, nor evil, nor pleasure, nor aversion, nor truth, nor illusion. *The twenty gates of the void are without foundation.*

In the void, the concept of the void does not exist. When one has eliminated all things, what remains is the one body of Buddha that fills heaven, earth, and the whole universe.

The nature of Buddha is one; just so his essence. To express this differently, there is not Buddha on one side and a demon on the other, or "your" true nature on one side and "my" true nature on the other. Everyone is Buddha; everyone is demon. Pfft! I'm Buddha. Pfft! I'm demon. Appearing unconcerned, I pinch a jewel and there I am: a thief. Nothing is changed whether an inspector catches me in the act, a policeman arrests me, or I am punished: I am a true thief.

Man is a very strange being. This one is a devout man when he chants namu amida butsu and a shady character when he engages in dishonest conduct in his business. This one does zazen, but when he's no longer doing zazen he smokes, gambles, and drinks alcohol. Others say they're on the way to do zazen, but turn around en route to go to the movies. All these men, whether doing zazen, practicing business, going to the movies or stealing from a shop window, all are part of the same body, like wax figures. With wax, one can equally as well mold a Buddha as a demon. A marionette can become any sort of person, hence this poem: "From the box he carries around his neck, the puppet master says he's going to bring us a Buddha, but it's a demon that appears." It's also said, "Buddha and demon, same face." Buddha is everywhere; the demon is everywhere. There where is Buddha, there also is demon. So, with a blow of the fist let's rid ourselves of all that and simultaneously chase away Buddha and demon, for the substance of Buddha is of one nature.

Nothing can escape from unity, because all things are one. It's said in the *Kongyō-kyō*[1]: "All characteristics are without character, such is the true reality." The least action on our part contains the universe, participates in the entire universe. Thus, each day we accomplish an infinite task, vast as the universe. This is why, from the point of view of time, the present moment is eternity. We breathe in, the whole universe breathes in. When we breathe out, the whole universe breathes out. The work of the eyes is that of the entire world, the same with hearing, taste, touch and consciousness. Here and now we create the world. It's said in the texts: "I myself, together with all animate and inanimate beings of the universe, become the Way. All grasses, tress, regions, lands, without exception, become Buddha." We participate in the work of the entire universe, a task that does not admit of mediocrity.

When we eat dishes we are offered, we need not eat them competely to judge their taste. For example, when we're served koyadofu cooked in shitake broth and seasoned with soy sauce and sugar, if we taste just a little broth we can tell if the whole dish is salty or sweet. Tasting a tiny piece of shitake, we can judge the taste of the entire dish. In short, we know an entire dish through a little taste. *The nature of Buddha is one; just so his essence.* It is true reality because all of its aspects are without aspect. It has neither form nor fragrance and since it has no characteristics, there is nothing.

The king Daibonten-ō wished to measure himself against the Buddha. He placed himself behind him, but since he measured only one foot one inch tall, he reached only the buttocks. Through his supernatural powers he raised himself to two feet, nine inches, but he still only reached the buttocks. Then, by increasing his powers tenfold he enlarged himself again and again. Finally, he reached the top of the head, but was unsuccessful in seeing the top of the skull, because it is here that is found the distinctive mark of the Buddha, that consists precisely in not being seen. This mark is the symbol of the Buddha, all of whose characteristics are without character.

You'd think from what's recounted in the sutras that radio existed in the most distant times. One day, Shākyamuni's disciple Mou-lien,[3] wished to test the range of the Buddha's voice. He set off toward the east and walked straight forward without stopping. Although he covered considerable distance, still he heard the Buddha's voice. Using one of his supernatural powers, he managed to go beyond some thousand myriads of Buddha lands and reached a country flying the banner of the Buddha Kōmyo. Mou-lien arrived right in the middle of a meal. The great iron bowls were filled with rice and, plop! he fell like a drop of water onto the edge of a bowl. The Buddha of this country measured eighty yujūn, with a yujūn[6] representing forty leagues.[7] He was therefore twelve thousand eight hundred kilometers tall. This was truly a large Buddha. He couldn't even have seated himself on our terrestrial globe; he would have hung it on his belt like a medicine box. This Buddha was surrounded by his disciples, who were arhats[8] and in all points similar to this Buddha. Their bowls as well were so large that all of Japan could have been put inside. It was on the rim of one of these that Mou-lien landed.

The arhat saw this, and paid close attention to what seemed to him to be a tiny insect. To observe it more closely, he picked it up delicately between thumb and forefinger. He saw that it had a shaved head, wore a *kesa* and had every appearance of being a monk. The arhat said, "World Honored One, a monk insect has come to visit us. What can be the causes and conditions of his coming? Can there be monk insects?" The Buddha responded, "Well, well. Beyond some thousand myriads of Buddha lands, there is a world named Saha[9] in which resides the Venerated and World Honored One, Shākyamuni. This man that you see is a powerful disciple of this Buddha. He wanted to measure the range of the Buddha' s voice, and thus he's arrived here in our world. However, he's exhausted his powers without exhausting the voice of the Buddha." After having heard the teaching of this Buddha, Mou-lien returned to our earth. They say that Shākyamuni, the World Honored One, heard the Buddha Kōmyo across space at precisely the same moment, just as if by radio.

The universe is one: *The nature of Buddha is one; just so his essence.* All form is non-form, true reality is always the same and never discontinuous. This uninterrupted flow of life is you and is me. How can an ordinary man whose life is limited to the contents of his billfold be aware of this flow? It's only by dying that one truly understands the continuous flow of life.

If we reconsider things from the standpoint of the dead, we see very well that *the nature of Buddha is one; just so his essence.* It is our illusions that create disorder and confusion. At the moment of death, there is no longer good and evil, neither existence nor non-existence. All that is only dreams and illusions.

57

Activity of mind is the base, it creates phenomena as dust.
Both leave traces on the mirror.
Wiped clear, it regains its original brilliance.
No longer obscured by the dust of mind activity and phenomena, true
  reality appears.
Alas! The Dharma is in decline, evil reigns in this age.
Beings lack virtue and control their passions with difficulty.
The more distant the Saint grows from us, the more profound the heresies.
Demons are powerful, the Dharma weak, and hate wreaks havoc.
When Buddha's doctrine of sudden awakening makes itself known,
Their frustration is that they cannot smash it like a tile.

The Last Period of the Dharma

Activity of mind is the base, it creates phenomena as dust. The mind is a conjurer that creates belief in the existence of a subject. It produces dreams and phantasms that create the illusion of an object. Phenomena are the perceptible world, this world's dust.

Both leave traces on the mirror. The mind and phenomena are reflected in the mirror of our true nature, obscuring it, when it is fundamentally pure and without stain. Subject/object, truth/illusion, existence/nonexistence, good/evil, body/mind: all these dualisms are stains, the same as the twenty gates of the void and the non-void.

Wiped clear, it regains its original brilliance. The dirty marks are nothing. When all trace of root, of mind, of subject and object, is eliminated, the mirror recovers its brilliance. The instant the rain ceases and the clouds scatter, the blue sky appears and suddenly the horizon reveals a thousand mountains. *No longer obscured by the dust of mind activity and phenomena, true reality appears.* Zazen exhausts the fabrication of objects appearing through our innate delusion. Then, for the first time truth appears. We discover the truth that all things lack essence and there is nothing to cling to.

Alas! The Dharma is in decline, evil reigns in this age. The Buddha Dharma evolves in three successive stages: a period when the Dharma is correctly taught and practiced, followed by a period when it is distorted or counterfeit, and finally by a period of degradation and decline. The correct dharma is that which Shākyamuni taught during his lifetime. He unified the Dharma through his strong personality and was the engine of its propagation. This man was a leader of fantastic strength who carried everyone in his wake. Decline was indicated from the moment of his death. In his lifetime, they abstained from drinking alcohol, but from the moment he entered nirvana, the thought arose that perhaps there was nothing so terrible about that after all.

Then the doctrine appeared. They drafted what was called Dharma, the Abhidharma[1] or canon of Buddhist scriptures. During Shākyamuni's lifetime, no doctrine was necessary. Only after his death was it established based on his teachings. Still, the doctrine is not solely theoretical, although some monks follow only the dogma. Dharma is based upon three principles that are called the Three Treasures: The Buddha (the teacher), the Dharma (the teachings), and the Sangha (the community).

Little by little, they lost sight of the Buddha's force of personality. Next, the disciples who had direct contact with Shākyamuni disappeared, then the disciples of the disciples. From generation to generation, as a result of cutting the whiskey with water, they ended up with a colorless and tasteless liquid. As time rolled on, the perfume that had emanated from the Buddha dissipated and the Dharma degenerated. *Alas! The Dharma is in decline, evil reigns in this age.*

In the final stage, the Dharma is vanquished by passions. The further it is distant from us, the weaker it becomes and the more the share of our happiness dwindles. Men no longer control themselves and become difficult to manage.

The more distant the Saint grows from us, the more profound the heresies. Demons are powerful, the Dharma weak, and hate wreaks havoc. To the extent that Shākyamuni is further from us, the demons draw nearer. They are numberless and of every kind. There are demons of melancholy, of desires, of greed, of sloth, of fear, of doubt, of remorse, of anger, of profit, of pride. Because the Dharma has been distorted and falsified, they are powerful. The true Dharma weakens, the passions intensify and hate rages everywhere.

When Buddha's doctrine of sudden awakening makes itself known, their frustration is that they cannot smash it like a tile. Sudden awakening is the teaching according to which each man, just as he is, is Buddha. One renounces destroying it because it is indestructible, and one cannot destroy it because the demons exist. Where are these demons? Where do they come from? We will find out in the next verse.

58

Actions arise from the mind, spawning retribution on the body.
There's no point in complaining or blaming others.

How to Hold the Reins

Actions arise from the mind, spawning retribution on the body. In other words, we reap what we sow. Each individual constructs his own world and lives in the universe that he himself has created. Even if we appear to live in the same world, the perception of it differs for each one of us. What we judge to be good or bad depends solely on the manner in which we personally view things. The robber and the robbed see the world differently. The same is true for the person who gives and the person who receives. Seated in the dōjō side by side in zazen, each one's world is different. Satisfaction is read on the face of one and humility on another. This is why monks depart humbly to seek their food by virtue of an ancestral tradition of poverty that permits them to live freely in this world.

Actions arise from the mind. The mind deceives both itself and us. It's the author of our false views about life's affairs. The *Hannya Shingyō* speaks of ten-dō-mu-sō, the untruths and illusions for which we alone are responsible.

Offer a precious object to a cat and all he'll say is "meow... what's that thing? ... meow." Though it is a diamond, he'll not move the tip of his nose. The donkey would respond, "hee-haw . . ." and the cow, "moo . . ." What we call a treasure is the product of our illusions.

Most men consider gold a treasure. In my case, although I also belong to the human race, this is not so. Shākyamuni said, "Gold is a venomous serpent." How stupid to elect money a god of happiness! And the money one borrows? Does it bring happiness? Everything depends on the manner in which we see things. Happiness is at the root of unhappiness and, conversely, happiness is founded upon unhappiness.

Phantoms and ghosts, torments and illusions are merely projections of the mind. When our manner of seeing changes, they disappear completely and nothing remains. This is why we say that the passions give birth to Awakening. From our flesh is born unhappiness, and from our flesh is born the Buddha Dharma.

Buddha nature is not the stuffing with which we garnish a meat pie. Our body is not stuffed with buddha nature: it is buddha nature. Each cell of our body is, without exception, the basic material of the passions. In short, this body is made of passions, and the problem is to know how to make use of it. This mass of flesh is the burden we must carry all our lives. If there were no flesh, we couldn't do zazen. Without this inconvenient thing, we couldn't work. If we destroyed it, we could no longer do anything. So there is no other solution except to take it in hand and guide it by embracing the objective of bringing it to the highest point of its capacity. Thus, from the passions will be born awakening and the inconvenient load will become completely tolerable.

If this mass of passions becomes an overpowering force, it drags us forward implacably, with in most cases no possibility of resisting. The human being has all sorts of natural appetites, sexual and other, without which he wouldn't exist. And add to these greed, anger, stupidity, discontent, and doubt. Passions are without number, but when we learn how to recognize them and how to make use of them, they finish by no longer weighing anything.

"With the rust that comes from the body, one fashions a red prisoner's coat," says a proverb. Let's say that we row our own boat and reap what we sow. "I didn't mean to do that, but under the impulse of the moment . . ." What's done is done. In two or three seconds an irresistible desire to steal something arises . . . zip! That's it . . . and one spends two or three years in a cell. *Actions arise from the mind, spawning retribution upon the body.*

"I didn't intend to steal and wouldn't have if his negligence hadn't pushed me to it. It's not my fault, he's the guilty one." We always wish to push the fault off onto someone else. *There's no point in complaining or blaming others.*

He wasn't longing for a watch or a wallet, but the wallet sticking out of a pocket winked at him, and the watch ticked and drew his attention. The temptation was too strong and he gave them a new home. The negligent owner was the guilty one. "It's the girl who tempted me with her red lips, her makeup, her curls, and her bewitching regard. I didn't do anything at all; I just felt desire rise and I couldn't resist." We always wish to attribute our faults to someone else, when in reality the seed of the evil is in our own self. No matter how great the seductive power of the other might be, if the seed weren't there in us, it would have no effect. Go ahead and see if you can seduce a pine tree or a rock! The moon remains indifferent to your charm. This seed of seduction is within you, and all it takes is an impulse for it to germinate. From then on, anything can happen, but it depends upon our vision of reality. Dōgen says in the Gakudōyōjin-shū: 'It's to hold the truth in aversion and to seek illusion." I think man loves illusion; he loves to be deceived.

However that may be, things are what they are. Let's return to our foremost mission and find again our panoramic view. Let's take our self in hand and learn to know it. It is said in Fukanzazengi, "Learn to withdraw, turning the light inward, illuminating the self." That means that over there, there is nothing. Everything is here. Mencius said, "Everything, absolutely all, is within us."

59

To avoid creating a karma of uninterrupted suffering,
Do not slander the teachings of the true Buddha Dharma.

To Slander the Buddha Dharma

To avoid creating a karma of uninterrupted suffering. Wherever one may be and whatever one may do, suffering never ceases. It's daily hell. Even illness and misery grant some moments of concession, but there's no respite in the present case; the harassment is continual. Not the slightest spot of repose in time or space. Unless you wish to know such pain, don't slander the teaching of the true Buddha Dharma.

To slander the Buddha Dharma is to denigrate yourself: "I'm a poor excuse of a guy, there's no buddha nature in me. Guys like me can't know awakening." When we thus belittle ourselves, we profane our self and debase the true Dharma.

Shākyamuni taught us to understand our real nature: "Know yourself, know your buddha nature and you will know that you also are Buddha." In fact, to realize that one is oneself Buddha is to understand the teaching of the true Dharma. Conversely, to depreciate oneself by considering that there is no resemblance between one's self and Buddha is to slander the Dharma.

Commentary

The Jōfukyō[1] chapter of the Lotus Sutra illustrates this aspect of the Dharma. The bodhisattva Jōfukyō prostrated to everyone he met, saying "I would never dare to disrespect you. Surely you are all to become buddhas." He profoundly respected all men because they were Buddha. They responded to his words with abuse, threw stones at him, and beat him with sticks. He moved away and cried, "I will never scorn you because one day you will practice and infallibly realize your condition of Buddha." Countless kalpas flowed by before he was understood. All the men that he venerated despite their insults are now gathered around him, for the bodhisattva Jōfukyō who taught this aspect of the dharma was none other than Shākyamuni.

I am Buddha, just as I am. If I do not respect myself, I commit a sacrilege. "I earn ten thousand yen a month, maybe it's not much, but even so, with my ten thousand yen I am Buddha. I am a complete ten thousand yen Buddha." In Buddhism, it makes no difference whether one earns ten thousand or fifty thousand yen. Ten thousand yen is ten thousand yen, a hundred thousand yen is a hundred thousand yen. What does the salary matter? Just as one is, one is Buddha. In the *Hōkyo Zanmai* it is said. "When inverted thinking stops, the affirming mind naturally accords." Such is satori. To understand is to realize one's true reality.

Let's seize ourselves, the ultimate of ourselves, our genuine ego, never mind what name we give it. It's critical to grasp it, for just as it is, it is buddha nature. Everything that sees the self as inferior, belittles and debases it, is wrong. All desecration of the self scorns the Dharma and in consequence the mind lives a veritable hell with no respite.

To seize our true nature, we must know how to mark the places where a pause is necessary. It's not good to always run after something. To pause does not mean to stagnate. To pause is to find pacification, tranquility of spirit, peace of mind within ourself. The young girl finds contentment in her condition as a young girl and, become a woman, in her womanly condition, then as a grandmother and finally in death. Most often the girl is in a hurry to become a woman and when she's a woman she wants to be a mother. The servant is bored with cooking rice and wishes to immediately be the proprietress, but become proprietress she finds the work too hard. Let the servant fully enjoy her condition as servant, the young girl her condition as young girl. The essential thing is to live fully: we are what we do.

One day I received a postcard from a policeman telling me that he did his best to live fully "his condition" of police inspector. Reading his card, I couldn't help laughing. Exactly so! He had perfectly assimilated my teaching. To become Buddha is to become completely oneself. When one is not oneself, life becomes hell. A schoolboy who imitates adults by smoking is a ghost of a schoolboy. Not being oneself, just as one is, is to despise the teaching of the true Buddha Dharma. "Even if I earn but one go, I am a samurai." I fully live my life as a warrior even though I must clench my teeth against an empty stomach. It's an interesting aspect of the Japanese soul: if I get a thousand go and yet I'm not authentically myself I ridicule the teaching of the true Dharma and my life becomes a hell without remission.

60

The lion makes his home within the thick foliage of the sandalwood forest
Where no other trees grow.

Authentic men

Long ago, the temple of Kisshō-ji at Komagome was called "Sandalwood Forest."[1] The name signified that only highly accomplished men lived within this temple. They had personalities with clear and pure contours like all those who seize their self and carry it without letting go. When we don't have our self well in hand, we act only in imitation of others. On the contrary, the one who is at one with himself is like the man in the poem: "In the lion dance, he doesn't beat the drum or play the flute, he becomes the back paws."

When one performs as a horse's hind hooves, one must fulfill perfectly one's role as hind hooves. It goes without saying that not just anyone is capable of playing the role of Atsumori or Kumagai in the Kabuki play Ichinotani, but without the horses one cannot perform the piece. Moreover, when the front feet advance the hind feet mustn't remain still. It's only when the rear feet walk in perfect harmony that the play succeeds. In the lion dance,[2] it's not enough to beat the drum and play the flute for the play to succeed. The hind feet must also play their role perfectly.

"Within the thick foliage of the sandalwood forest where no other trees grow." In this forest live only men who have found their true ego. The one in charge of housework plays his role perfectly and realizes his self in the act of wielding the dust cloth. Each is identified with what he does. Each one is completely concentrated and one with the action he performs, whether in the kitchen, at the great bell,[3] the taiko drum, the mokugyo, or sutra reading. In this forest of sandalwood, dense and deep, grow no other species of trees. Solely those who have realized their true nature live thus. We call them lions.

61

Alone, he prowls in the silence and tranquility of the forest.
All other animals, having fled, stay away.
A band of lion cubs follows him.
At three years of age their roar is already powerful.

Even if a hundred thousand jackals wished to pursue the king of the
    Dharma,
These monsters would yap in vain.

Alone with oneself

Lions are alone. No one sees them, so they don't remain on guard. In general, when we know we're being observed, we make an effort, but when no one is watching we let ourselves go. A lion does not comport itself like a little mouse. *Alone, he prowls in the silence and tranquility of the forest.* The lion lives in a world that belongs to him. The rabbit gambols and . . . hop! hop! . . . clears out, for he's always on guard and acts only in step with others' attention. The world where the lion lives has been described often:

> Pearl of dew, pure light . . .
> Three thousand worlds, treasures revealed . . .
> High solitary pine . . .
> Majestic mountain, sovereign of heaven and earth . . ."

Whatever the chosen images may be, they evoke the place where one is alone in the silence of oneself. One must be able to find the calm and silence of the forest, no matter where, even right in the middle of a boulevard. The winds of the eight directions may blow, one does not stir; praise or criticism, joy or anger, one is indifferent to the passions. When the lion roars, the ordinary feathered or furred animals, rabbits, mice, foxes or badgers, run off as far as they can go. When one has seized his self, no one approaches.

The young lions follow the way of the old ones: *At three years their roar is already powerful.* They roar like their parents, though the intonation is still lacking. They do not yet live fully conscious of their role as lions.

Even if a hundred thousand jackals wished to pursue the king of the Dharma, these monsters would yap in vain. The jackal resembles the fox, but the king of the Dharma is the lion. The Dharma has only one master, not two, much less three. Even supposing that a hundred thousand jackals imitated the lion's roar, they could go on opening their muzzles and crying as much as they wished, their voices would not carry. It's also said in the *Nehangyō*,[1] "Were the jackal to imitate the roar of the lion, a hundred, a thousand, years would pass before he acquired his cry. In contrast, a little three-year-old lion cub roars like his parents." The lion's roar cannot be imitated. You must be a lion yourself to roar like him. The lion is the image for buddha nature. The Buddha Dharma teaches how to become a lion, how to authentically live our true nature.

62

The sudden perfect doctrine is without human inclinations
If you have unresolved doubts, you must struggle with them.

A New Vision of Life

The sudden perfect doctrine is without human inclinations. By considering all things equally, we free ourselves from sectarian opinions that require that this be Tendai[1] or that be Shingon.[2] One does not base oneself on fallacious concepts that suggest that hell is bad and the Buddha is good. In truth, if one is satisfied with his life in hell, why not stay there? Likewise, if someone pretends to be Buddha and gives himself important airs, it's only a vast imposture. He who thinks he has satori is completely in error. I always repeat it in vain, but can't ever repeat it enough: concepts are illusions.

The Tendai approach proceeds by chronological stages and levels of understanding—the teaching of the three baskets, the general doctrine, the special doctrine and the perfect doctrine. The three baskets mean the Hinayana sutras. The general doctrine straddles the Hinayana and the Mahayana. The special doctrine clearly affirms that it's definitely Mahayana. As for the perfect doctrine, it is absolutely not specific. It is sufficient to rediscover one's true nature.

This point is illustrated in the "Faith and Understanding" chapter of the *Lotus Sutra*. It's the story of a man abducted from his family when a very young child. He lived miserably by begging until his father found him again. In the intervening time, his father had made a huge fortune and lived in opulence. Being humble and poor, the young vagrant thought it was a dream. He entered his father's house as a domestic servant, and then climbed the rungs to the point where he became steward. After long years, he suddenly realized that he was the owner of this immense fortune. "But then," he said to himself, "I've always been rich! Even when I held out my chipped begging bowl, I wasn't poor! My poverty was a dream!" Now that he had become rich, he clearly understood his true condition. In looking back over his life, he understood that fundamentally illusions have no existence: there is nothing. The return to one's normal condition is to be oneself, because just as one is, one is Buddha. No being exists that does not possess buddha nature. If we reflect for a moment upon our society, can we say that one man is better placed than another? A boss certainly has more worries than his clerk. When the latter goes off to run errands, he talks with his buddies, offers himself little extras, and life is beautiful! You can't tell which one is happier. But if we look more closely, if the errand boy wants to earn ten or fifty thousand yen a month, he is exactly like a beggar who takes to the road with his chipped bowl, dreaming of becoming rich. When we make the mistake of considering things from a materialist point of view, we devalue our own nature.

To Depart from the Forefront

The sudden perfect doctrine is unrelated to human feelings. Unlike the situation with the ordinary man, the perception of the world is not accomplished via the ordinary emotions. For that man, it's better to be rich than poor and employer than employee. He prefers what is good to what is bad. This fashion of thinking is of an affective nature. When one transcends emotions and preferences, the vision of reality is totally different and phenomena appear from a dramatically opposed angle.

Poverty gave me lack of care. I inherited only debts from my parents, yet despite this I am king of my kingdom, a king who travels on foot, carrying with him his treasures and his estate. I am at home everywhere. When they ask my address, I reply: "Komazawa University." Immediately they ask, "Isn't that your office address?" These days, people think you work at a university to put a salary in your pocket. I don't go to Komazawa University to earn my living. It's the place where I work, which is to say, where I fulfill my mission. Then, say, I go to Sojiji, and people ask. "Is that also your work?" I don't set myself up anywhere. I'm here, I go there, and from there I go elsewhere. I advance from one point to another, for I have no house to which to return. Without care, I take to the road toward my ultimate dwelling. It's simply for convenience' sake that I leave companions and furnishings in place to serve me as reference points along the road.

My stepfather borrowed huge amounts of money against what he'd receive if his stepson didn't survive the Russo-Japanese war. He pawned my life, but having survived the war, upon my return I paid off his debts. May heaven forgive me, on the day I made the final payment I raved with happiness and shouted to the four winds that now I was the only master on board!

If my parents had left me a fortune, I would have squandered it and no doubt turned out badly. Without forcing my body to take exercise, it was trained all by itself to support everything and to abstain from rich foods. Whatever the torture might be—water, fire, poverty—it passed all tests without ever showing the faintest sign of weakness. Let's not conclude hastily that it's good luck to be poor, but no better training exists for forging character and toughening the body. When one has responsibility for a wife and children the situation differs greatly depending on whether one inherits a fortune or not. The parents' money can pay for your spouse's wardrobe or the children's schooling. All you need to do is place an order. Without fortune, you must draw against the end of the month and cope all alone.

If I'd had money, I would have studied at a universally recognized university, earning a degree, or perhaps even two doctoral degrees. Since I was poor, I had only four years of primary school, but I was resourceful. I entered a technical school along with students who'd come out of secondary school. They had knowledge of English, while I had none. One day I asked one of them about the meaning of some words. The student replied, "What is written there is "I don't know." I still remember that experience. I was already about thirty years old and had to study together in the same class as eighteen and nineteen year olds. There were many shameful experiences, though I could do nothing about it because I had finished only four years of elementary school. Nevertheless, I felt immense joy in pursuing studies that I owed only to myself.

You can think me a bit crazy and that I've a curious manner of seeing things and understanding happiness, but this is precisely the meaning of the phrase: *There are no preferences in the sudden perfect doctrine.* Thus, the one who takes advantage of his parents' money to make his studies feels less satisfaction than the poor person who must suffer to pay his own way. Life is not a tranquil river; its waters are turbulent and rush headlong. One laughs, one cries, they knock you head over heels and carry you away, but one feels immense happiness when one succeeds in traversing it.

When someone asks me if it's a bad thing to be rich, I don't know how to answer. Perhaps it's better to have parents with a fortune? I don't know. According to current opinion, we're favored when we have rich parents and not favored when our parents are poor. It's also said that hell is a horrible place, paradise a place of delights and the world here below deceiving. All these opinions are only conventional ideas worth nothing. Buddha is reality just as it is, with its jumble of illusions, hell, paradise, and Buddha. *There are no preferences in the sudden perfect doctrine.* This absolutely must be understood.

To Seek Buddha

The perfect doctrine teaches us to grasp our self, to strengthen it and not profane it. The man who, no matter where, when or how, has his feet firmly planted on the ground is seated on a lotus in the most noble, perfect, elevated posture of himself. If he does not debase this posture, Buddha is there where he is. Buddha is not something inaccessible; Buddha is oneself. Therefore, "satori" is the awareness of one's self nature. To give reprimands is to give them to oneself, to seek Buddha is to seek yourself. If we don't understand that, we don't cease chasing after something and no matter how far we may go, we will find nothing elsewhere than in ourselves. Buddha is not at the ends of the universe.

Where then is the source of Buddha? The perfect doctrine tells us to return to the source of ourselves to find Buddha. In the Lotus Sutra, the lotus flower symbolizes the perfect doctrine The lotus has the singularity of not developing its seed after the fall of the petals, but rather at the very interior of the flower. A lotus flower is at the same time flower and fruit, cause and effect. Flower and fruit are one. It is the same for man. The ordinary man is not on one side and the Buddha on the other, they are one. The starving person who devours food in secret is at one and the same time both the starving one and Buddha.

One day when I went to give a lecture at a school, it turned out that the director was totally disinterested and closed off to my teaching. The only one with whom I found a resonance was the clerk who waited in the entry to greet me and stood before me as I got out of my car. Completely terrified, he said to me, "We're happy that you've come, we were waiting for you." As for the director, my presence was manifestly disagreeable to him, but since he had no valid reason to cancel a lecture that had become a tradition under his predecessor and to which had been invited members of the municipal council and distinguished persons from the prefecture, he had to deal with the bad luck willingly, telling himself that enduring the lecture was part of the job he was paid to do.

This is also certainly what the teaching personnel thought. I saw them reading books placed on top of the brochures that had been distributed. I was up on a platform and could observe them at leisure. If they'd been novices, I would have been irritated and called them "impious barbarians!" But I have a sense of profit, so I was magnanimous. I made no remarks because I thought that their attendance at my lecture would bring them a bonus at the end of the month. My lecture would also be a gift souvenir for the clerk. He stayed outside the room, making himself small so that he could listen from the doorway. He was on my wavelength.

If he was attuned to me, that does not mean he was more remarkable than the others, for in terms of human value one cannot know. In a class, it's cause for disquiet when no student surpasses the master. If such were the case, masters would finally disappear completely, dwindling down like the tail of a mouse. The ideal teaching is when, of five students following a professor's course, five become stronger than he. Unhappily, insignificant professors are more and more numerous in our schools. Their teaching consists of conjuring tricks to pocket a salary at the end of the month. If not, they make multiple copies and sell them as expensively as possible. The students who buy the course and, on top of that, attend it, really show great indulgence. This is not my way of teaching at all. You have to do zazen. If you don't straighten the spinal column . . . kyōsaku! If you doze . . . crack! . . . crack! I strike. It's a whole other world.

Human beings are arbitrarily categorized according to social level, wealth or state of health, and portions of happiness or unhappiness reckoned according to these givens, when in truth every man can become Buddha if he rises to be a fierce guardian of himself, and takes hold of his self to carry it to the highest dimension. This is what it means to become Buddha and what the perfect doctrine teaches us. It's not necessary to have free time or propitious occasions. We seize ourselves here and now in the state we're in.

63

Humble mountain monk that I am, I have no personal point of view,
Fearing that my practice might fall into a rut of nihilism or eternalism.

An All Encompassing Doctrine

In the preceding verse, Yōka Daishi said, *If you have unresolved doubts, you must struggle with them.* Now he adds: *Humble mountain monk that*

I am, I have no personal point of view. The doctrine that he is expressing is located beyond himself and his point of view. He has tested it and knows that it is good. Expressions of modesty like "mountain monk" or "country monk" indicate self-effacement through the pejorative sense of a rustic and ignorant man good only for digging potatoes.

Using contemporary language, we could call the perfect doctrine proposed by Yōka "all-encompassing." It brings hell and Buddha together into one, encompasses the whole universe in a single glance and uncovers satori while contemplating illusions. Nevertheless, unless the perfect doctrine is authentic, it is to be feared that our practice may fall into the trap of nihilism or eternalism. In Buddhism, each assertion, whether positive or negative, is an illusion.

The nihilist position is held by the simplistic mind that limits its thoughts to the impermanence of all things: yesterday is not today and today is not tomorrow. Yesterday I stole something, but given the ephemeral nature of all phenomena, logically today I am no longer a thief. Thus there are people who make a blank slate of their past in the name of impermanence.

The eternalist position considers exclusively the evidence of the chain of causality. Transmitted from parent to child, it prolongs itself in him without discontinuity. That's to say I am born Sawaki and will always remain Sawaki. But has this child who inherited a rich patrimony at birth profited from the gifts he received? He was always first in his class at school, but look at him now at the age of fifty. He has a red nose and the puffy, fat face of a drunkard. Where are the praises and congratulations of yesteryear?

We must distance ourselves from all extreme positions. This is the sense I give to the word "all-encompassing"—to not allow oneself to be carried away by either the current of nihilism or that of eternalism and to consider that nihilism is eternalism and eternalism, nihilism. The chain of causality of all phenomena is dependent upon their impermanence and because they rise and perish from instant to instant, this impermanence is in itself a chain of causality. Thus there is combination and amalgamation of the two.

In the *Shōmankyō*,[1] it's said that the impermanence of phenomena is a negative vision and that the chain of causality is a positive vision because it leads to deliverance from the cycle of rebirths, to nirvana. These two extremes finally join at one stroke when one thrusts them into the receptacle that we call hishiryō.[2] It is the nature of an all-encompassing doctrine to embrace great contradictions and to reconcile extremes. Such is the perfect teaching. Let us add that it is beyond illusory conceptions, though this does not mean that one suddenly becomes a balloon that flies away into the heavens, no longer remembering anything. On the contrary, it means that the doctrine has become our self, our state of being, that our consciousness is hishiryō and that we are without deceptive thoughts. This doctrine that embraces all things must penetrate our guts right to the innermost depths of ourselves. If not, it's to be feared that our practice *might fall into a rut of nihilism or eternalism.*

Jiun Songja of Katsuragi[3] wrote: "The ordinary man sees all phenomena and the Buddha Dharma through his ego, producer of karmic acts, and through his heart, creator of attachments. This is the reason he falls into extremes." In the Shōbōgenzō, Dōgen recounts the tale of the good man and the wicked man. One had acted for the good all his life, while the other had always acted evilly. At the moment of death, they each had a premonitory dream. The good man was warned of his fall into hell and the evil man of his rebirth in the kingdom of heaven. The latter exclaimed, " What luck! I've done nothing but evil all my life, yet still I get good results!" From this he concluded that a bad action didn't inevitably produce bad fruit. At that moment, the sky darkened, the portent collapsed, and the wicked man was hurled head first into hell. The good man, who couldn't remember having committed a single evil action in his entire life, said to himself: "Certainly the karmic consequence of an act is not limited to one life." He traced time back to its origin and saw that in effect his fall into hell was justified by evil actions in his former lives. He concluded from this that the Buddha was right. Immediately, the portent collapsed and he found himself in the kingdom of heaven.

64

Right and wrong are neither right nor wrong,
But be off by a hair and you are a thousand miles distant.
Right, one becomes Buddha like the daughter of the naga king.
Wrong, one is thrown living into hell like Zenshō.

Error of a millimeter, divergence by ten meters

When the perfect doctrine penetrates to the depths of our guts, *right and wrong are neither right nor wrong.* Right and wrong are concepts worked out by our mind. Right and wrong are functions of time, place, and circumstances. What one estimates to be right or wrong differs according to the era or the country. It's evident that fundamentally the relative values of right/wrong, true/false have no existence in and of themselves.

But be off by a hair and you are a thousand miles distant. A very small error can create great damage. In archery, an error of a millimeter when the arrow is loosed by the bow translates into being off by ten meters upon reaching the target.

Right, one becomes Buddha like the daughter of the naga king.[1] This appears in the Lotus Sutra in the chapter devoted to the bodhisattva Devadatta. One day when the bodhisattva Manjusri[2] was lecturing in the palace of the king of the nagas, the young princess heard him and at that moment became Buddha. It would seem that the young girl had immediately realized her true self nature. Within the doctrine of sudden awakening, beings do not differ, all can suddenly become Buddha.

Wrong, one is thrown living into hell like Zenshō.[3] This is about a monk in Shākyamuni's community who questioned his words and fell immediately head first into hell.

65

During long years I have amassed learning,
Studied the commentaries and consulted the sutras.
Without rest I have analyzed words and signs,
Counting the grains of sand in the sea, I have exhausted myself in vain.
The Buddha has severely reprimanded me.
What good is it to count the treasures of others?

To wear out your bones for nothing

This verse poses the problem of intellectual learning and methods for teaching the Buddha Dharma: *During long years I have amassed learning, studied the commentaries and consulted the sutras.* I also thought the Buddha Dharma was written in a book. I bought books that I courageously read, but the more I learned, the less I retained. Now they bore me prodigiously. All these books and periodicals on Buddhism continuously go over and over the same things.

Yōka Daishi also had searched in texts, notes, glosses, and exegeses: *Without rest I have analyzed words and signs.* One never sees the end of it. *Counting the grains of sand in the sea, I have exhausted myself in vain.* It's a task to wear out one's bones. *The Buddha has severely reprimanded me. What good is it to count the treasures of others?* Dōgen says exactly the same thing in Gakudōyōjinshū: " It is of no benefit to count the treasures of others from morning to evening." You're the equivalent of a loan shark's clerk who counts the coins that don't belong to him.

What's the good method? What must we do to comprehend? Someone answered the question this way: " A mute bites into a bitter fruit." He grimaces and groans. Anyone who has ever personally experienced a bitter fruit understands immediately. The mute's mime is enough—his face puckers, he blinks, opens his mouth and emits a bizarre sound. Words are powerless to describe an unknown taste. In fact, words are not needed; to understand perfectly you must bite into some bitter fruit and taste it for yourself.

The Buddha Dharma is to "do," to oneself become Buddha. If we don't become aware of this imperative, then we must call on ancient texts and decipher classical languages such as Sanskrit, Pali, and Tibetan. Even so, at the price of enormous effort we would not have better understanding of the Buddha Dharma. It's thus that Yōka arrived at his question: "What good is it?" He got reprimanded for doing things halfway and making use of completely ineffective stratagems.

66

I have gone astray on dead-end roads and experienced the futility of my efforts.

So many years wasted in wandering for nothing in the dusts of the world!

When a spiritual line becomes corrupted, knowledge and comprehension become mistaken.

We cannot gain access to the perfect awakening of the Buddha.

Vagabond in the World of Dust

I have gone astray on dead-end roads and experienced the futility of my efforts. We blindly launch ourselves upon roads that lead nowhere, then back track and start off again by chance in another direction. Our entire life goes by as we turn in a never-ending circle. Correctly practicing the Buddha Way, one goes straight ahead without hesitation, with neither retreat nor detour.

Once we realize the impermanence of the things of this life, the everyday becomes a matter of great importance, not something one throws away on trifles. Dōgen says in Gakudōyōjinshū, "The mind of awakening has many names, but all express a single mind. The patriarch Nagārjuna[1] said: The mind that sees in the process of creation/destruction the impermanence of all things is also called the mind of awakening." Denouncing false masters, Dōgen adds, "They throw away the root and run after the leaves." Yōka also warns us, "*Seize the root, don't worry about the branches.*" Now, reviewing his past, he realizes that his practice of the Buddha Dharma has not been truly faithful, or perfectly suited to himself. *I have gone astray on dead-end roads and experienced the futility of my efforts.*

So many years wasted in wandering for nothing in the dusts of the world! This dusty world is where we are prey to emotions and passions stirred up by the five desires and six consciousnesses. *When a spiritual line becomes corrupted, knowledge and comprehension become mistaken. We cannot gain access to the perfect awakening of the Buddha.* The ordinary man outside the Way has a deformed nature. Because his true self is distorted, his reasoning and judgment become aberrant. Seeking correct awakening outside of the mind, or hoping for a rebirth elsewhere, is wishing to grasp a phantom. You disregard your true nature, and like Yōka Daishi you commit innumerable errors that prevent you from attaining the perfect awakening of the Buddha.

67

*The Two Vehicles have energy, but do not have the mind of the Way.
Heretics have intelligence, but do not have wisdom.*

Spiritual Lines

These two verses develop and clarify the preceding verse. *The Two Vehicles have energy, but do not have the mind of the Way,* thus it is that *when a spiritual line becomes corrupted, knowledge and comprehension become mistaken.* Previous understandings can be troublesome; even if one says a thing is good, such is not always the case. A father who is a thief won't think his son's acted badly if he's adroitly pilfered something, even if the thing is without value.

It is very interesting to observe the spiritual lineage of a man, what I will call his "education." If you want to teach him that it's stupid to accept something that he already has too much of, you can say, " What an idiot you are, rejoicing because someone's given you something you've no idea what to do with. You have the mentality of a beggar." Or, instead: "You must not accept anything, that's bad!" These two approaches belong to two spiritual lineages. If they teach you that to die for nothing is stupid, you'll say to yourself, "Right! I'll die like a dog; I'm getting out." On the other hand, suppose your father welcomes you back by saying, "Ah! Here you are back, did you care so much about your precious life?" That's as good as saying that it would have been better to die. In the Hagakure, written by Yamamoto Tsunetomo, a warrior of Hizen, there is a saying: "The way of the samurai is the way of dying."

The children in Satsuma played at jumping off a cliff, and at the moment of throwing themselves into space, they sang: "Do you want to weep or do you want to leap? Don't weep, leap!" They always leaped, preferring to die rather than to whimper and refuse. Men think that they will change humanity thanks to education. The goal seems to me extremely valid, but if they teach you that it's sufficient to weep in order not to leap, when the moment arrives in which you will be compelled to leap, you will know only how to groan and weep. The objectives and the methods for attaining them must be perfectly matched.

The Two Vehicles have energy, but do not have the mind of the Way. Heretics have intelligence, but do not have wisdom. In these two lines, energy and wisdom parallel one another. By energy, one means the ardor and courage that permit one to diligently complete an effort without slackening. It takes much courage to stop doing evil and to pursue good. But however great this courage may be, it must be well utilized or it has no value. It also takes courage to steal or to brawl. In the world of thieves and brawlers, those who have courage enjoy great prestige, just as in the world of drinkers, the one who holds his liquor best, or in the world of runners, the swiftest.

A competition of "mochi drinkers" takes place in Kyūshu. Mochi is a paste of steamed rice that has been pounded and molded and rolled into the shape of a gooseneck and whose end is coated with soy sauce. The contestant swallows the paste without a break, making the sound of "gloup . . . gloup" in his throat. "I drank two liters . . . well, I drank two and a half . . ." He who outdoes the others is the hero of the festival. He's very proud. He commands respect in the world of mochi drinkers.

The Two Vehicles are the shōmon-engaku.[1] The Hinayana doesn't have the mind of the Way because it seeks individual salvation. To lack compassion for others is to not have the mind of the Way. The mind of the Way is the perfect fusion of self and others. When egoism and altruism do not merge, it's not the mind of the Way. You are my life; I am your life. If you don't experience this feeling of total fusion, you don't have the mind of the Way. Even if you have a perfect practice, ardent and unremitting, if you limit your objective to escaping your own torments, you do not have the mind of the Way.

The one who wishes to individually escape his own suffering, to obtain deliverance and safety for himself, belongs completely to the Hinayana class. Looking at a girl promotes desire, eating a good dish tempts one to eat too much, and drinking alcohol promotes drunkenness, so in order to avoid danger one covers one's eyes, ears, and mouth like the monkeys in the fable who refused to see, hear, or speak. One flees the hostile and menacing world, cuts off the temptations of society, shuts oneself up in a box, mummifying oneself. One acts for oneself, in one's personal interest. Such are the Two Vehicles. Certainly, one battles valiantly and without remission, but no matter how great the ardor, if it doesn't embrace the universe, it is not employed in the spirit of the Way. It is a terribly narrow and stingy view.

There is nothing narrow about the mind of the Way. You and I are identical, equal and without difference. To regard oneself is to regard the other. This is the meaning of the Way and the spirit of the Mahayana. I make your suffering mine. There is no interval or gap between self and other. There is total fusion with the Buddha and this feeling goes for all the beings of creation. When the mind of the Way is lacking, there is discontinuity between oneself and all beings. This is individualistic behavior, a very small thing.

The following event took place in Tōtomi Province (a portion of present-day Shizuoka Prefecture), in the village of Asabamura where a great assembly of Sōtō monks from all over the country gathered in 1915 for a ninety-day retreat. I accompanied Oka Sotan Roshi as his personal attendant,[2] when he went there as guest teacher.[3] In the morning, we heard a reading from Shōbōgenzō, and in the afternoon, a commentary on the text. Oka Sōtan Roshi had a very dark complexion and his face was devastated by pockmarks. His eyes were sunk into the depths of their sockets and his nose was twice as prominent as mine. It was a frightful face. He wore little eyeglasses in the old style perched on his high nose, and above the glasses his unmoving regard transfixed you. He was terrifying.

One day a monk asked for a private interview. In this circumstance, it is customary to spread out your zagu[4] outside the fusuma[5] and do sanpai.[6] From the moment you've prostrated, your lips dry out, your throat knots up, and you can no longer emit a sound. If it's the case of an indulgent superior like me, everything quickly works out, but it was another matter with old Oka Sōtan Roshi. You were paralyzed by his terrible face, and above all, his steady eyes above the glasses. His lips were compressed into an inverted "v" and when he opened them a deep voice emerged from his entrails: " Hum . . . what's it about?" It gave you gooseflesh.

The monk to whom this question was addressed responded with reverential dread: "I would like to know what's most important?" Oka Roshi responded: "What? . . . The most important? . . . For whom?" "For me . . . " "What? For you? For you alone . . . doesn't matter . . . that's without importance . . . Ha! . . . Ha! . . . Ha!" When he laughed, you'd have thought it was a demon breathing poisonous vapors, a fighting cock disemboweling a pullet. I was in the next room where I heard everything, and it stopped me dead in my tracks.

If it was frightful, was it because of his formidable appearance . . . the unique, brutal and cruel attack . . . or my own fragility? The fact remains that his manner of expressing himself was effective. The majority of people take on great airs for the sake of discussing the Shōbōgenzō," Zanmai ō zanmai," the true Dharma or the scope of Buddhism, but insofar as they themselves are concerned, have they found interior peace? When one acts for oneself, one is Small Vehicle. Whether you work for the nation, society, the Way, or no matter who or what, if it's to obtain personal advantage, it is not the mind of the Way. The mind of the Way is to set aside your self on behalf of the whole body of the Way, of the country, parents, brothers and sisters, husbands and wives, of the entire society.

The adept Hinayana person practices with ardor, to the point of sacrificing his life, but it's finally for personal ends, for his own satori. In sum, he wishes to alone touch the message. They say that the Hinayana is the Buddha Dharma. The practices certainly have the appearance of it: strict diet, erudition, and profound learning. Yet all that is destined for oneself, and oneself is a very little thing, totally insignificant. When one acts in one's own interest, one does not have the mind of the Way. That which is not the mind of the Way is not the Buddha Dharma.

The completely self-absorbed Hinayana adept is not available to others and cannot experience the mind of great compassion. He does nothing for others. The mind of great compassion is to devote oneself to one's parents, to live in harmony with one's husband or wife, to be loyal to one's friends, and to be the friend of one's brothers and sisters. In multiple fashions it transforms all things.

Heretics have intelligence, but do not have wisdom. The word "heretic" smells of sulfur and we immediately picture grimacing faces, yet there are also pretty faces among them. To be a heretic means to be outside the Way. A heretic is every person who, with erroneous reasoning, seeks a reward for his merits, affirms that life exists (or doesn't exist) after death, and preaches false and arbitrary dogmatic theories.

Limitless causality

A well-known clairvoyant described what he saw as happening after the passing of eighty thousand kalpas. For example, persons who had been a bird eighty thousand kalpas earlier would be reborn in the kingdom of heaven. Thus, the one who today imitates the behavior of a bird will go to heaven. This is called the heresy of imitating a bird.

We have hair on our head. Some say it's good to plaster it with oil, some say the contrary. My barber joked the other day while shaving my head, "What a pity to shave off such beautiful hair!" I have no particular feeling about my hair, except that I don't feel comfortable going for more than five days without shaving it off. I never catch cold. They say that the hairs are passions and they must be cut off so "they" don't grow. Someone even recommended using a depilatory. Others also say that clothes are passions and so to escape from passions we should go naked. In this case, we're speaking of the heresy of nudity.

It's a heresy to assign limits to that which does not have them. Today they say that what we see under a microscope is the truth. "Look here! The cell of a camellia leaf is identical to a human cell!" Is it identical or not? It would be good to reflect and ask oneself if a man and a camellia leaf are truly identical. The same goes for the sardine and the turnip: both are living organisms, but the sardine swims and the turnip does not.

Astronomy interests me and I've read a quantity of books on the subject. I don't have scientific learning and at the beginning, to be able to even comprehend them, I had to work out a plan of action. I began by attacking primary school manuals, continued with those of grammar school, and finished by reaching the college level. Little by little,

I plumbed the depths of knowledge and finished by understanding everything. However, since these books stank of boredom, I immediately forgot what I'd read, although I was very interested. To say that I understood astronomy is completely false. Everything was clear at the primary level, but I lost my footing upon arriving at the college level and no longer understood anything. "According to the theory of Scholar So-and-So . . . but according to that of . . . one is unaware of . . ." I perceived that what I'd understood clearly in astronomy as explained to children was a deceit, an arbitrary simplification, a construction of concepts and, sum total, a heresy. They had wished to give limits to the limitless. It is heresy to not accept that the limitless is incommensurable, whether it is infinitely large or infinitely small.

In the ancient texts, lacking wisdom signified not believing in the chain of causality, that is to say, in the unlimited, in perpetual change. We are merely an image on a spool of film that unrolls indefinitely. Always changing, the journey continues. We are able to grasp only a miniscule fragment of the limitless, and we wish to apply this minute part to the whole universe and draw conclusions from it. Such an attitude lacks wisdom, for as soon as we place limits upon the unlimited, even provisionally, even if only to render it comprehensible, it escapes us completely.

In 1877, a company was founded with the goal of utilizing hydroelectric energy to make cars run between Beppu and Oita city. It failed. These days nothing any longer astonishes us in the realm of discoveries, but at that time most people had trouble understanding that water can create fire. In the same way, when man began to fly, they thought it was the magician Tenjiku Tokubee.[7] They wondered how such a marvel could be produced. Today it seems normal to hear planes constantly flying overhead.

It is absolutely necessary that we thoroughly understand that the phenomenal world is without limits. If not, tears are spilled when something unexpected comes along. The flood that carries us along is limitless and so it's natural that in the course of the voyage many things arrive. Once one has become clearly conscious of the unlimited, one can no longer remain unaware of it.

These days, the world of diplomacy is consulted to know if one should be prepared to make war or to make peace. Whatever decision is made, wisdom requires that one be ready. Dōgen wrote in Gakudōyōjinshū: "The Buddha Dharma is without equal or superior, it's for this that one seeks it." The one who aspires to become a great bodhisattva takes as guide the mind of the Dharma and of wisdom.

The Two Vehicles have energy, but do not have the mind of the Way. Heretics have intelligence, but do not have wisdom. By placing oneself under the protection of these two guardians, mind of the Way and wisdom, one tastes the subtle flavors of life and enjoys it fully. The mind of the Dharma allows one to forget one's ego on behalf of the world and other beings. Wisdom breaks the encircling limits. When one enters into the limitless, one has access to infinite causality, there where the endless expanse of the Buddha Dharma resides. In truth, Mahayana Buddhism has the mind of the Way and of wisdom.

68

One who is foolish or naïve is fooled by an empty fist or an index finger

A Creative Life

He who does not follow the mind of the Way and of wisdom is a fool. To be a fool is to be unable to adapt to change. They also say that stupidity is the dimming of reason. It is essential that we understand the eternal truth, but to grasp merely a single aspect and to always sound one note is pure foolishness. You see only one side of things, like a beast of burden wearing blinders or a man with a plank on his shoulder. It's boring to always play the same old refrain, and he who is not capable of renewing his repertoire, of recreating himself within an unlimited and always new world, is an imbecile. It's practice that leads to living a creative life. The great Mahayana vehicle rolls on the road of life.

Naïveté is for children. Little children are naïve because they don't understand the why of things, but when the naïveté is associated with stupidity, it becomes infantilism and from then on it's no longer a question of children, but of puerile louts who understand nothing of the actuality and reality of life . . . *fooled by an empty fist or an index finger.* You stick out a finger and say to him: "The lion's going to eat you!" He's immediately terrorized like a young child.

In Kyūshū there lived a certain Uramachi Kane. He saw a scary play about a ghost story in which the ghost appeared at the sound of a drum. Then, one evening, he saw what appeared to be phantoms dressed in blue robes approaching, crying "Hoo! . . . Hoo! . . . Hoo!" It was a band of little good-for-nothings come to frighten him. Kane challenged them: "Hola! Are you ghosts? You look a lot like them!" He regarded them closely and then said, "No, you are false ghosts because I hear no drum!" Kane certainly wasn't lacking in sangfroid, and those who came to intimidate him were stuck with their expenses.

In our society we let ourselves be fooled by an empty fist: "Someone told me that Somebody was on the road to success? No, he got chucked out . . ." The truth is that in one case as in another, there's some good.

"The moon in the water, it appears and disappears." Or you might say, " The moon in the water, it disappears and reappears." There is a song that says, "Saigyō, whether an ox or a child may be changed from one to the other, in the end all are no more than a broken earthenware doll from Fushimi." In Buddhist terms, we would say that in addition to the five aggregates,[2] the twelve links of causation,[3] and the eighteen worlds[4] that represent the three categories of the production of phenomena, innumerable empty fists are manifested under an infinity of forms through which we produce happiness, unhappiness, love, hate, beauty, ugliness, purity, impurity and so many other things. Money? What use is it when you're at death's door? A woman's beauty? Without her skin, she resembles a frog. What's left of health? What remains of a rich man who's been stripped of his gold? Men let themselves be fooled by an empty fist. It's not astonishing that they commit crimes. One person feels the assurance of a man who has wealth; the other's deepest nature is twisted out of shape because he doesn't have it. They are all ignorant fools who allow themselves be taken in by appearances.

69

He takes the finger for the moon and makes an effort for nothing.
He forges strange chimeras from the phenomena his senses perceive.
The one who does not see a single phenomenon is identical with the Buddha.
He truly merits being called Kanjizai.

To Make Fissures Disappear

He takes the finger for the moon and makes an effort for nothing. When you ask where the moon is, your eyes follow the direction indicated by the finger and don't stop at the finger. In many Zen temples, the location where sutras are stored is designated by a plaque on which just two characters are written: "finger" and "moon." This means that one doesn't stop at the finger that points out the Way, but that one extends the line up to the moon. Unhappily, this finger always finishes by being itself invested with powers.

He forges strange chimeras from the phenomena his senses perceive. He confuses the sense organ, its perception and the object perceived, from which arise the awarenesses: the eye and color, the ear and sound, the nose and odor, the tongue and taste, the body and the sensation of warmth and cold. When our perception of phenomena mixes the subjective with reality, the result is a haze, a mixture of highs and lows, of good and bad fortunes, of joys and sorrows. If you don't free yourself from them, you fabricate all sorts of bizarre mental constructions that lead to ruin. You float or drown at the mercy of deceitful concepts.

The one who does not see a single phenomenon is identical with the Buddha. From the moment you embrace all things, not resting on a single aspect, chimeras, sufferings, and joys disappear. As it is said in the *Hannya Shingyō*: "Avalokiteshara Bodhisattva, when deeply practicing prajna paramita, clearly saw that all five aggregates are empty, and thus relieved all suffering."[1] This is what is meant by the phrase, *He truly merits being called Kanjizai* ("one who observes freely," Skt. Avalokiteshvara).

Manzan Oshō[2] cites the following fable: "As they battled, two bulls covered with mud fell into the sea and, since then, they have given no further signs of life." The bulls symbolize our likes and our dislikes, the pungent and the bland, riches and poverty. Once fallen into the sea, the differences between them vanish and they are reunited. In truth, when one understands that all things are equal, one no longer makes value judgments. A stove becomes a reviled object if you catch a cold when you leave an overheated room, and a venerated object when the cold wind lashes you and, chilled to the bone, you find refuge next to it. Is a spicy dish of which we grow tired preferable to another that at the outset seems bland, but whose subtle flavor we discover little by little?

The one who does not see a single phenomenon is identical to the Buddha. He embraces all aspects, rejecting none. No matter which way he turns he encounters no obstacle and never meets an impasse. *He truly merits being called Kanjizai.*

70

With clarity of understanding, the emptiness of karma's shackles appears. Without it, karmic debts remain due.

To Transcend the Present

With clarity of understanding, the emptiness of karma's shackles appears. I'm often questioned as follows: "Does the principle of causality exist within Buddhism?" I reply, "Pinch the end of your nose and you'll know." How regrettable to hear constant talk about luck, fortune, and destiny! What does "to have luck"mean? Is it luck to inherit a fortune? Let's think of all those whom money condemns to vegetate like cripples all their life. Is it luck to have good health? "I was born with bad karma, I have no health!" So why not go ahead and die? It's because we cherish ourselves that we speak of good luck or bad luck. Man thinks only of his own person, and this is why he talks so much nonsense.

One day a student asked me if I had played sports. I replied that I'd always lived in poverty and so had never had the leisure or the means to practice a sport. In fact, I had the good luck to avoid doing so, because I had to work a lot. I worked as a layman in the kitchens of Eiheji and didn't have a penny for transportation, so I went on foot from the prefecture of Echizen to Shoshinji in Kyūshū and when I left Soshinji to practice at Entsuji, I walked from Kyūshū to Tanba.

During the Russo-Japanese War, I marched with a pack on my back from the port of Darien as far as Mukden, following the railway line. Solidly packed on my back I carried: food rations for a week, a hundred and fifty cartridges, a signal device with arms that had flags, a blanket, a greatcoat, a change of clothing, and shoes. I believe that I "played sports" to excess. I can't say whether it's good or bad luck, but thanks to this my legs enjoy good health.

When one limits one's vision to the immediate present, one finds it detestable enough to make one weep. In this regard, Takayama Chogyū wrote: "We must absolutely transcend the present." That's to say, situate ourself beyond happiness and unhappiness. They say that it's a terrible trial to lose one's fortune, but wealthy parents raise their children in a hothouse and when the money disappears they wilt like morning glories in the first breeze. In fact, the parents' ruin permits the children to prove their courage in the face of difficulties, and this will have the happy result of strengthening their character and their solidity will be of benefit to them. What's worth more, wealth or poverty? Happiness or unhappiness? No formula gives the answer. In consequence, by transcending the present, we can place ourselves beyond good and evil and take events as they come. It's the mind of hishiryō, situated outside of that which is rationally measurable.

In the first section of The Song of Awakening it was written, *When we awaken to the Dharma-body, there is nothing.* Even considering the wisest of human beings, they seem somehow to be caught up and tangled in things, suspended in mid-air, as it were. In this suspended state they cannot go up or go down, and hang there in this peculiar situation, weeping and rejoicing. It's essential that they grasp their true self in order to have a total vision of reality and be able to say, "Now I know where I am."

With clarity of understanding, the emptiness of karma's shackles appears. It would be a grave error to imagine that one can act badly with impunity or that doing good is useless. This would be to deny the truth and fall into nihilism. What they call luck-bad luck, fortune-bad fortune has no substance, no self-existence. Whatever the epoch and the place, from good emerges an evil and from an evil a good. To aid someone financially produces beneficent effects that later on become harmful since the beneficiary is a person weakened by the assistance. In contrast, he could also invest the money and make a fortune.

One day an impudent student, interested in something that was none of his business, asked me: "Why do you spend your life blathering and walking about?" I answered him that I blather because I want to. As for my gait, whether you call it that of a spiritual guide or something else doesn't matter. I've no idea whether I guide anybody at all, but it's not the results that count, it's to "do." Moreover, I don't have time to think about the "whys." I travel my road and what I have to do now, I do; what I have to say, I say, period. That's all. If it so happens that I'm bad, I apologize. As the saying goes, "It is old Saiō's horse—from the good comes evil, from an evil a good."

The Crown Prince Ajase

The *Kanmuryōjugyō* sutra[2] relates in detail the causes and conditions that determined the destiny of King Ajase.[3] King Bimbasara and his wife Idaikebunin keenly desired a child. They consulted a soothsayer who told them: "You don't have a child because your future child is presently a hermit on the mountain where he fulfills his practice. As long as he lives, he will not inhabit your body."

It might take years and years to wait for the death of this hermit! After deliberating with his vassals, the king determined to kill him. Very strangely, as soon as the act was accomplished the queen's belly began to swell. They called the soothsayer again, asking him to read the child's future in the eight signs. He told them, "Even if you had not killed the hermit, he would have come, but by reason of this crime the unborn child has become his parents' enemy. There is no other solution but to kill him." So they piled up sabers that the baby landed upon at birth. He escaped unscathed except for one toe that was cut off. Such were the circumstances of the birth of King Ajase.

How could such an adorable baby be their principal enemy? Since he had escaped death, they raised him and eventually named him Crown Prince Ajase. In the meantime, King Bimbasara was converted to Buddhism, which he practiced fervently. Living at the same time as a member of Shākyamuni's community was a certain Devadatta.[4] He had provoked a schism among the monks and had succeeded in attracting a great number of disciples to his cause. He wished to become head of the order and in order to accomplish this would have to eliminate the master. Since one has to live and at the moment he had not a crust to eat, he set out to attract the favor of Prince Ajase and busied himself in persuading him of their common interest: "If you do away with your father, you become master of the kingdom, and if I kill the Buddha, I become master of the Buddhist order. We two will hold all the power." The crown prince replied, " You're talking nonsense!" and refused the proposition. Devadatta insisted, "You say you love your parents, but what about your missing toe? Didn't they see an enemy in you when you were born?" Little by little, he revealed to Ajase the causes and conditions of his birth and ended by convincing him. Thus King Bimbasara found himself in a prison cell encircled by seven walls. Immediately, a disciple of Shākyamuni named Venerable Mokuren used his unequaled and unsurpassed supernatural powers to pass through the seven walls, bringing to King Bimbasara the teachings of the Dharma, and Shākyamuni sent the Venerable Furuna[5] as a deputy to assist him in his task.

A nun named Rengeshiki, also with supernatural powers, appeared in the cell. In actual fact, it was the queen Idaikebunin. She had smeared her body with various forms of cosmetics and the king, licking them off, filled his stomach with nutrients. She also wore delicious pastries disguised as jewels. The jailor dared not intervene, intimidated by the unparalleled distinction of Her Royal Highness.

In this way the king maintained his life. Not only did he not die of hunger, he put on weight and radiated good health. One day the crown prince, now King Ajase, asked for news of Bimbasara, " I suppose he's dead?" He was answered that the king still lived. Very surprised, Ajase immediately visited the premises and confirmed that in fact his father lived and was in splendid shape. "Who's been feeding him?" he growled at the jailor. The jailor told how the king received the teachings of the Dharma thanks to the supernatural powers of the Buddha and intervention of the Venerable Mokuren, who suddenly entered the cell. "The queen comes to visit him every day and the king licks her body and eats her jewels. If things continue like this, there's no fear he'll ever die!"

A living father was a living enemy. Ajase drew his sword, deciding on the spot to kill his mother, but his two vassals, Gekkō and Giba, intervened and reprimanded him. The business is reported in the Kankyō Wasan: "King Ajase demonstrated great anger, saying his mother had behaved like a bandit and he was going to punish her as she merited. He drew his sword and departed to kill her. Giba and Gekkō tried to dissuade him by respectfully telling him that such a crime was not worthy of a king and that to kill his father or his mother was a base and vulgar act that led to a rebirth in a world inferior to the vilest caste in society." To put it directly, king though he was, he would be afflicted by torments, since this is the punishment of all those who commit matricide or patricide. The texts report that from then on Ajase was converted to Buddhism.

In light of these events, we see clearly that the road of happiness was transformed into unhappiness and that this unhappiness became happiness.

The *Kanmuryōjugyō* sutra explains that the Buddha had manifested his supernatural powers to Queen Idaikebunin when she was imprisoned in her cell. It's also evident that the revelation of the Buddha was sudden in the case of Bimbasara and Ajase. The sutras report numerous confirmations of sudden awakening. As though in a dream, we live in a world devoid of substance, empty, and we struggle in vain within illusory concepts. Like a dog that runs after a clod of dirt, we pursue shadows, have pleasures and desires, for nothing. We are always running after something or fleeing something. Happiness and unhappiness are illusions. He who wakes from the dream understands that the chains of actions are fundamentally empty. If we do not deeply comprehend the fundamental non-existence of the hindrances, we must forever carry the burden of our punishment: we must pay our debts.

In the Lotus Sutra, there is a chapter dedicated to Devadatta in which the Buddha renders homage to him. This man was not a simple criminal. He was one of the greatest masters and propagators of the Buddha's teaching. He transcended his acts. This chapter also celebrates the daughter of the dragon king, become Buddha at a time when she had fallen into the bad path of the animals. What does it mean to become Buddha? It is to grasp one's true nature, here and now, just as it is. As I constantly repeat, it's to be oneself in oneself, by oneself. To grasp one's true nature also applies to nations. For contemporary Japan, to become Buddha is to embrace its true identity with an assured and courageous gait, without deluding itself with concepts. Without seeking to elevate itself in the hierarchy of nations: one is oneself, just as one is. For Thailand to become Buddha is also to grasp its true identity, though this is different from Japan. Your Buddha and mine are not identical. If one doesn't encounter his true self, life becomes an endless quest. One runs from one side to the other, chasing shadows. The game of blind man's bluff never concludes and must always begin again so long as one is not "released from his debts."

71

Though hungry, they do not eat the royal feast they are offered.
Sick, they consult the King of Physicians, but do not follow his prescription.

To Run after a Shadow

Though hungry, they do not eat the royal feast they are offered. Sick, they consult the King of Physicians, but do not follow his prescriptions. If we refuse to taste the banquet, our stomach remains empty and even when we consult the best doctor, if we don't follow his prescription we don't get well. It's a question of nourishing oneself with the Buddha Dharma and practicing it very correctly with the best masters.

We must stop destroying our true nature. Dōgen Zenji says. "All men are furnished with a rich and opulent nature." Just as he is, man is Buddha. He adds, "However, not practicing, they are not aware of it and cannot awake." Only zazen permits this grasping of one's self. A mysterious alchemy operates through zazen, so that we discover our true self, in itself and by itself. If our self doesn't recover its real essence, we will continue our game of blind man's bluff. To put it another way, to do zazen is to raise the scarf that covers our eyes.

Some enterprises offer their workers training, but before they've finished, these same workers abandon them to go elsewhere. "Come join us, you'll get a better salary!" Later, however, the realization dawns that although they began at a good salary they've received no raises since they joined that company. If they'd stayed with the original enterprise, their living conditions would now be much better. They were happy at the prospect of getting an extra 500 yen. And how much candy does that buy? Besides, when business slows, they're let go. This is behaving like a dog at which someone has thrown a stone, who runs after the stone instead of biting the person who threw it. Thus, for a few pennies more, one loses his "self."

By partaking of the royal feast, we realize our true self. We discover that there is no difference between self and Buddha. Satori is the revelation of the true self. Some encounter the correct Dharma, follow the teaching of a true master, and perfectly understand the doctrine without the slightest dust or false idea that might tarnish their perfect comprehension. Still, their knowledge remains purely intellectual. They comprehend that these are excellent things, yet say, "I don't eat that, I don't like it." They recognize all the benefits of zazen, but say, "I don't like doing zazen, it hurts my knees." So much for them. Their ailment is the loss of the true self. "Where am I? Where am I?" They suffer from being unable to grasp their true nature. They go to the best doctors and demand a remedy that will help them drive their true self out from under cover so as to become themselves, to find their true identity. The doctor prescribes a potion, but they don't drink it. It is a mental malady that makes us lose sight of ourselves, and of which we must be cured.

In the Lotus Sutra, there is a parable illustrating the loss of self. Someone had his hand pierced by an arrow. Before this accident, he had never been conscious of the existence of his hand. It was by losing the free use of his hand that he realized that he had it. Little by little, he could move it, then get it to function normally, and he realized how much a hand merited recognition. Up to then, he'd been unaware that he was equipped with a hand that functioned by itself, freely.

Fundamentally, we function freely but, curiously, the sick man doesn't agree to function without getting a medal or a reward. The human being cannot live without acting, so it's normal for him to have activities, but much less normal that they lead nowhere. Well now, the sick man who suffers from the loss of self turns in a circle without ever arriving. "Where am I? Where am I, then?" If he'd take a swallow of medicine, he'd know. By doing zazen, he'd intimately encounter his self in the depths of himself. How can he be cured if he doesn't take care of himself? He does not enter into himself; rather, he circles around himself pursuing fantasies.

72

Within this world of desires, it is the power of seeing and knowing that
    permits the practice of zen.
The lotus that blooms in the fire is indestructible.
Though having committed a capital crime, Yuse realized the unborn,
Became immediately a Buddha, and remains so now.

The Three Worlds and Twenty-five Existences
Within this world of desires, it is the power of seeing and knowing that permits the practice of zen. Ancient buddhism distinguished three worlds[1] in which the conditions of existence of all beings unfold: the world of desires, the world of form, and the formless world. The world of desires is that of dissipation and agitation that does not lend itself to meditation and where *zen* doesn't exist. One gives oneself over

to pleasures, gives free rein to one's numberless passions, succumbs to sexual desire, to food and to sleep, among other things. The world of form is that of cultural pleasures that give rise to the senses. The formless world has its origin in this and reaches beyond it to attain a strictly spiritual sphere where the senses no longer intervene.

The lowest level is hell, where man is prey to furious primitive and barbarous impulses. Dogs bite and do battle over a bitch, but men, policed by civilization, burn with jealousy and destroy themselves in their struggle to let nothing become evident to others. This type of behavior disappears to the degree that one raises oneself toward the world of form, favorable to concentration. The first four stages of *zen* belong to the world of form. Suffering caused by sexual appetites, desire for a woman, or the scaldings of anger, arises from the world of desires, while to admire the cherry trees in bloom and works of art are part of the pleasures of the senses. Nevertheless, there are gradations in the world of form. To love grilled eel, tempura, or bamboo shoots is situated at the bottom of the scale of values. The more one elevates oneself toward the formless world, the more subtle and refined become one's pleasures, to the point of disappearing completely. The formless world also consists of four stages, the ultimate level characterized by the total absence of discrimination: the "without character-without no-character." Existence then becomes pure clarity. Theoretically speaking, progression comes about gradually from the lowest level to the highest.

There is no *zen* in the world of desires. Even though we may sit in zazen posture, in actuality we are very far from what is called zazen. There is something that occupies the mind, something extra that is introduced just before the present moment. Your thought acts as a calculator; you ask yourself if the business you are preoccupied with is profitable or not. You think of the pretty girl you've just met or about your end of the year balance sheet. Even if you say that you do zazen, this agitation of thought has nothing to do with samadhi.

Long ago, a visiting monk from a teaching school asked Gako Daiji Zenji: " *Zen* doesn't exist in the world of desires, then why do you do zazen?" To conceive of the three worlds as superimposed stages like those of a silk farm is to have a topographical view. Or you imagine them like stars on an astronomical map. Such a vision is erroneous and under no circumstances religious. You unfold a map of the heavens to locate paradise and scrutinize the sky to discover it, but such a place does not exist.

You will find the three worlds when you recognize them within your own life, for it is our conditions of existence that they call "the three worlds and the twenty-five varieties." In fact, since they are un-limited, one cannot count them. In the three worlds, we distinguish twenty-five forms of existence within which rebirth can be realized. These are: the four continents,[2] the four bad roads,[3] the six heavens of the world of desires,[4] three additional heavens, the four heavens of the world of form, and the four domains of the formless world. Each day, within our daily life we transmigrate into one or the other of these worlds. Sometimes we are ravenous demons, sometimes a brute. The ravenous demon appears when a servant takes advantage of the mistress' inattention to gulp down a bit of food. This goes for me, too. One day when I was a young monk, I pounced like a predator upon some cakes that the cook had just taken out of the oven. Panicked at being caught in the midst of my thievery, I swallowed a scorching hot cake in one mouthful.

Long ago, at Eiheiji, there was a monk who was crazy about mochi. His visitors knew this and so they were accustomed to mak-ing offerings of very good soft cakes. In those days, the monks held a mondo[7] to decide who would get to eat the mochi. One monk would say to another, "Please give me the mochi." The other monk then asked, "Are you qualified to eat the mochi?" to which the first replied, "Yes, yes, of course I am," and a debate would begin between the two opponents. The winning monk would eat the cakes. One day, this particular monk sensed that his adversary was too strong for him, so he seized the cakes and took flight, pursued by the adversary. On the brink of being overtaken, the monk swallowed the mochi so greedily that they stuck in his throat. They say he died with a ladle at his mouth, trying to wash them down with the water of the Hakusan. This is an explicit example of persons in the realm of desire.

The principal axis of life can be rice cakes as well as women, alcohol, or something else. You know your blood pressure is too high so you shouldn't drink and smoke, but you continue despite your doctor's warnings. It's thus that one dances in a circle within the world of desires. Since one doesn't make an exit from its enclosure, one can't find true freedom on the outside.

This is why the monk asked Gako Osho, "Why do you practice zazen?" and Gako replied, "You only know that there is no *zen in* the world of desire. You don't know that the world of desire doesn't exist in *zen*." I have been familiar with this sort of question and answer since I was very young. Within zazen, there is no world of desire; there is nothing. Therefore, in zazen we must be strong and courageous and just sit. If you sit with some an expectation of results, you are sitting in the world of desire and such activity is not zazen. Zazen is not zazen at all if you practice it for the sake of obtaining satori.

In the World of Zazen, No Desires

When one desires satori, one begs for glory. In zazen, one wishes for nothing, neither money, nor honors, nor even life. Nothing. It's in simply doing zazen that the hishiryō state of consciousness appears, thought beyond thought, beyond all rational thought. It is evident that by simply doing zazen, there is no longer a barrier. It's enough simply to practice the Way of the Buddha. In zazen, the world of desires no longer exists, one transcends the three worlds, and beyond the three worlds there is the power of wisdom. Doing zazen, one obtains wisdom. However, the zazen must be perfectly correct, not done just any old way.

Essentially, the method rests upon being prepared to undergo the test to the end. When zazen and daily life can no longer be dissociated, wisdom manifests and we understand that in the world of *zen* there are no desires. And it is very difficult to practice zazen when you yourself belong to this world of desires. Among men, some are intelligent, others stupid, and their faculties are infinitely varied, but whatever they may be, it is essential that they prove to have courage. Truthfully speaking, courage is required to practice *zen* by transcending the world of desires, this world in which we live.

The lotus that blooms in the fire is indestructible. Nor is the life of this lotus any easier, and it's a terrible test for it. Fire is the symbol of beings' existence in this world filled with cares, illusions, and temptations. The Lotus Sutra relates the parable of the burning house[8] to illustrate the three worlds. Yōka uses the example of Yuse to demonstrate the same notion.

Though having committed a capital crime, Yuse realized the unborn, became immediately a Buddha, and remains so now. This story is related in the *Jōgō-kyō*. Long ago, in very distant times, in the era of the Buddha "Pure Light Without Stain" in the world of "Multiple Perfumes," lived a monk named Yuse. He was astonishingly beautiful and a young married woman fell in love with him. She became melancholy and began to dwindle away. These days, we would have immediately diagnosed her illness, but in those days they knew nothing about the malady of listlessness. Nevertheless, her nurse made inquiries and while chatting discovered that the young woman was completely captivated by the monk. She immediately hurried to tell the girl's mother, who tried unsuccessfully to convince her daughter to forget the monk. Days passed and the young woman continued to waste away. She was so piteous that her mother finally acceded to her desires. One day when Yuse came to beg, she invited him inside and asked him to teach the sutras to her sick daughter. The young woman immediately became better and little by little recovered her health. The two people became friends and the day came when Yuse broke the precept forbidding illicit love. The husband became an inconvenience, so with the complicity of the nurse, Yuse resolved to do away with him. But from the moment he'd accomplished the crime he was overwhelmed by remorse. He had the feeling that he was awaking from a dream. He suddenly realized that he, a monk, had just broken the two most important precepts: he had committed adultery and murder. What to do? He went to consult the bodhisattva Bikkutara, confessed his crimes to him and told him the whole business, omitting nothing. Bikkutara said to him, "Don't be anxious. Thanks to my powers, I give you the gift of non-fear." He entered into the concentration called Seal of the Dharma[9] and produced the incommensurable Buddha, then said, " All phenomena are reflections in a mirror, like the moon in water. The ordinary man suffers stupidly in his mind by making discriminations between madness, anger, and love." The shadows in the mirror and the reflection of the moon in the water look real, but have no existence in themselves. Why make distinctions? The ordinary man is a fool who imparts reality to that which does not have it.

This is how the monk Yuse, obtaining the magical metamorphosis of all the buddhas, awakened to the fact that reality was a dream, a film. Before the roll of film was developed, he saw nothing. He discovered life the way one discovers the images on a film after it's been developed. In the blink of an eye, he saw the past, the present, the future and, for the first time, he comprehended the unborn. To put it another way, he awoke to immortal life. Yuse became the Buddha Hōgetsu, protector of the Buddha lands. He discerned the incommensurable past that still exists now: *became immediately a Buddha and remains so now.* Which sends us back to a previous phrase: *With clarity of understanding, the emptiness of karma's shackles appears.* The lion roars a doctrine without fear.

73

The lion roars a doctrine without fear,
Alas! How pitiful are these confused and limited spirits!

A Single Word Fills the Universe

The lion roars a doctrine without fear. The Buddha Dharma is speech without fear. In our world, we ceaselessly employ vague language: "It's possible that . . . perhaps . . . probably . . ." In the Buddha Dharma there is no place for doubt or hesitation: things are or they are not. It's true or false. Zero or five out of five. Nothing is blurred or equivocal. As the adage says, "A single word exhausts the ten directions." This is the lion's mode of being when he roars the doctrine of non-fear.

In this world, people are like kids playing at being bride and bridegroom, without knowing exactly what these are. They pretend to do a wedding ceremony, saying they are offering feasts for an auspicious occasion.

In the same way, though people talk about what true reality and delusions are, they do not know what satori or ignorance are. kids in their play who say, "Our baby was born, please accept red rice to celebrate its birth," adults in this world do the same of play-acting.

Prince Shōtōku said: "In this world, all is vanity, only the Buddha is real." In fact, everything is a lie in our human society. Men call "happiness" that which is merely a parody of happiness, because they are unaware of true and profound happiness. They merely have an impression of being happy, and in pursuit of this fallacious happiness they exhaust their energy for nothing. They waste their life.

The Nihon-gaishi[1] describes Tairo no Kiyomori's climb to power that culminated in a "high position at Court" and describes the splendor of his zenith. Despite the power he enjoyed, he caught a fever and died. He left a stupid and cowardly son who abandoned both family and vassals to take flight at the mere sound of the rapids in the Fujikawa River. He found refuge in the vicinity of the capital, but was soon attacked and defeated by Kiso Yoshinaka. Once again, he fled successfully by sea but, pursued by Kuro Hangan and Minamoto Noriyori, he was re-captured in the bay of Dan-no-ura. This was the downfall and annihilation of the Taira clan. The whole story illustrates that the splendor and glory of Kiyomori was nothing but rubbish. There is a poem that says:

> I thought that this world was a world forever. I didn't
> imagine that it could wax and wane like the moon.

The prestige of the Fujiwara[2] also only lasted for a time. All these people quarrel and move about at the zero level and since their happiness or unhappiness belongs to the same level, even if they talk of satori or illusions, all their actions remain zero.

Ōbaku Oshō[3] said, "All of you, no matter who
...e dregs!" One knows nothing else; one finds it
...harma, like the roar of the lion, is a true voice.
...the cry of life, a sonorous voice that fills heaven
...word exhausts the ten directions." It resounds in
...erse; it *shatters the skulls of the beasts that hear it.*

... day some students were brought together to participate in
... elocution contest. Curious to know their oratorical gifts, I went to
glance out of the window. What I perceived was a fellow who spoke
abundantly, scratching his head, but who upon sighting me at the
window, hid his face behind his hand. His voice sounded like the
whimper of a tiny dog that flees at the sight of a bulldog. Even a
bulldog with its powerful bark would flee like a cur when hearing the
cry of the lion. The roar of the lion must break the animals' eardrums
and tear open their heart. Thanks to this, the thinking of men can
change completely.

The Buddha and the Dharma end up becoming banalities, and
satori and the truth, clichés. The Buddha Dharma is transformed
into hazy concepts. Hell may create fear, and paradise rejoicing, but
they're no longer more than words empty of substance. It's no longer
the contents, but the packaging, that creates fear. Words become like
children's toys and men let themselves be fooled by *an empty fist.*

Zero or Five Out of Five

Alas! How pitiful are these confused and limited spirits! The mind is
blinded by a cloud of thick smoke, and in this obscurity, like an idiot
deprived of discernment, it no longer distinguishes anything. Concepts have a thick skin. No one is any longer even aware of what has
value and what has not. We establish a norm and define everything
with reference to it: "He pays big taxes, so he must be wealthy." We

see no difference as to whether the money was inherited or personally acquired. Well, it's blindness to be vain about an inherited fortune that's shrinking like untanned leather, and one must expect to suffer great torments when one reaches the bottom of the slope. They say someone's grandfather was great, but what about now? He got into trouble and now has nothing. To say, "A delicacy remains a delicacy, even when spoiled," is like saying, "I have a good pair of shoes that used to fit." It means nothing.

Living upon the heights in conservative towns in Kyūshū, the descendents of samurai families look down with prejudice upon the common people, saying, "You are chonin" (mere townspeople). Even the Minister of Finance is looked down upon as a kind of merchant because his job is to calculate revenue and expenses. Even though they profess to be the descendants of samurai, these families have no money, are greedy and cowardly, holding their lives dear. Such people are not samurai, despite their fixed concept that the samurai class is higher than that of town dwellers. In reality, there is no such fixed concept, and those caught up in such fixed concepts have *"confused and limited spirits."*

In the same manner, we conceptualize satori. Hence Jōshū's[4] famous kōan on the buddha nature of a dog,[5] that some guy once demonstrated by going about on all fours and barking. We consider that a high functionary is a man of value, but if he clings to his function to get job security and a good retirement, like any old college professor, he is merely a vulgarized high functionary. There's no longer anything remarkable about his case. Curiously, man fabricates attachments, even on the subject of satori and illusions. All the folk chained to their ideas struggle in the zero sphere. Their slightest movements always aim at raising themselves in society. Some are even so insignificant as to offer gifts to the person who helps them climb, and wallow in thanks. What a pity!

I've always done my best to remain outside social success. I think the degree of excellence obtainable by a man is nothing much. I've decided to frequent society plainly and unadorned, without attachments or accessories. Some say that when I was young I gave edifying sermons, but that these days my talk is too simple and flat. When I was young, it appears that I had some charm and a well-modulated voice. In the zero world, a modulated voice is one that modulates the confusion of human sentiments and it has no rapport with the Buddha Dharma. For expressing emotions, we have excellent naniwa-bushi[6] and joruri[7] artists.

The Buddha Dharma is the sphere of the absolute highest degree. Dim and dense minds situated below zero are blind to the Buddha and the Dharma. If they were to glimpse it, if only for a moment, they would be astonished at having lived up until then at ten thousand degrees below zero, and would say to themselves, "How have I been able to not only pass through zero, but go beyond?" For with a leap, in an instant, they find themselves at the absolute highest degree. Certainly, it is difficult. One can do nothing about that, it's the principle of the Buddha Dharma. The Buddha Dharma is the doctrine without fear that the lion roars, and each one of its words has authority.

Lecturers begin their talks by utilizing a strange formula in which they thank their auditors for lending them their ears. I've never said such things. That is the manner of expressing oneself in the zero world. I don't employ these formulas, not because they are stupid, but because they are useless. To make the cry of the truth of the Way heard, we need not solicit the friendly attention of the audience. It does not enter into consideration whether one speaks to a single person or a half-empty hall.

At one time, Hōtan Oshō[8] was studying at Miidera Temple. At the outset, his master had a full hall, but little by little the audience thinned, until the day came when he found himself alone. The master said to him, "Since you're the only one here, I'm going to discontinue these lectures. If you want me to continue my teaching, get some people to come." "In that case," answered Hōtan as he left, "I'll return tomorrow with lots of people." The next day Hōtan was there, but still alone. "So," said his master, "you're still alone today?" "Absolutely not, there's a crowd, " responded Hōtan seriously and he began to install Fushima puppets in the seats. "But these are puppets!" exclaimed the master. Hōtan replied, " All those who came here before aren't worth any more than these puppets. I alone am listening to you, but that's enough." One is not qualified to hear the Buddha Dharma unless one has absolute confidence in oneself.

One day when my audience consisted of two persons, I spoke so loudly that those passing in the corridor opened the door, curious to see whom I was scolding. When Sawaki roars the dharma, it changes nothing if one or ten thousand are present. Too bad if I address a large audience, but however numerous, they hear only the "dregs." Nevertheless, it's a great error and absurdity to beg the audience to pay attention to the Buddha Dharma's cry of truth, like a bad actor might offer biscuits to his spectators so they'd listen to him.

74

They comprehend only that grave faults are an obstacle to awakening,
And are incapable of penetrating the Buddha's secret.

Transgressions Make No Sense

What is the cause of their incomprehension? *They comprehend only that grave faults are an obstacle to awakening, and are incapable of pen-*

etrating the Buddha's secret.

This verse picks up again the theme of the preceding one: *Though having committed a capital crime, Yuse realized the unborn, became immediately Buddha, and remains so now.* In Buddhism, one considers as a grave fault the transgression of the four most important prohibitions: murder, theft, illicit love, and lying. These precepts are common to both Hinayana and Mahayana traditions; they are also rules of conduct accepted by all human societies. Ordinary minds understand that the violation of a prohibition prevents awakening, but don't have the key that permits them to gain access to the secret of the Buddha. When we hear the words, "secret of Buddha Dharma," we tend to think that this secret key can make our crimes disappear. To think there is such a desirable secret key is the cause of mistakes.

In our tradition, from the very beginning it was said, "There is no violation of the precepts forever," which means there are no precepts that we may ever violate. When told that we should not kill life, it was viewed as a rigid regulation, so that to kill even an insect was a crime. When the time came that one could observe sour milk under the microscope, they perceived with horror that the liquid wriggled with bacilli, and exclaimed, "Oh, I've drunk living beings! They've gone to my stomach. I've committed a sin and I will be punished! Namu amida butsu . . ." They refused to ingest milk products, even to look after themselves. From the point of view of life, our entire universe is a living organism. All is life. Even the Sun and the Moon are living. You and I, one another, die each instant. In sum, the one who comprehends death awakens to the unborn.

The one who awakens to the unborn does not have the feeling of being born and in consequence the feeling of being in life. When life has neither initial nor final term, it becomes impossible, even if one wishes it, to carry out harm to the great life of the universe. Even if someone wielding the celebrated sword made by Masamune tries to kill all living beings, it isn't possible to kill anyone, because no one is born.

The secret of Buddhism is the total and absolute transparency of all things. You and I become clear and transparent, and it's the same with the past, present, and future. Satori is to become transparent. In this transparent clarity of original existence, the forms that one says exist are without form. Differentiation poses no obstacle to the equality of all things, and the equality of all things poses no obstacle to differentiation.

I'm questioned very often on the subject of the precepts: "Must one observe them?" This is not the angle from which they should be considered. The precepts must burst forth from our very depths, for it's there that the secret of the Buddha lives. One also calls this secret "calming and tranquility." One pierces the secret when one becomes Buddha oneself, just as one is, and when one is no longer anything but one with him. If there is no longer a space between the Buddha and the self, it no longer makes sense to violate the precepts. Being no longer anything other than united with the universe as a single body, it's obvious that there's no longer anything to run away from or to pursue. When the mind is totally gathered into itself during zazen, it discovers the secret of the Buddha and, within the secret of the Buddha, to break or not to break the precepts has no meaning. In the world of "absolute highest degree," problems of levels or categories do not exist: all becomes equal, without classes, without ranks, without degrees.

"If one breaks a precept, isn't one going straight to hell? Can one be cleared if a lawyer pleads your case before the court?" It's not at all a question of this. When one is fully within the absolute highest degree world, life continues, all fresh and teeming. The secret of the Buddha is illustrated in another parable in the following verses.

75

Two monks became guilty of lewdness and murder
And Upali, no more enlightened than a firefly, merely aggravated their
* guilt.*
The great Vimalakirti immediately melted their doubts
Like frost and snow beneath a blazing sun.

The power of deliverance is inconceivable,
With limitless marvelous functions as numberless as the sands of the
* Ganges.*
Would one dare renounce offering it the gift of our four possessions
When ten thousand pieces of gold would not suffice?

Where Is the Error?

Two monks became guilty of lewdness and murder. Upali, no more enlightened than a firefly, merely aggravated their guilt. This story is recounted in the *Yuimagyō*.[1]

At the hour of the siesta, two monks were deep in sleep. But was it a dream or was it reality? They violated their vow of chastity with a girl from the neighborhood. When they suddenly opened their eyes, the young girl took fright and fled. As she ran away she fell from a rocky escarpment and was killed. Her death had not been their intention, but they felt responsible. Tormented by guilt, they no longer kept their seat and could no longer concentrate. How could they confess their fault to Shākyamuni? They decided to go and seek counsel from the venerable Upali,[2] the great specialist in the precepts. To their great shame, they recounted all that had happened. "Here's what we've done!" they said, confused and filled with remorse. The venerable Upali, in a solemn and learned tone, explained to them that to take a being's life was a grave fault, the gravest of all according to the Great Vehicle, the Mahayana, and that from the Hinayana point of view that favored personal salvation, the capital crime was that of the flesh. In the present case, they had violated the prohibitions against both murder and lechery. Upon hearing the verdict, the two monks began to shake in terror.

Vimalakirti, who had meanwhile arrived upon the scene, said to the venerable Upali, "Upali, there's no need to augment the guilt of these two monks." By toting up their crimes, Upali had aggravated still more the fright of the monks, already overwhelmed by remorse, just as if he'd added fuel to a fire. Vimalakirti said to him, "By crushing them on the spot, you trouble their mind and overwhelm them. You ought not to act thus." He added, "Upali, the character of the fault is neither inside, outside, nor between the two." The Buddha had taught that if the mind is soiled, the being is soiled and that it's sufficient to eliminate the stains for the being to once again become pure. As soon as the mind has recovered its purity, where is the sin to be found? Moreover, supposing that the mind has been cleansed and the mind is pure, where then is the mind to be found? No more is it inside, nor outside, nor between the two.

This case is identical. We can locate neither the mind nor the sin. Wouldn't it be the same for all conditioned phenomena? In fact, the same applies to all the dharmas. Without exception, their true character is without characteristic, and thus without impurity. What one calls crime, sin, or fault are only concepts, dust gathered along the road. The *Daichidoron*[3] also says, "Which one is the father? the mother? the child? the sin? the merit?" Bodhidharma said, "There is no merit." We also have the example of Devadatta,[4] whom Shākyamuni considered as his master.

Theoretically, Devadatta was a veritable scoundrel, yet he's presented to us in the Lotus Sutra as a perfectly awakened one, and as such, he's invested with the ten titles of praise that designate a Buddha: "Thus Come, Worthy of Offerings, Perfectly Aware, Well Provided in Science and Practice, Well Gone, Knowing the World, Without Superior, Tamer of Men, Master of Men and Gods, the Venerable Awakened One." So Devadatta was not merely a vulgar criminal. Shākyamuni said that he had attained true awakening in a past life due to Devadatta's instruction.

Alone on stage, Devadatta and Shākyamuni each play their role. Which is the father? the mother? the child? What is a gain? What an injury? Nothing is fixed. Vimalakirti demonstrated it masterfully, and the two monks awakened at the instant when the bonds of doubt were cut.

When at one blow one dismisses the underlying multiples of one, it remains one. One and zero have the same nature; they function in the same manner and in the same places. They differ only in the use to which one puts them. Zero becomes a value and a value becomes zero. There are also people who fall into hell while reciting namu amida butsu or while doing zazen.

Inversely, some zeros have become buddhas while preparing miso[5] and others have found awakening in the toilet. There are also some who practice the Way of the Buddha while keeping accounts.

Like frost and snow beneath a blazing sun. When one suddenly enters into the world of unity, sin disappears. *The power of deliverance is inconceivable.* It transforms the mere nothing into something, and dust into gold. A unique sound resounds in the whole universe of the ten directions.

With limitless marvelous functions as numberless as the sands of the Ganges. Whether we are asleep or awake, in motion or still, seated or dancing, the secret of the Buddha operates in all the realms of daily life, whether highs or lows.

Would one dare renounce offering it the gift of our four possessions?[6] A monk is authorized to receive four articles: clothing, food, bedding, and medicine. If an ordinary man were to receive offerings of these, his karma would be to be born as a cow in a future life, and he would bear the weight of this karma until he'd paid for them. The sutras have left us numerous stories on the subject of the "fruits" of actions. In our world, one who receives what he'd normally obtain by the sweat of his brow has a debt of gratitude toward his benefactor and becomes obligated to him.

There is an interesting story about the origins of Madam Mari's four servants. On festival days they carried their mistress' palanquin, and on ordinary days, the sewage from the toilets. Long ago in a previous life, these porters had been monks. At that time, they lived withdrawn at a mountain temple where they practiced the Buddha Way, but since there was no one in the vicinity to give them alms, they were dying of hunger.

To remedy their desperate circumstances, they decided that one of them would remain at the temple to pretend to do zazen and carry out pure conduct, while the other three would go down into the valley to beg. Arriving in the village, they said to the people: "Up there on the mountain lives a saintly man of great compassion, who does zazen every day. If you make gifts to him, you will obtain immense and infinite merit." Thus they spread the rumor about a monk on the mountain who was a true sage.

Their eloquent lie awakened Madame Mari's faith. She climbed the mountain to offer a quantity of food to the holy man. The four monks rejoiced, eating their fill and saying to one another: "This is it! It's in the bag!" Shākyamuni was immediately informed about it, and the four monks found themselves to be porters carrying Madame Mari's palanquin and sewage. When one lives in the zero world, the world of frozen concepts prior to achieving the fluidity of the water of Buddha wisdom, it is a fault to receive the gift of the four articles. In contrast, in the world of oneness would one *dare renounce offering it the gift of our four possessions?*

At Tendoji, a high government official asked Nyojō Zenji to give a formal dharma discourse for his father's memorial ceremony. After the speech, the official offered Nyojō Zenji a large amount of money, but Nyojō Zenji said, "If you had understood what I said, I could receive your offering", meaning that the official wasn't qualified to make such a donation. Nyojō Zenji did not receive the offering. There are few masters who examine a patron's understanding of the dharma when the person offers a donation. In fact, today a priest with such an attitude would never receive offerings.

When ten thousand pieces of gold would not suffice. This phrase perfectly expresses the conditions of life in the world of oneness. Hyakujō Zenji[8] also utilizes this image in Hyakujō-roku: "Beyond the dual nature of being and non-being, there is nowhere that dust can fall. If one does not live with the notion of purity and if conceptual thought resides nowhere, were one to dispense ten thousand pieces of gold daily, one could not exhaust his treasure." This quote demonstrates that its author had the roar of the lion for teaching the doctrine without fear whose limitless effect penetrates the entire universe.

76

Grinding our bones to powder or cutting our body into pieces could not
repay it.
A single word well understood surpasses ten thousand words.

Below zero

Grinding our bones to powder or cutting our body into pieces could not repay it. Dōgen utilizes the same expression in Gakudōyōjin-shū: "Numerous are the men who from ancient times have ground their bones and broken the body. But among them are very few who have transmitted the Dharma. Also numerous are those who have practiced austerities and rare those who have realized awakening." We imagine that to put an end to one's life is a terrible test. In fact, it's not so difficult. There are lovers who commit suicide, trapped persons who throw themselves into wells, and others who, entangled in their debts, see no other way out than to end life.

During the Russo-Japanese War, many combatants like me acted as if death was of no importance. They said that I had courage, but in fact I made war, and death was part of that. Such a thing has nothing to do with satori.

When I recently traveled to Manchuria, I coined an expression suitable to Manchuria: "below zero" (below zero Centigrade, or the freezing point.) It became pretty popular. It's also apparent that the world of zero isn't limited to Manchuria. Within the world below zero we find innumerable specimens: the rich, the great, the powerful, and leading figures in the university or in society. Man absolutely must pass beyond this barrier of zero.

We even sacrifice our lives for this zero world. We wander at random, we depart and return and death arrives before we've stopped turning in circles. I call the one who lives thus a common man. Even though he might pass his life in reciting namu amida butsu or in sitting zazen, he is no whit less a common man who will always end up falling into hell. For a human being, the essential thing is to go above zero. If not, whatever he may engage in, sacrificing his life, earning money or becoming a scholar, will have no value. If he makes money, it will be his master, and he will serve it by spending his life watching over his strongbox. A guy who risks his life at every turn is also below zero.

We must leap over the barrier of zero. *This tranquil man of the Way, who has attained awakening and ceased studying and acting* has passed through *the gate of unconditioned reality that one clears at a leap, entering the land of the Buddha.* That which is beyond zero bears no name—it is the truth. This thing without name that we call true reality must be sought after. We have also seen previously that *in our dream, we clearly distinguish the six destinies. After awakening, all is empty, not even the universe remains. There is neither unhappiness nor happiness, neither loss nor gain. In the peace of extinction there is nothing to seek.*

This signifies that everything found below zero is in the realm of the dream. We have also seen that to cut through the illusions of this world is to *seize the root.* To put it another way, the man who turned in a circle without ever getting anywhere now points himself in the right direction. The ultimate end of the Buddha's teaching is to make men leap over the barrier of zero, were it only once. This is truly the "great business" of Buddhism.

Once we've leaped over the barrier of zero and clearly realized this "great business," it becomes evident that it's not by speaking that one has arrived: *A single word well understood surpasses ten thousand words.* Pure Land Buddhists might say that chanting namu amida butsu while a person is below zero is polluted practice.

Keizan Zenji,[1] in a paragraph in the Denkō-roku dedicated to Nyojō Zenji,[2] describes a kōan that was posed to him by Setchō: "How can something which has never been soiled be cleaned?" Nyojō pondered this question day and night. A year went by and suddenly he understood and experienced great satori. "I have hit upon that which is not soiled!" Originally, man is pure and without stain. Therefore, there is nothing to be purified. When we go beyond even satori, there is no distinction between satori and delusion. When we go beyond zero, there is no delusion to avoid and no satori to seek after.

In the world below zero, there is not much difference between a janitor and the company director. When a person goes beyond zero, he is great, even if a janitor. This is what "the self is itself Buddha" (sokushin sokubutsu) means; then all things are equal.

To do this, the powers of the scholar, of money or of rank are of no use. Without knowing themselves, intellectuals handle a pen with skill, yet they only lean upon words and the point of their pen to say terribly obscure things about man, whom they manipulate like a toy. But all that still has no connection with their nature. Dōgen Zenji wrote in the Bendōwa chapter of Shōbōgenzō, "Doctrinal texts and rituals have multiplied in abundance and the practice has suffered because of it." We so complicate the things of this world that the truth disappears. We can no longer even grasp it. In all this jumble of phenomena, philosophies, sciences, not to mention the 84,000 sutras, how does one discover this unrivaled truth, this word that transcends ten thousand words? If one doesn't find it, there's no other solution than to throw oneself into the drudgery of reading a mountain of books.

This reminds me of a riddle I heard in Manchuria: "My daughter is my mother, my granddaughter is my younger sister, my father is my son, my wife is the mother of my father." I turned these family connections over and over in my mind without being able to unravel them, but I told myself that after all it was a good exercise for training myself to seize the truth of a tangled affair. I had to find the key. From the moment that I understood that the daughter from my wife's first marriage had married my father, the family relations held no further secrets. In effect, since my wife's daughter is also my daughter and had married my father, she becomes my mother. The child born of this marriage is my granddaughter and at the same time my father's daughter, that is to say, my younger sister. My father who married my daughter is my son, for my daughter's mother who in reality is my wife becomes the mother of my father. If you don't uncover the basic fact upon which this whole story turns, you comprehend nothing.

The same goes for the Buddha Dharma. It must be seized in its living actuality. Though we might know everything about the history, geography, science, dates and statistics of Buddhism, we will turn in a circle without finding an exit and will go to our graves never having understood the meaning of the word Buddha in the expression "the Buddha Dharma."

Without question, we must find the key to the riddle, that one word that, well understood, surpasses ten thousand words. However, no precise word exists. It's only a question of the truth. One could just as well name it Buddha, satori, true reality, nirvana, or "to attain comprehension of the highest wisdom," perfect and supreme illumination or awakening. It matters little what term we use. It's just *that*, without name. When we've understood this unique and true thing, all problems resolve of themselves. *A single word well understood surpasses ten thousand words.*

77

It is lord of all existences, none surpass it.
All buddhas, as numerous as the sands of the Ganges, bear witness to it.
Now I understand the nature of the mani jewel,
It accords with those who receive it in trust.

One perceives clearly that there's nothing at all,
Neither man nor Buddha.
The myriad universes are bubbles in the ocean,
The saints and sages, lightning flashes in the sky.

A Day, a Life

It is the lord of all existences, none surpass it. It's a question of the tranquil man who, having leaped over the bar of zero, has attained awakening and has ceased studying and acting. A noble personage, no one equals him, no one is superior to him. More simply stated, it's a question of having oneself understood one's true nature and completely become one's self, just as one is. A monk is not a semblance of a monk, an artisan is not a false artisan. By completely becoming one's true nature, there's no longer a problem. One becomes completely Buddha. Becoming Buddha, the entire universe is Buddha. But when one doesn't enter his true nature, all is illusion. Even as Prime Minister, one remains the prisoner of illusions. Whatever one may do and wherever one may go, one advances pushing an illusion before oneself. No one is more worthy or noble than the one who has understood his true nature: *It is lord of all existences, none surpass it.*

All buddhas, as numerous as the sands of the Ganges, bear witness to it. The expression "sands of the Ganges" is a poetic image denoting a number beyond anything that can be counted. These innumerable buddhas represent the target of our quest. If we grasp the Buddha Dharma in its living actuality, we are in unison with all the buddhas, however numerous they may be. When one is perfectly in unison, there are no longer problems.

Now I understand the nature of the mani jewel. Yōka Daishi proclaims it with assurance. After having known personal suffering, he has sought the difficult Buddha Dharma, followed an authentic teaching, questioned the greatest masters and encountered the correct Dharma, thanks to which he has leaped over the bar of zero. This verse resounds with joy and self-confidence.

It accords with all those who receive it in trust. Thanks to the power and merit of faith, whoever believes in it lives in harmony with it. If he encounters an authentic master, pays attention to the correct Dharma and knowing that *a single word well understood surpasses ten thousand words,* does not wander about in the zone below zero, this man will find peace and tranquility. Even if he has not leaped over the bar of zero through his own strength, he will receive all the benefits accorded to all the buddhas, as numerous as the sands of the Ganges. Such is the merit of faith.

To have faith is not to believe in a God or a Buddha exterior to oneself. Faith is to live God or Buddha within oneself. It's to be in unison with him when one bows down to him. When you firmly believe in the teachings of Shākyamuni, without experiencing doubt, you are fulfilled. That's to say, you have discovered the magic jewel. One day becomes a motionless century, one day includes immutable eternity, one day is a life. I will add that it's a day when the arbitrary no longer exists, a day no longer adulterated.

One perceives clearly that there is nothing at all. A text says: "To know that one has understood is inevitably to remain in ignorance." Another says: "Before satori, one is in illusion, after satori one sees that there's no longer satori." When the mind becomes illuminated, neither light nor shadows exist, and when one realizes his true buddha nature, there is no longer Buddha and no longer self. It's what one calls the sanmai[1] state of consciousness. In the Sōtō Zen branch of Buddhism, during zazen one very precisely realizes this state of consciousness, provided one doesn't do zazen to obtain satori, but is just simply sitting without seeking anything.

In this state of mind, *neither man nor Buddha* exists any longer. The myriad universes are *bubbles in the ocean*, the sages and saints *lightning flashes in the sky.* The universe? What's that? The ego, Buddha, illusions, satori, the ordinary man, the saint, what do these words mean? To give a name to something belongs to the world of relativity, which is to say, the world below zero.

They say that someone is a remarkable man. Yes, certainly he is remarkable, but in the world below zero. Yet, in that world nothing is truly significant. I think that even the fact that "a lie seems okay" is really nothing special and, at any rate, it's just one more error. If robber and robbed belong to the world below zero, that can't be too serious. Nothing important exists in that world. Nevertheless, he who steals commits a doubly immoral act.

To cross beyond zero is to elevate oneself above our world. It's to go beyond ignorance and reach where *neither man nor Buddha* exists. It's an illusion to think that there are men on one side and on the other a savior Buddha who will come to the aid of all living beings.

"The weather today is fabulous!" or "What rotten weather!" This type of conversation belongs to the zero world. As the poem says,

> The morning glory understands nothing of the morning star,
> that there be neither God nor Buddha does not cause it to
> weep.

From the moment one crosses the threshold of zero, there is no longer discontinuity between oneself and the universe, so when I inhale, I inhale the universe and when I exhale, I exhale the universe. Each day I am the in-breath and out-breath of all the universes, as numerous as the sands of the Ganges.

This extremely important thing that must be grasped is the unique truth. Where to discover it? This unique truth is found in the vegetable that is a vegetable and nothing other than a vegetable, just as the rice is rice, the in-breath is the in-breath, the out-breath the out-breath, I am I and you are you. I constantly repeat, "Cease fire! Cease destroying yourself!" This being, that is; that being, this is. *The sages and saints, lightning flashes in the sky.* Like the lightning flashes, one cannot grasp them. It is useless to seek the Buddha; he is part of the dream. The moment you think you've caught him—pfft!—he's gone.

78

Even if our heads were crushed by a turning iron wheel,
The perfect light of concentration and wisdom would not vanish.

Though the sun may cool and the moon warm,
Mara's hordes cannot destroy the true teaching.
The high chariot drawn by an elephant tranquilly advances.
How could a praying mantis deflect it from its course?
The great elephant does not frequent rabbit runs.
Great awakening is not concerned with little details.
Do not calculate the vastness of the sky by peering at it through a straw.
Friend, if you have not yet clearly understood, I have given you here the
   key.

Great and Noble as the Ocean

Even if our heads were crushed by a turning iron wheel . . . We live in disorder and confusion. We adore, we detest, we exult, we despair, we have too much work or too little. Whatever our daily hubbub is, even if the ground shakes beneath our feet and our universe collapses, since the myriad universes are only bubbles in the ocean, we should remain forgiving, in the manner of the ocean. However, it's easier to write about remaining unshakeable when an iron wheel begins to turn on our heads than it is to live it. It's like teaching swimming outside the water. To have the experience is something else. A gangster executing his first hold-up understands this well. He wears a mask, aims his revolver, changes his voice and says, "Your cash or I shoot!" But his teeth are chattering and his knees are shaking. One can do nothing about it, that's the way it is. A real problem.

One day a thief entered the shop of a woodcutter I know who had left the door open to the back courtyard since it was summer and hot. Suddenly, the chest of drawers began to squeak. The owner's son awoke with a start and shouted, "Thief! Thief!" Caught in the act, the frightened thief fled. The son, beside himself, threw himself into pursuit and caught up to him. At bay, the thief pulled a knife and as the young man lunged at him, he stabbed him in the ribs. The two bodies rolled on the ground together. The terrified father arrived on the scene at this moment. He saw that his son was getting the worst of it, so he seized a stick of wood and brought it down with all his strength on the robber's head, shouting, "Filthy beast!" He struck so hard that not only did the robber's head burst, but he also broke his son's. The two of them died on the spot.

A crowd of stupefied gawkers gathered around the immobilized father. The police arrived, investigated, and determined that nothing had been stolen from the woodcutter's house. It was all just the result of a tragic encounter among three persons who had simultaneously lost their composure. This lamentable little news item is only one example of the innumerable dramas arising among people in the zero world. They immediately get their back up and grow angry over little things of no importance. Likewise, they burst into tears over trifles.

It's obvious that one must go beyond the zero world.

Ryōkan[1] felt unlimited compassion for beings. One day a thief entered his place, making a great noise and not even covering a sneeze. Ryōkan sank down on his mat, held his breath and pretended to be asleep. He said to himself that he had nothing to steal and that the sole thing that might interest the thief was the mat. The thief, who had at that moment reached the same conclusion, began to pull on the mat. Ryōkan, stiff as a corpse, let himself be rolled off and plundered. The robber fled. Ryōkan listened to the sound of his steps as they faded away and died out into the night. "He must be contented," he said to himself. He sneezed and rose to warm himself. As he neared the window, he saw the shining moon and composed this poem: "Left by the thief, the moon through the window."

Ryōkan exhibited extraordinary composure. This is how we ought to be, tranquil and at ease in all circumstances, but this tranquility does not just come of itself.

To Grasp the Unique Truth

During the Meiji era a great monk of the Shin-shū[2] tradition, named Shichiri Kōjun, lived at Hakata. One day a thief entered his house and said, "Give me your money!" Shichiri answered, "If it's money you want, I've got plenty!" and handed him a wad of at least a hundred one yen bills, wrapped in a little square of silk used for the tea ceremony, and which a pious person had just brought him as an offering. He offered it to the thief just as it was. The man said to him, "Abbot, you're generous, can I take it all?" "Certainly, certainly," Shichiri responded. As the thief was leaving, the abbot called him back: "Hey! Wait a minute! Your clothing looks very thin to me, and as cold as it is out, you'll catch cold. Yesterday someone gave me a good cloak that originally belonged to someone now deceased. It's your size and it will fit you very well. Wait, I'm going to look for it." Shichiri brought back the clothing, carefully wrapped in tissue paper. The thief was again leaving when the abbot called to him again, "Hey! Wait!" The thief wondered what more he wished to give him. "I've nothing more to give you, but when one receives a gift one must thank the person who offers it!" This anecdote is witness to Shichiri's mastery of self.

The thief continued his activities and was finally caught by the police. When interrogated, he confessed all his misdeeds, including his theft at the temple. Shichiri was summoned to the police station. "Are you aware that you've committed an infraction by assisting a thief and that you're liable for a severe punishment?" Astounded, Shichiri answered, " Yes, but no thief entered my place!" They brought in the robber: "Here's the one who confessed the theft. Don't you recognize him?" It really was his man. Without turning a hair, Shichiri responded, "Certainly I know him! He came to the temple one day. Let me see, when was it? Didn't I give him some money and didn't he thank me for it?" Thief though he was, these words affected the man like an electric shock. Stunned and as if under the effect of a drug, without realizing it he said, "I thank you."

The thief began to sweat out all the dirty waters of the zero world, and then felt a great relief. He'd just leaped over the bar of zero. Satori isn't as difficult as our Buddhist scholars would have us believe, nor does it stink of boredom like university chit-chat. The thief had never encountered a man like Shichiri. It was as if this extraordinary human specimen generated an electric current and he'd been hooked up to it. Now he saw and experienced things just like him. One might say that it was as if his old bamboo pipe, blocked due to humidity, had been suddenly unblocked and let the air circulate freely. The world had completely changed. He became a model prisoner during his incarceration and benefited from a pardon due to an amnesty issued on the occasion of the funeral of the dowager empress Eishō.

As soon as he was freed, he presented himself at the temple to thank Shichiri. He hadn't passed an hour or a day in prison without thanking him and venerating him in his thoughts. The infinite gratitude that he experienced transformed his life. No matter what the daily hardships, he never had a sad air and never complained. In fact, this was why he'd been given a pardon. He begged Shichiri to accept him as a disciple. Shichiri immediately responded, "Agreed! Come along then!" He was put in charge of the temple treasury and in his entire life never committed the slightest error.

The perfect light of concentration and wisdom would not vanish. We have already talked about concentration and wisdom in a previous chapter. When the two unite in perfect communion, we discover the unique truth, this single word that, well understood, goes beyond a hundred thousand words, the indestructible truth against which one can do nothing.

Though the sun may cool and the moon warm, Mara's hordes cannot destroy the true teaching. A man who steps beyond zero transcends ten thousand words and from that moment on, he walks the daily road with great strides, head high. Since there is no thing or person that can be his obstacle, he enjoys total freedom. *The high chariot drawn by an elephant tranquilly advances. How could a praying mantis deflect it from its course?* The heavy, calm gait of the elephant evokes power and serene strength. What can a little insect do to prevent his passage, even if it stretches to its full height?

The great elephant does not frequent rabbit runs. Great awakening is not concerned with little details. In truth, man's great and supreme liberty manifests when he has passed through zero. A caution is addressed to those who have not yet had the experience and allow themselves to criticize everything: *Do not calculate the vastness of the sky by peering at it through a straw.* What good is it to judge others through one's self, the absence of illusions through one's own illusions, non-acting through one's activities and the conditions of a world to which one doesn't belong, and knows nothing of?

Shōdōka ends with this line: *Friend, if you have not yet clearly understood, I give you here the key.* The term "friend" that opens the poem, reappears here and reverberates in us like an echo: "Friend, don't you see?"

Shōdōka makes us leap over the wall that encloses us in the zero world. Beyond the words of the poem, Yōka wants to inspire in us the inexpressible. He says the essential things that can be expressed by language and awakens within us a profound resonance.

Notes On Sawaki's Commentary

1

1. **Tōzan Ryokai** (Tung-shan Liang-chieh, 807–859): Ch'an (Jpn. Zen) master. Author of the *San-mei-k'o* (Jpn. *Hōkyō Zanmai*) "Samadhi of the Precious Mirror"'"

2. **Ten directions**: north, south, east, west, north-east, north-west, south-east, south-west, zenith and nadir, i.e., space in its totality

3. **Three times** (Jpn. sanze): three periods of time—past, present, future

4. **Shinran Shōnin** (1173–1262): founder of the Jōdo shin-shu or True Pure Land school of Japanese Buddhism. He thought that faith in the power of Amida Buddha is more important than the number of times one recites his name. (Namu Amida Butsu) He rejected the monastic rules of the traditional Jōdo sect and authorized his monks to eat meat, live like lay people, and marry.

5. **Amida** (Skt. Amitabha): made 48 vows as his promise to assist all beings without distinction.

6. **Cosmic cycle** (Skt. Kalpa): 4,320,000 of our years. Each cycle divides into four periods: creation of the worlds, duration of the life cycle of existing worlds, destruction of the worlds, and duration of chaos.

7. **Satori**: Zen term designating the direct experience of Awakening. The word derives from the verb satoru—to perceive, understand, comprehend, realize.

8. **Hishiryō**: lit. without judgment, no thinking. Signifies that reflection carried out by analyzing something through differentiating its characteristics is totally unsuited to producing knowledge of true reality.

9. *Shijūnishōgyō* (Sutra in Forty-two Chapters): sutra translated from Sanskrit into Chinese during years 58–75 CE. It may have been the first Buddhist writing introduced into China and translated into Chinese.

10. **Daitō Kokushi** (1281–1337): Rinzai Zen monk.

11. **Kunisada Chūji** (1810–1850): defender of oppressed peasants and a poplar hero at the end of the Edo period.

12. **Banzuin Chōbei** (d. 1651): chivalrous person and renowned swordsman who put into practice the moral code of the warrior.

13. **Dōgen Zenji** (also Dōgen Kigen or Eihei Dōgen, 1200–1253): Introduced the tradition of the Sōtō School into Japan. He is considered to be one of Japan's greatest thinkers, and is venerated by all schools of Buddhism. Author of Shōbōgenzō, his principle work, as well as many others.

14. **Gakudōyōjin-shu** (Advice to Students of the Way): Compiled by his student, Ejō, this work sets out ten subjects for study by beginners on the Way.

15. **Keizan Jōkin** (1268–1325): fourth patriarch of Sōtō Zen in Japan, founder of Sōji-ji, one of Japanese Sōtō's two head temples.

16. **Zazen Yōjin-ki** (Measures to Respect During Zazen): Celebrated text by Keizan.

2

1. **Shōken Kōtaikō** (1850–1914): wife of the Emperor Meiji
2. **Miyamoto Musashi** (1584–1645): celebrated swordsman. Author of Gorin no shō (Treatise on the Five Rings).
3. **Dōkukōdō:** "The Way of the One Who Goes Alone."
4. See Chapter 18.
5. **Bushidō:** "The Way of the Warrior."
6. **The Dharma Wheel** (Skt. Dharma-chakra): symbol of the teaching of the Buddha, it was set into motion when the Buddha gave his first sermon after his Awakening. It is one of the Eight Jewels and one of the eight symbols which indicate the Buddha.
7. **Tenrinjō-ō** (Skt. Chakravarti-raja) "kings who turn the wheel": ideal kings in Indian mythology. They rule the four continents that surround Mt. Sumeru, turning the wheels they have received from heaven.
8. **Kinshi kunshō:** a decoration awarded to the soldiers wounded in war, as well as those of great achievement. It was begun during the Meiji period (1868–1912), continued until the end of World War II and was accompanied by a pension.
9. **Dharma body** (Skt. Dharmakaya, Jpn. Hosshin): the true nature of Buddha, the essence of the universe, expressing the identity of the Buddha with all forms of existence. It is unchanging, beyond time, without distinctive sign, exempt from all forms of duality.
10. **Yoshida Shōin** (1830–1859): patriot at the end of the Edo period. A partisan of the Emperor, a well-read expert on military affairs, he founded a school to spread western learning and participated in a failed assassination attempt on a counselor of the Shōgun who was supposed to sign the final treaty opening Japan to foreign commerce.

11. **Yamato:** old Japan

12. **Kōan** (chin. kung-an): at its origin, a Chinese term signifying "precedent in a legal proceeding, a decree that became a statute." In the Zen tradition: a statement, question, anecdote, or dialogue that cannot be understood by relying on analytical thought. Meditation on a kōan leads to transcending logical thought and to experiencing the non-dual nature of true reality.

13. **Joshū Jūshin** (Chin. Chao-chou, Ts'ung-shen, 778–897): one of the greatest Ch'an (Jpn. Zen) masters. His words possessed great power, and it was said that they were able to cut through the thoughts and blind sentiments of his students like a sharp sword.

14. **Tenjō tenge yuiga dokuson:** a Japanese phrase that witnesses to a grasp of total awareness of the identity of the self and the true nature of the universe. The one who has knowledge of this truth has, according to the colorful language of Zen, "swallowed the universe."

15. **Kobayashi Issa** (1763–1827): poet who devoted himself to haiku.

16. **i-shin-den-shin:** Japanese phrase meaning literally: "transmission from heart-mind to heart-mind." A central concept of Zen philosophy, it is drawn from the "*The Sutra of the Sixth Patriarch*," by Hui-neng (Jpn. Enō)

17. **Hagakure:** work composed by Yamamoto Tsunetomo around 1700, following conversations he had with the daimyo of the fief of Saga. The author's intention was to battle against the decline of the spirit of bushidō. Its distinguishing characteristic is to wish to persuade warriors of the beauty of death, considered to be the crowning moment of their life. It found numerous readers again during the Second World War.

3

1. **Shākyamuni:** lit. " sage of the Shākya lineage," surname given to Siddhartha Gautama of the Shākya clan, founder of Buddhism. He was born in 566 or 563 BCE and lived for 80 years. The historical Buddha, he's designated by the name Shākyamuni to distinguish him from the innumerable transcendental buddhas who are the many manifestations of the one and unique principle of Buddha.

2. **Ananda:** cousin and great disciple of Shākyamuni, renowned for his exceptional memory that allowed him to retain all of the teachings of the Buddha. He succeeded Kāshyapa in leading the community.

3. **Ajase** (Skt. Ajātashatru): King of Magadha. He reigned during the final eight years of Shākyamuni's life, about 494–462 BCE. See Chapter 70.

4. **Geta:** Japanese wooden clogs.

5. **Kitō:** esoteric ritual common both to Shintoism and Buddhism, performed in the case of illness or natural catastrophe.

4

1. **Skandha** (Skt.): group, aggregate. The five components that together form an individual living being: form, sensation, perception, formation, consciousness.

2. **Six roots** (Jpn. rokken): The five sense organs plus consciousness are considered as the roots of earthly desires.

3. **Isan no keisaku** (Collection of the Words of Master Isan): Isan Reiyū (Chin. Kuei-shan Ling-yu or Wei-shan Ling-yu) (771–853) was a celebrated Ch'an master in southern China. A community of 1,500 members was grouped around him and the origin of a great monastery on Mt. Kuei-shan.

4. **Shokusanjin:** Nom de plume of Ota Nampo (1749–1823): accomplished in both Chinese and Japanese culture, he was the author of poetry in the Chinese style, essays, entertainments, comic novels. Wrote also under the nom de plume of Neboke Sensei ("The badly awakened master").

5

1. **Hannya shingyō:** abbreviation of *Maka Hannya Haramitsu Shingyō.* "Sutra of the Heart of Great Perfect Wisdom." One of Mahayana Buddhism's most important sutras, it takes on a particular importance in Zen, for it offers a clear and concise formulation of the doctrine of emptiness.

2. **Karma** (Skt., lit. "act"): Buddhism gives it the sense of mental, physical, or verbal actions. Each action, good or bad, has a latent influence on the life of a being. The law of karmic causality operates in the three phases of existence: past, present, and future. Each act is a seed of another act to come. One harvests the fruits of karma in the form of joy or suffering, according to the nature of one's acts and thoughts.

3. **Lotus Sutra** (Skt. *Saddharmapundarika sutra*): "Sutra of the Lotus of the Good Law." One of Mahayana Buddhism's principal sutras. The Tendai and Nichiren schools in particular stress its doctrines. It is considered as the sutra of the complete teaching of the Buddha. It is said to be a sermon pronounced on Vulture Peak at the end of his life, but it was transcribed only toward the year 200 CE.

4. **The four elements:** According to ancient Indian belief, earth, water, fire, and wind are the components of all life in the universe. Buddhism adds space, whose function is to integrate and harmonize the other elements.

5. *Fugen-kyō* (complete title: *Kan Fugen bosatsu gyōbō-kyō*): "Sutra of the Meditation on the Bodhisattva Fugen." It is considered as the conclusion of the Lotus Sutra, prolonging the final chapter dedicated to the bodhisattva Fugen, who has made a vow to propagate the teaching of the Buddha after his death.

6. **Sange:** to acknowledge one's errors. At the beginning of Buddhism, a meeting was held twice a month, during which all those who had violated the precepts apologized before the community. This act was called sange.

7. **Sanshō shima** ("three obstacles and four demons"): The three obstacles are: (1) Bonnō-shō, worldly desires; (2) Gō-shō, karma; (3) Hō-shō, the retribution for acts committed in wicked paths. The four demons are: (1) On-ma, the five aggregates; (2) Bonnō-ma, the passions; (3) Shi-ma, death; (4) Tenji-ma, the oppression of power.

8. **Avichi** (Skt.) "Hell of incessant suffering": the eighth and most terrible of the eight burning hells.

9. **Ksana** (Jpn. setsuma): a moment, an instant.

10. **Yamaoka Tesshū** (1830–1888): a politician.

11. **Kōkujō:** the second of the eight hot hells, to which go those who have lied, slandered, spoken ill of others, engaged in idle talk, as well as dishonest civil servants.

6

1. **Nyorai zen:** Nyorai (skt. Tathagata), lit. "thus come"; one of the ten appellations or ten epithets applied to a Buddha.

2. **Kyōsaku** (lit. "awakening stick"): Flat stick that one uses to strike the shoulders of practitioners seated in zazen. It aids in overcoming fatigue, eliminates tensions, and increases concentration. It is used to help and not to punish. It symbolizes the sword of wisdom.

3. **"Clouds and water"** (Jpn. Unsui): Novices in Zen monasteries. To take the clouds and water as a model for one's life is an idea that goes back to Taoism.

4. **Sesshin** ("concentration of mind"): days devoted to rigorous and intense practice of zazen.

5. **Hell** (Skt. Naraka): The lowest of the wrong paths. As a state of life, hell is a condition of extreme mental or physical suffering, characterized by a destructive drive.

6. **Greed** (Skt. preta Jpn. gaki): The preta originated as spirits of the dead in ancient India. Incorporated into Buddhism, the word signifies "hungry ghost" since the spirits of the dead were considered to be such. Greed is the second of the wrong paths. In this state, one is consumed by insatiable desires for food, wealth, power, etc.

7. **Animality** (jap. chikushō) : the third of the six wrong paths. A state where one is mastered by instinctive desires and where one loses all notion of reason or morality.

8. **Anger** (Jpn shūra): Originally, the asuras were quarrelsome demons in Indian mythology. They live in a constant state of anger. A person in this condition cannot stand being inferior to others in any arena whatsoever.

9. **Humanity** (Jpn. ningen): fifth of the six paths. It is the state in which, thanks to reason, one controls his instinctive desires and where one acts in a human fashion.

10. **The world of heaven** (Jpn. tenjōkai): the sixth of the six paths. State of temporary happiness.

11. **Shōmon** (Skt. shravaka): lit. "those who hear the voice" Disciples of the Buddha who hear his teaching and make every effort to attain Awakening, but for personal ends, for their own salvation.

12. **Engaku** (Skt. pratyekabuddha): lit. "arrived at awakening by oneself." Originally, this designated a person who has retired from this world and seeks awakening alone in a forest.

13. **Bodhisattva** (Skt.): lit. "awakened being." The one who aspires to the state of Buddhahood, but who renounces entering nirvana as long as all beings are not saved. The virtue that brings about his/her action is compassion sustained by knowledge and wisdom. The bodhisattva devotes him/herself entirely to helping others.

14. **Hinayana**: lit. "small vehicle." Originally a negative, belittling term created by followers of the Mahayana ("great vehicle") to designate early Buddhism.

15. **Paramita** (Skt.): lit. "which has obtained the other shore." Generally translated as "perfection" because these practices lead to perfection.

16. **Shōjin** (Jpn.): diligence, energy.

17. **Fukanzazengi**: "Universally Recommended Instructions for Zazen."

18. **Bendōwa**: "Talk on the Wholehearted Practice of the Way."

19. **Zanmai o zanmai**: "The samadhi king of samadhis."

20. **Zazen Yōjin-ki**: "Points to Watch in Zazen."

21. **Gasshō** (lit. "palms together"): Zen gesture and saying that expresses a greeting, a request, thanks, respect.

22. **Hakama**: skirt that is part of the garb of a warrior.

23. **Shikantaza** (lit. "just sitting"): According to Dōgen, the state characterized by a sustained attention which fixes itself on no object and does not attach to any contents of thought or support such as kōans. It is simply to do zazen for the sake of zazen.

24. **Kinhin**: Zen exercise that consists of slow and concentrated walking between two periods of zazen.

25. **Kakusoku** (Jpn.): "kaku" to perceive, "soku" to touch.

26. **Sōtō**: a principal school of Japanese Zen, along with the Rinzai. Founded in Japan by Dōgen, it particularly emphasizes shikantaza, while the Rinzai school teaches meditation on kōans.

7

1. **Nothing** (Jpn. Mu; chin. wu): lit. "nothing, not, un-, is not, has not, not of": It is employed in the sense of "absence of" thought, desires, character, attachment, own nature, etc.

2. **Takuan**: dried radish pickled in salt and bran, part of the daily nourishment of Zen monks. It's the nickname given to himself by the great Rinzai master, Sōhō (1573–1645). He also made a name for himself in poetry thanks to his waka, in painting and calligraphy, and the Way of Tea. He wrote a celebrated letter on the spirit of kendō ("Way of the Sword") to Yagyū Munenori.

8

1. **Gankai** (Chin. Yanhui, 514–483 BCE): a disciple of Confucius.

2. **Heike Monogatari**: narrates the events of the years 1165–1185, the splendor and fall of the Taira clan, defeated by the Minamoto. The tale was written in the thirteenth century.

3. **Ryōkan** (1758-1831): Zen monk of the Sōtō school. After twelve years of training, he settled in a hermitage and devoted himself to poetry: haiku, waka, and poetry in the Chinese style. His poems are the expression of his experience of Zen. They are among the most beautiful Zen poems in Japanese literature.

4. **Gō**: equals 0.18 liters of rice. The salary of warriors was calculated in measures of rice.

5. **Koku**: equals 180 liters.

6. **Sōkushin jōbutsu:** lit. "the body is identical to the Buddha." Famous saying by Kūkai, founder of the Shingon School.

7. **Kannon** (Skt. Avalokiteshvara): "perceiver of the cries of the worlds." According to the Lotus Sutra, this is a bodhisattva who, through his profound compassion, takes on thirty-three different forms and manifests everywhere in the world to save beings from danger and suffering.

9

1. **Shoen** (Jpn.): lit: "relations, links"—interdependent, causal links. Phenomena and beings exist or manifest only as a function of their relations with beings and phenomena. Fundamental Buddhist doctrine of the interdependence of all things.

2. *Yuikyōgyō* "Sutra of the last teachings of the Buddha": This is purported to have been the last sermon given by Shākyamuni to his disciples prior to his death. Precepts to observe in order to control the sense organs and to regulate one's mind. It is particularly valued in the Zen school and was translated into Chinese by Kumarajiva.

10

1. **Sōzan Daishi** (Chn. Ts'ao-shan Pen-chi, 840-901): Ch'an master that, in collaboration with his master Tōzan Ryōkai (Chn. Tung-shan Liang-chieh) founded the Ts'ao Tung (Jpn. Sōtō) school that draws its name from the first characters of the founders' names.

2. *Kegon-kyō* (Skt. *Avatamsaka Sutra*): fundamental text of the Kegon School. It teaches that all things are in constant relation and give birth one to another.

3. **Ninomiya Sontoku** (1787–1856): specialist in rural economy at the end of the Edo period.

4. **Mujū** or **Ichien** or **Dokyū** (1236–1312): Rinzai monk and author of Shaseki-shū (Collection of Sand and Stone), a collection of legends and stories, often full of humor, and very much appreciated by Zen masters.

5. **Toba Sōjō** or **Kakujō** (1053–1140): painter monk. Tradition attributes to him four scrolls representing animals. Monkeys, rabbits, frogs etc. are shown in action, caricaturing human customs.

6. **Hell:** according to certain sutras there are eight burning hells, or principal hells, or eight freezing hells.

11

1. **Jizō** (Skt. Kshitigarbha) "maternal bosom of the earth" Originally, god of the Earth in Indian mythology. In Buddhism, he is venerated as a bodhisattva. Faith in Jizō spread to Japan among the common people in the twelfth century. He rescues people from the torments of hell, aids dead children, and protects travelers. One finds his stone statue at crossroads, where he is represented as a monk on pilgrimage, carrying the six-ringed staff.

2. **Iroha:** according to tradition it was supposed to have been composed by Kūkai (774–835), but it is first encountered in a sutra from the eleventh century. This poem is composed in such a fashion that all the sounds of the Japanese syllabary figure in it, each one employed only on a single occasion. It was used to teach writing to children.

3. **Namu amida butsu** ("Homage to Amida Buddha"): Invocation utilized by the Pure Land schools that affirm it is possible to be reborn in the Pure Land by reciting this phrase.

4. **Gosui** (Jpn.): five signs of decay which appear when a celestial

being's life is coming to an end: (1) his clothing wears out; (2) the flowers on his head fade; (3) his body becomes dirty and smells bad; (4) his armpits sweat; (5) he doesn't feel happy, no matter where he is.

5. ***Kongō Hannya Haramitsu-kyō*** (Skt. *Vajracchedika prajna paramita sutra*) (Diamond Sutra): Sutra translated into Chinese by Kumarajiva. It reports Shākyamuni's discourse on the constant flux of all phenomena and on the principle of non-substantiality. Fundamental sutra for Zen.

6. **Cf. Hannya shingyō:** "a.noku.ta.ra.san.myaku.san.bo.dai."

7. **Sōtōba** (Chn. Sou-tchan or Sou Tong-p'o, 1025–1101): One of the most celebrated poets of the Song dynasty. He practiced Ch'an.

12

1. **Fugu** (Jpn.): globe fish which contains a deadly poison. A Japanese saying equivalent to the English saying: "Honey is sweet, but the bee stings."

2. **Kagura:** songs and dances executed before the gods.

13

1. **Eihei-ji** ("Monastery of Eternal Peace"): one of the two principal monasteries of the Japanese Sōtō school. It was founded by Dōgen in 1244 as Daibutsuji and renamed Eiheiji in 1246.

2. **Sen** (Jpn.): quarter of a yen.

3. ***Daiichido-ron*** (skt. *Mahāprajnāpāramitā-shāstrā*) (Treatise on the Sutra of Perfect Wisdom): one of the principal works of Nāgarjuna, commentary on the *Makahannya Haramitsu* sutra. The only version remaining is that in Chinese, translated by Kumarajiva. French translation by Étienne Lamotte.

4. In China, during the epoch from the Hegemonies of the fifth century BCE, two kingdoms of the southeast, Wu and Yue, dominated political life, after having vanquished the neighboring kingdoms. Then they fought among themselves and Yue absorbed Wu.

5. **Chindon-ya:** musicians in gaudy costumes making a stir in the street to attract clients to a store, etc.

6. **Kanzan Kokushi** (Kanzan Egen or Musō Daishi, 1277–1360): Rinzai Zen master. He spent many years in the mountains where he worked during the day as a laborer and passed his nights in zazen. He became abbot of one of the great Zen monasteries in Kyōto.

15

1. **Mani jewel** (Skt. cintamani): according to a Chinese legend, a pearl that fulfills all the desires of the one who possesses it.

2. **Daichi Zenji** (Daichi Sokei, 1290–1366): Sōtō Zen monk and poet. His work includes some "remarks," Goroku, and a collection of poems, Kaninshū ("Drought and Flood").

3. **Gyōsan:** lit. "form-mountain."

4. See Chapter 10.

16

1. Cf. *Hannya shingyō*: Shiki soku ze kū, kū soku ze shiki.

2. **Meiji-jidai** (1868–1912): period characterized by the opening of Japan to the West and by its efforts to develop industry and the economy.

3. **Tokugawa-jidai** or **Edo-jidai** (1660–1868): period when power was held by the Tokugawa Shogun, characterized by the closing of Japan to foreign commerce, and a feudally structured society.

17

1. The eye of the Buddha perceives the nature of the life of the past, present, and future. The eye of the Dharma is what permits the bodhisattvas to penetrate all the teachings in order to save human beings. The eye of wisdom is the possibility of perceiving that all phenomena are without substance. The divine eye is the capacity to see beyond physical limits, darkness, distance, or obstacle. The eye of the flesh is that of common mortals who distinguish colors and forms.

18

1. One of the numerous comparisons utilized to express the emptiness of all conditioned phenomena: magic, mirage, reflection of the moon in the water, echo, dream, shadow, reflection in the mirror, metamorphosis, bubble of water, lightning, cloud etc.
2. **Nanzen-ji:** Rinzai Zen monastery. It possesses a great number of archives and frescoes.
3. **Obaku Kiun** (Chn. Huang-po Xiyun, died 850): one of the great Ch'an masters, successor of P'ai-chang Huai-hai (Jpn. Hyakujō Ekai) and master of Linchi I-hsuan (Jpn. Rinzai) He was the precursor of the Rinzai school.

19

1. **Arhat** (Jpn. Rakan) "he who is worthy of a religion": He represents the Hinayana ideal because he has attained the highest degree of perfection in his practice: he has erased his impurities, satisfied his vows and put down his load: his mind is truly liberated. The Mahayana reproaches him for being an egoistic saint.

2. **Zōga Sōzu** (917–1003): Japanese monk of the Tendai school, he was born into the illustrious Tachibana family during the Heian period.

3. **Hieizan**: mountain near Kyōto where in the ninth century Saichō founded the mother house of the Tendai sect and which became the principal center of Buddhism in medieval Japan.

20

1. **The three bodies** (Skt. trikaya): Concept adopted by the Mahayana to organize the different concepts of the Buddha that appear in the sutras. As regards Zen, the three bodies designate three levels of reality that form a whole because they are in constant relation with one another.

2. **Dharma body** (Skt. dharma-kaya, jpn. hosshin): the truth or fundamental law, the cosmic consciousness that eludes rationalization.

3. **Reward body** (Skt. sambogha-kaya, Jpn. hōjin) or wisdom body: reward for having brought to term the bodhisattva practices; permits transmission.

4. **Practice body** (Skt. nirmana-kaya, Jpn. ōjin) or body of metamorphosis: the physical form under which a Buddha appears in the world in order to save beings, incarnated by Shākyamuni.

5. **Enō Zenshi** (Chn. Hui-neng, 638–713): sixth patriarch, one of the most important Ch'an masters. He gave the Indian Buddhist tradition its specifically Chinese face. He had numerous disciples who were the source of all the great Ch'an lines of transmission. Yōka Daishi went to his monastery of Pao-lin to meet him, and Hui-neng confirmed his profound enlightenment. Hui-neng is the author of the sole work in Chinese that has acquired the title

of "sutra"—"The platform sutra on the treasure of the dharma", which includes certain of the most profound passages in all Ch'an literature.

6. **"Thusness"** (Skt. tathatā, Jpn. shinnyo): lit. "the truth, it is thus." As translated by Étienne Lamotte , "the true manner of being," which is absence of own nature, without birth or destruction, equal for all. Buddhist texts have a stock of synonyms: own nature of matter, emptiness/non-emptiness, absolute, point of the real, true buddha nature, non-duality, true reality, ultimate reality, unthinkable, indefinable, inconceivable, essential truth, etc. It is the nature of all things, inherent in all beings, even the insentient.

7. **Namu amida butsu** ("homage to Amida Buddha"): written in six characters: na-mu-a-mi-da-butsu.

8. **Sekitō Daishi** (Chn. Shi-t'ou Hsi-ch'ien, 700–790) Ch'an master and author of *Sandōkai* ("Harmony of difference and unity"), one of the four texts which are the objects of recitation in Sōtō Zen monasteries—*Sandōkai, Hōkyō zanmai, Shinjinmei, Shōdōka.* Sōan: grass hermitage.

9. **Manzan Zuihō** (1683–1769): Japanese Sōtō monk.

10. **Hishiryō:** "rationally incommensurable," state of awareness: thought/no thought, beyond thinking.

11. **Eight liberations** (Skt. ashta-vimoksha, Jpn. hachi ge, hachi gedatsu, hachi haisha): the eight ways of meditation for removing various attachments

12. Cf. chap. 7. **Six roads** (Jpn. rokudō) : conditions of existence. (hell, greediness, animality, anger, human, divine): The one who lives in these states is dominated by his reactions to external stimuli and is thus never truly free.

13. **Zanmai** (Skt. samādhi): in Mahayana Buddhism designates interior equilibrium, calm, concentration of mind. Non-dualistic

state of awareness, the disappearance of all distinctions between subject and object.

14. **Tenjiku Tokubei** (1618?–1686?): a merchant, he embarked at the age of fifteen on a ship headed for India. He stayed there for three years, then on his return left for Macao where he remained for two years. He wrote an account of his travels relating the marvelous things he had witnessed. The account has disappeared, but it was the source of numerous popular entertainments in the eighteenth century.

21

1. **Bashō** (1644–1694): the most celebrated poet of haiku (17 syllables in three lines; 5-7-5). He enjoyed great renown during his lifetime as well as after his death. He expressed the beauty of the simplest aspects of daily life and states of soul of high elevation in a form of poetry that, before him, was a simple amusement. He has left an important body of work, including the collection, Oku no hosomichi (Narrow Road to the Deep North).

2. **Saigō Takamori** (1822–1877): descended from a family of warriors from the fiefdom of Satsuma, he was a celebrated hero at the time of the battles that took place at the end of the Edo period, between the fiefdoms and the central government of the Tokugawa shogun.

3. **Tōgō Heihachiro** (1847–1904): born of a family of warriors from the fiefdom of Satsuma, he made a career in the navy, commanded the fleet during the Russo-Japanese War and was named admiral in 1904.

4. **Miroku** (Skt. Maitreya): lit. "he who loves," incarnation of universal love. Belief in Maitreya developed in Mahayana

Buddhism, particularly in Tibet. He would succeed Shākyamuni as the future Buddha. He would reappear in this world in 30,000 years, or according to other texts, 5 billion, 670 million years, following the death of Shākyamuni.

22

1. See Chapter 8.

24

1. **Fukakusa no Gensu** (1623–1668): Nichiren monk, historian, and poet. He withdrew into a hermitage for 32 years and led an austere life, welcoming with kindness all those who wished to study with him. He is known as a poet in the Chinese and Japanese styles. His poems have been collected in the Sōzan-shu (Collection of the Grassy Hills) and the Fusō in'itsu-den (Biography of the hermits of Japan.)

25

1. **Tenkei Denson** (1648–1735) Japanese Sōtō monk.
2. See note, Chapter 10.
3. **Takuan Oshō**: see Chapter 7, note 2.
4. **Natsume Sōseki** (1867–1916): novelist recognized as one of the writers representative of modern Japanese literature. His work seeks to recreate a truly Japanese esthetic. He explored human consciousness and expressed the solitude and difficulty of being. Among his most well-known novels are I Am a Cat, The Gate, The Poor Heart of Men.
5. *Hannya shingyō*: "Kan-ji-zai-bo-satsu."
6. *Sandōkai* (Chn. *Ts'an-t'ung-chi*): of Sekitō Kisen (Chn. Shih-t'ou),

the *Hōkyō zanmai* (Chn. *San-mei-ko*) of Tōzan and the *Shōdōka* are three of the four texts recited in Sōtō Zen monasteries, the fourth being the *Shinjinmei* (Chin. *Hsin-hsin-ming*) of Sōsan (Chin. Seng-ts'an).

26

1. **Enō** (see chapter 20, note 5) Jpn. mu itchi motsu: lit. "not a thing." Celebrated Zen phrase, it indicates that no phenomenon has substance.

2. **Seigen Gyōshi** (Chn. Qingyuan Xingsi, 660?–740) Nangaku Ejō (Nanyue Huairang, 677-744): two eminent disciples of Enō (Chn. Hui-neng) Each is the founder of a great Ch'an lineage.

27

1. **Daichi Zenji:** see Chapter 15.
2. **Kiang Hou** (Jpn. Kōko).
3. **Hui-neng:** see chapter 20, note 5.
4. **Kanzan Egen:** see chapter 13.
5. **Ingen Ryūki** (Chn. Yinyuan Longch'i, 1592–1673): master of the Lin-chi (Jpn. Rinzai) school of Zen, came to Japan in 1654 and founded there the Obaku school of Zen. His teachings have been collected in many works.

28

1. The complete formula is gyō-jū-za-ga: lit. "while walking, sitting, standing, lying down." Expression indicating that Zen must be practiced in all circumstances of daily life and that it does not limit itself to the posture of zazen.

2. **Kamakura-jidai** (1185–1333): also called the Middle Ages. Era

marked by the installation in power of the military and decline of the control of the Imperial Court. It is also the period when Zen Buddhism appeared in Japan, to play an important role in the mentality of the warriors of the Middle Ages.

3. **Kunisada Chūji** (1810–1856): popular hero at the end of the Edo period.

4. **Banzuin Chōbei** (?–1651): chivalrous character who became a literary theme exploited by storytellers. He put into practice the code of the warrior (bushidō) and was a remarkable swordsman. He died assassinated in the bath at the home of his adversary.

29

1. **Nentō** (Skt. Dipankara): lit: "Torch-burner" Legendary Buddha who symbolizes the ensemble of the Buddhas of the past. According to tradition, he was at least 96 meters tall and was said to have lived 100,000 years.

2. **Ninniku** (Skt. Kshāntivādin-rishi): Name of Shākyamuni when he was practicing austerities in a previous life.

3. **Diamond concentration** (Jpn. kongō-zanmai, Skt. vajra sāmadhi): The highest level of the eight concentrations. It is characterized by the total absence of obstacles, only impassiveness and keenness of mind exist.

4. See Chapter 24

5. **Miura Dōsun** (?–1516): Born of a warrior lineage, he participated in a plot to overthrow the power of the Hōjōs and was defeated.

30

1. **Shiguseigan:** lit. "the four great vows" of the bodhisattva that one recites after zazen in zen monasteries. They are as old as Mahayana Buddhism:

Sentient beings are numberless, I vow to free them.

Delusions are inexhaustible, I vow to end them.

Dharma gates are boundless, I vow to enter them.

The Buddha Way is unsurpassable, I vow to realize it.

2. **Dōgo Enchi** (Chn. Taowu Yuanchi, 769–853) Ch'an master, successor of Yakusan Igen.

3. **Shinran:** see Chapter 13.

4. **Kanzan:** see Chapter 13, note 6.

31

1. **Kassan** (Chn. Chia-shan, 815–881): Cha'n master.

2. **Jōsan** (chin. Ting-shan): Ch'an master

3. Differing sets of kanji are both Romanized as "shiki," with different meanings: "form" and "color."

4. **Kaga no Chiyo** (1703–1775): poetess, author of haiku. She left two collections of poetry: Poems of the Nun Chiyo and Song of the Pines.

32

1. **Sushi:** balls of rice, sometimes filled with raw fish, wrapped in dried seaweed.

2. **Daichi Zenji:** see chapters 15 and17.

3. **Ōishi Yoshio** (1649–1703): leader of the 47 samurai condemned to commit suicide by hara-kiri. In Edo castle, his lord, Asano, had struck with his weapon Kira Yoshinaka following a humiliation and in consequence was condemned to death by suicide. Yoshio and 46 warriors who remained loyal to Asano decided to avenge their master and kill Yoshinaka, then give themselves up to the authorities.

4. **Kusunoki Masahige** (?–1336): participated in the 1336 failed uprising unleashed by the emperor Go-Daigo against the shogunate government. Defeated, he committed suicide on the field of battle. Masahige's exemplary loyalty and his integrity were cited as an example up to the end of World War II.

34

1. **Satta** (skt. sattva) or **Makasatta**: Shākyamuni's name in a previous existence. This story is told in the *Konkōmyō Saishōō*, (Sutra of Golden Light)
2. **Yaksha** (Skt.): originally, beings who served Kubera, the god of Wealth in Indian mythology. In certain sutras, they are described as ugly and cruel beings that eat human flesh.

35

1. **Kāshyapa** or **Mahākāshapa** (Skt.): one of the great disciples of Shākyamuni, celebrated for his ascetic discipline and moral rigor. He ensured the direction of the community after the death of the Buddha.
2. **Sōchō (Chn. Seng-chao)** (374 or 378–414) Taoist who became a monk after reading The Teachings of Vimalakirti.

36

1. See Chapter 11.
2. **Tettsū Gikai** (1219–1309): disciple of Koun Ejō, Dōgen's successor. At his death, Ejō named him the third head of Eihei-ji Monastery, but another disciple, Gien, who had received transmission of the precepts from Ejō, also claimed succession. The conflict terminated with the expulsion of Gikai from Eihei-ji.

37

1. **Kokan**: old saying. "Ko," barbarians from the west of China. "Kan," the China of the Han. What difference does it make if suffering comes from the north or the south?

2. *Daijōkishin-ron* (Skt. *Mahāyānashroddotpāda-shāstra*): lit. "Treatise on the Awakening of the Faith in the Mahayana." Known in its Chinese version of 557, it's considered a purely Chinese work. It explains the great ideas of the doctrine and gives authority to Zen.

3. **Shigetsu Zenji** or **Ein**: Sōtō monk from the middle of the eighteenth century.

4. **Tendai** (Chn. T'ien-t'ai): school introduced into Japan in the eighth century. Its doctrine is based on the Lotus Sutra.

5. **Kusha**: school introduced into Japan in the seventh century. It taught that the self is without substance, but that phenomena exist in reality. It analyzed all things into 75 phenomena divided into 5 categories.

6. **Kotatsu**: traditional heating apparatus, a sort of foot-warmer set into a lowered area underneath a cloth-covered table.

7. **Murakami Senjō** (1851–1929): scholar and monk of the Otani branch of the Jōdō shin-shū school. He published numerous works, including a History of Buddhism. He sustained a thesis according to which Mahayana Buddhism was not practiced by the Buddha. This thesis created a scandal, and he had to renounce his status as a monk.

38

1. *Hannya shingyō*: see chapter 5, note 1.

2. **Musō Soseki** (1275–1351): "Kokushi" is an honorific title given

to a Buddhist master who has had an emperor of Japan as a student. A celebrated master of the Rinzai school, Musō was one of the major authors of the "Literature of the Five Mountains." His best-known work is Muchū mondo, "Dream Conversations."

3. **Hotoke** (Jpn., Buddha), (Skt. and Pali: lit. "the Awakened.")

39

1. **Precepts** (jpn. kai, skt. shila): precepts or rules of discipline. "To receive the precepts" (Jpn. jukai): action of receiving and recognizing the Buddhist rules. The ceremony in the course of which one pledges to respect the rules of the Way signifies an official adherence to Buddhism. Jukai is considered an important step on the road of awakening.

2. The five fundamental precepts are the same for Hinayana and Mahayana Buddhism.

3. The eight or ten precepts are those of ancient Buddhism.

4. **Three treasures** (Jpn. sanpō or sanbō, Skt. trisatna): during the ordination ceremony the initiate pledges to serve the three treasures.

5. **Threefold pure precepts** (Jpn. sanjujōkai): to abstain from what is unwholesome, to do what is wholesome, to benefit all beings.

6. The ten precepts of the Mahayana bodhisattva are those that Zen monks observe.

7. **Kobayashi Issa** (1763–1827): poet devoted to haiku. He left numerous collections of poetry, including Ora ga haru (My Springtime.)

8. **Bodhidharma** (Skt.) (Jpn. Bodaidaruma or Daruma; Chn. Pu-ti-ta-mo, 470–543 CE) Twenty-eighth patriarch of the Indian lineage after Shākyamuni and first Chinese patriarch of Ch'an

(Jpn. Zen). After landing at Canton, he presented himself upon invitation to the emperor Wu of the Liang dynasty in Nanking. His teachings rested on the Mahayana sutras and the practice of meditation. Typically Chinese Ch'an resulted from the blending of Indian Buddhist dhyana (meditation) and Chinese Taoism.

9. **Hōnen Shōnin** (1133–1212): founder of the Jōdo (Pure Land) School in Japan. His most celebrated work is the Senchaku-shū, in which he states that what permits rebirth in the Pure Land is exclusively the recitation of the name of Amida (Namu Amida Butsu) and he demanded the "rejection, closing, ignoring, and abandonment" of all the sutras with the exception of the three Pure Land sutras.

10. *Alaya* (Skt. alaya-vijnāna; jpn. araya-shiki). This is the 8th of the nine consciousnesses, situated at a deeper level than ordinary consciousness. All the karma created in the course of the present and past life is stored there. This deep alaya forms the framework for an individual existence and, in turn, influences the functioning of the other consciousnesses.

11. **Nara-jidai:** era during which the capital was at Nara, 710–784.

12. **Ganjin** (Chin. Kien-tchen, 688–763): Tendai monk specializing in monastic discipline (Skt. vinaya)

13. **Dōkyō** (?–772): monk of the Hossō school. Introduced into the chapel of the imperial court, he had occasion to care for and gain the confidence of the empress, who had fallen ill. He involved himself in political affairs and distinguished himself for his uncommon ambition. He rose to the rank of minister and received the title of hōō ("king of the Dharma"), normally reserved for retiring emperors who had chosen to enter the religious life; then he tried to mount the throne. At the death of the empress, he was

chased from the court and exiled in the provinces.

14. **Sugawara no Michizane** (845–903): high dignitary during the Heian era, victim of intrigues and plotting of the Court.

15. See Introduction, Note 7.

16. **Bonmō-kyō** ("Brahma Net Sutra"), translated into Chinese by Kumarajiva in 406 . It details the precepts intended for Mahayana bodhisattvas. It was greatly valued in China and Japan and used to refute the Hinayana precepts.

17. **Unsui** (Jpn.): see Chapter 6, note 3.

18. **Miroku** (Skt. Maitreya): see Chapter 21, note 4.

19. **Prince Shōtoku** (574–622): made important reforms and governed wisely. He established diplomatic relations with China and opened the way for a great diffusion of Buddhism and Chinese culture.

20. **The three Mahayana sutras:** Prince Shōtoku wrote commentaries on the Lotus Sutra, the Shrimala Sutra, and the Teachings of Vimalakirti.

21. **Emperor Shōmu** (706–756): contributed greatly to the prosperity of Buddhism. He believed deeply in the protective power of Buddhism with respect to the nation. He had a temple and a convent for nuns built in each province.

22. **Kikuchi Taketoki** (1293–1334): born of a notable and powerful Kyūshū family. At the time of the civil wars, he joined the forces of the emperor Go-Daigo and was killed in battle.

23. **Takeda Shingen** (1521–1573): military governor of the province of Kai, participated in numerous battles during the period of the conflicts among the provinces and became a monk.

24. **Uesugi Kenshin** (1530–1578): military governor of the province of Echigo, he fought against Takeda Shingen, and became a monk.

25. **Daichi Zenji:** see Chapters 15, 17, 32.

40

1. **Zen monk's bowl** (Jpn. hatsu or hatchi): bowl made of wood or iron used for receiving food or alms, according to the tradition of the Indian monks who traveled the roads like Shākyamuni.

2. **Monk's staff** (Jpn. shakujō, lit. "metal staff"): Wooden staff with metal rings at the top that sound as one walks. The purpose of this ringing was to warn insects, snakes and little animals susceptible to being crushed by a monk, one of whose fundamental precepts is to avoid killing living creatures. The staff is part of the equipment of a monk who arrives at a monastery in the hope of following a master's teaching.

41

1. **Buson** (1716–1784): haiku poet and well-known painter. Thanks to his subtle sense of color and his delicate feeling for sounds, he knew how to translate the changing aspects of nature into clear images.

2. **Hakurakuten** (Chn. Po Chu-i, 772–846): T'ang era poet, one of the most celebrated Chinese poets. His work includes long narrative poems, realistic and satirical poems, and lyric poetry remarkable for its spoken tone and simple style.

42

1. **Gensha no Shibi** (Chn. Hsuan-sha Shih-pei or Xuansha Shibei, 835–908) Ch'an master, disciple of Seppō Gison (Chn. Hsueh-feng I-ts'un)

2. **Bodhidharma:** see Chapter 39, note 8.

3. **Eka** (Chn. Huik'o, 487–593): second patriarch of Ch'an, successor of Bodhidharma. He had the reputation of being well

read, very erudite in the domains of Confucian, Taoist, and Buddhist writings. Unsatisfied by his bookish understanding, he hoped that meditation would reveal to him the profound meaning of the Scriptures. After the death of Bodhidharma, he left the monastery and led a wandering life among simple workers in order to develop the virtue of humility. He then established himself at Yeh-tu, in the north of China, where he taught the Dharma in a somewhat unorthodox manner. The great success he encountered with his students awakened the jealousy of the traditional Buddhist monks. He had to flee to the south of China to escape pursuit and eventually returned to Chang-an, the capital of the empire. It is said that he was accused of heresy and executed at the age of one hundred and six.

4. *Kegon-kyō* (Skt. *Buddhāvatamsaka–sutra*) "Flower Garland Sutra": traditional text considered as the teaching that Shākyamuni pronounced immediately after his Awakening. It teaches that all things are in constant relation and give birth to one another: the one permeates the all and the all is contained in the one, where multiplicity finds its unity in the one.

5. **Hōkyō Zanmai** (Chn. San mei-k'o): see Introduction, note 15.

44

1. **Daichi Zenji:** see citations, Chapters 15, 17, 32, 39.

45

1. Jpn. (daijōbu; Chin. ta-chang-fu; Skt. mahāpurusa): This expression is a surname given to those who have awakened to the buddha nature. Étienne Lamotte, in The Teachings of Vimalakirti, translates it as "great man." A.L. Coles in Zen Poems of the Five

Mountains cites Jakushitsu Ginkō (1290–1367): "The practice of Zen is the business of solid persons (daijōbu). It is not within the reach of weak or over-delicate minds . . ." He remarks that the term "great man" can lead to confusion. Daijōbu is a being healthy of mind, morally sturdy, knowing how to free himself from the illnesses of passion that afflict the intellect and predilections of the ordinary man.

2. **Skandha:** see Chapter 4, note 1.

3. **Yamanaka Shikanosuke** (?–1577) : Warrior of the era of battles among the provinces. One of the faithful followers of the Amako family, which was then in decline and which he tried to restore.

4. **Koku:** see Chapter 8, note 5.

5. **Miyamoto Musashi:** See Chapter 2, Note 2.

6. **Yoshida Shōin** (1830–1859): Born of a family of warriors from Chōshū, he upheld the cause of the emperor and the thesis of the expulsion of strangers at the time of the opening of Japan to Western commerce.

7. **Sakura Sōgorō:** Head of the village of Kōzu in Shimōsa. The lord of the fief had raised the taxes to the point where they spread a great misery among the peasants. Sakura was chosen as a delegate by three hundred heads of villages to present a petition to the shogun in Edo. The lord of the fief avenged himself by crucifying Sakura and his wife and beheading his children. The lord was dispossessed of his lands and sent into exile.

8. **Way of the Warrior** (Jpn. bushidō).

46

1. Jpn. on-ri-issai-ten-dō-mu-sō- ku-gyō- ne-han.

2. **Māra** (Skt. , jpn. Tenma, Akuma, etc.) "Killer of life." Incarnation

of death, in Buddhism he symbolizes all the passions which enchain men. He is the king of the demons of the world of desires and the most redoubtable because he takes pleasure in manipulating men and making them act as he desires. He is considered as the symbol of the appetite for power.

3. **Ambrosia** (Skt. amrta, Jpn. kanrō): has two meanings. (1) immortality, (2) drink or medicine of immortality. Buddhist texts apply it above all in the first sense and make it a synonym for nirvana. The Jatakamāla speaks of a rain of ambrosia and the Milindapanha of the ambrosia with which the Buddha has watered the world. (See George Dumesnil, Festin d'Immortalité.)

4. **Shāriputra:** one of the principal disciples of Shākyamuni, considered as the wisest.

5. See Chapter 6.

6. Jpn. goshō.

7. **Icchantika** (Skt.) lit. "man without faith": He who lives without caring to reach Buddhahood, or who has great desires.

8. **Yakusan Igen Zenji** (Chin. Yueh-shan Wei-yen, 745?–834?) Ch'an master

9. Allusion to the three vehicles: Hinayana, Mahayana, Vajrayana. These distinctions developed after the death of Shākyamuni. The "vehicle" is the means utilized to travel the way of Awakening. According to Tibetan Buddhism, which has distinguished nine vehicles, the choice of vehicle depends both on the spiritual maturity of the individual and the capacities of the master.

47

1. **Manzan Oshō:** see Chapter 20.

2. **Wanshi Shōgaku Zenji** (Chn. Hung-chih Cheng-chueh,

1091–1157) master of the Sōtō school of Ch'an in China. He has left a Collection of Remarks (Wanshi kōroku). He is known above all for his celebrated discussion with Daie Sōkō (Chn. Ta-hui), master of the Lin-chi (Jpn. Rinzai) school of Ch'an on the difference in the methods advocated by the two schools for reaching awakening. At his death, Wanshi nevertheless entrusted the editing of his work to Daie Sōkō.

48

1. **Gasshō:** lit. "palms of the hands joined." A Zen expression designating a very old gesture of the hands common to numerous Eastern civilizations and which expresses greetings, a request, thanks, respect. This gesture spontaneously expresses awareness of the non-duality of phenomenon.
2. Jpn. Sanshōdōei.
3. *Hōkyō Zanmai*: see Introduction, note 15.
4. *Bonmo-kyō*: see Chapter 39, note 16.

49

1. **Rakugo:** a comic story that is both spoken and mimed.
2. **Naniwa:** form of popular music with a solo performer. It consists of a modulated recitation accompanied on the shamisen. It first appeared in the middle of the Edo period.
3. **Gidayu:** Recitation in episodes, executed by a narrator and a shamisen player in which are evoked the sentiments of the characters. It's sung in a tonality of great pathos. Furnishing an outlet for the feelings of the repressed masses, it enjoyed an immense success during the Edo period.
4. **Shamisen:** traditional 3-stringed guitar.

50

1. **Three worlds:** world of desires, world of form, and world of no-form.
2. **Sōzan Daishi:** see chapter 10.
3. *Daihatsunehan-kyō* (*Mahaparinirvana Sutra*, Sutra of Great Nirvana): Considered to be the last of Shākyamuni's sermons, a collection of Mahayana sutras dealing with buddha nature, immanent in all beings.

51

1. *Hōkyō Zanmai:* see Introduction, note 15.

52

1. The great wisdom (Skt. mahāprajna; Jpn. maka hannya).
2. CF. the *Hannya Shingyō:* " Jizai bosatsu."
3. Id. "shō-ken-go-on-kai-ku."
4. Id. "do-issai-ku-yaku. "
5. **Kanadaiba** or **Kanadeva** or **Aryadeva:** Fifteenth patriarch of the Indian lineage of Ch'an and a disciple of Nāgārjuna, the author of the Treatise on the Perfection of Great Wisdom (*Mahāprajnā paramita-shāstra*). He lived in the third century CE in Ceylon.

53

1. *Hōkyō Zanmai:* see Introduction, note 15.
2. *Sandōkai:* see Introductionm, note 14.
3. **Ikkyū Sōjun** (1394–1481): Rinzai Zen master. Excellent painter, calligrapher, and poet. One of the most popular Zen characters in Japan, due to the depth of his humor and his non-conformism in the style of the holy fool. Illegitimate son of the emperor Go-

Komatsu, he entered a monastery at the age of five. Endowed with great intelligence, he very early on composed poems in the classical Chinese style. One night on a boat, while plunged deep in meditation, he experienced Awakening upon hearing a crow's cry. He lived at first as a hermit, then in the isolation of his "Blind Donkey's Shed." Named by the emperor as abbot of Daitokuji in Kyōto, he preferred to live in a little temple in his native village where he taught the truth of *zen* in his unconventional manner to all people who visited him.

4. Lit. "Great mistress of Hell."

5. **Hakuin Zenji** (1686–1769): one of the most important masters of Rinzai Zen. He systematized kōan training and reaffirmed the importance of zazen, whose practice had become neglected in favor of intellectual study of Zen writings. He was a great painter, calligrapher, and remarkable sculptor. His watercolors are among the most celebrated works of Zen painting.

6. **Benkei:** legendary character who served Minamoto no Yoshitsune (1159–1189) during the wars between the Taira and the Minamoto. His exploits are recounted in numerous literary works belonging to the genre of warriors' tales. He is also a character in Nō and Kabuki dramas.

7. See Chapter 32, note 3.

54

1. **Kāshyapa** or **Mahākāshyapa** (Jpn. Kashō): see Chapter 35, note 1. He is considered to be the first patriarch of Indian lineage. He was the son of a rich Brahman and married at the urging of his parents, but the marriage was not consummated. With common accord, the two spouses donned the religious habit and each

went their own way. Kāshyapa encountered Shākyamuni, who conferred ordination upon him.

2. Jpn. angya.

3. **Zenkōji:** famous temple in Shinano.

4. **Shimokōbe Chōryū** (1624–1686): scholar within the movement of national studies.

5. **Keichū Ajari** (1640–1701) Buddhist monk and scholar of national studies

6. **Tokugawa Mitsukuni:** lord of the fief of Mito.

7. **Man'yōshū:** see Introduction, Note 27. The poems include funeral elegies, love poems, and miscellaneous poems.

8. Jpn. Juki.

9. Jpn. Menjū.

10. Jpn. Shisho.

11. **Hekigan-roku** (Blue Cliff Record): work of the Lin-chi (Rinzai) Ch'an master Yuan-wu K'o-chin (Jpn. Engo Kukugon, 1063–1135) See Introduction, note 18.

12. **Sōsan** (Chn. Seng-tsan, ?–606) According to tradition, he had leprosy when he encountered Eka. It is in the *Shinjinmei* (see Introduction) that there appeared for the first time the fusion between Taoism and Mahayana Buddhism that was characteristic of later Ch'an.

13. **Dōshin** (Chn. Tao-hsin, 580-651): he was said to have encountered Sōsan at the age of twenty and revealed himself to be a very brilliant student with a marked taste for meditation. He assembled numerous disciples around himself. Differing from his predecessors, who were still strongly attached to texts, he developed a tendency that was eventually revealed as characteristic of Ch'an: the rejection of scriptures in favor of the practice of meditation.

14. **Kōnin** or Gunin (Chn. Hung-jen, 601–674): founded the monastery of Mount Huang-mei (Jpn. Obai)

15. **Enō** (Chn. Hui-neng, 638–713) See Introduction, note 8.

16. See Chapter ll.

17. **Jinshū** (Chn. Shen-hsiu, (605?–706): defeated by Hui-neng in the competition in which they opposed one another for succession to the fifth patriarch, he nevertheless claimed succession and founded the Northern School of Ch'an. Legend would have it that he was a frightful character full of jealousy, who made an attempt on the life of Hui-neng. The sole definite historical fact is the decline that struck the Northern School after seven generations, while the Southern School founded by Hui-neng continued to prosper, giving birth to all the masters and streams of later Ch'an.

18. The Northern School, in reflection of its founder, insisted on the necessity for intellectual penetration of the sutras in order to be able to progressively approach Awakening.

19. The Southern School defends the idea that a brutal and intuitive plunge must be taken into the world of immediate experience that transcends intellect.

20. **Hōrin-ji** (Chn. Pao-lin-ssu): monastery constructed in 504 at Ts'ao-chi, near the port of Canton, where Hui-neng lived for awhile. It has since remained one of the best known monasteries in China.

21. **Seigen** (Chn. Ch'ing-yuan Hsing-ssu, 660–740): one of Hui-neng's successors, whose disciple was Sekito Kisen.

22. **Nangaku Ejō** (Chn. Nan-yueh Huai-jang, 677–744): another successor of Hui-neng and one of the greatest Ch'an masters during the T'ang era.

23. The robe: in the primitive Ch'an tradition, the disciple received the robe and begging bowl from his master as confirmation as successor in the Dharma. From whence comes the expression "the robe and bowl" in Zen literature to metaphorically indicate the "transmission outside the Scriptures."

24. Jpn. den-e.

55

1. **Tea ceremony:** Jpn. cha-no yu (lit. "hot water for tea") also called sadō or chadō, the Way of Tea. The custom of drinking tea infused from leaves would have been introduced from China in a very distant epoch, but it's Eisai Zenji of the Rinzai school who, upon his return from China in 1191, brought back Zen and at the same time the preparation of powdered green tea. It wasn't infused, but whipped in hot water. The monks used this beverage to stay awake. From the Zen point of view, tea is simply to pour the hot water on the powdered tea, nothing more. Zen is also simply to sit, nothing more. It's simple and at the same time difficult.

2. **Yōkan:** sweetened bean paste.

3. **Mujū Hōshi** or Dōkyō or Ichien (1226–1312): Japanese Rinzai monk. He traveled throughout Japan to follow the teaching of the masters of the different schools of Zen. He is the author of Shaseki-shū (Collection of Sand and Stone), a popular work grouping together the stories and legends full of humor with which the masters love to illustrate their teachings.

4. **Tendai Daishi** (Chn. T'ien-t'ai Te-shao, 891–972) Ch'an master.

56

1. See Chapter 11.

2. **Daibonten-ō** or Benten (Skt. Brahma): in Indian mythology, he was considered to be the personification of the fundamental principle of the universe (Brahman), and Buddhism made him one of the two principal tutelary gods, the second being Taishaku (Skt. Indra)

3. **Mou-lien** (Skt. Maudgalyāyana): one of Shākyamuni's principal disciples: known as the most advanced in the mastery of occult powers. He was born in a Brahman family and from childhood was Shāriputra's close friend. He died before Shākyamuni, killed by a hostile Brahman as he was begging for food.

4. **Buddha World** (Jpn. butsodo; Skt. buddhaksetra): field or domain where the activity and the influence of the Buddha are exercised.

5. **Komyō ō nyorai**: "King of Light," resides very far in the West in a land called "Banner of Light."

6. **yujun** (Skt. yōjana): unit of measure in ancient India, equal to the distance that the royal army was supposed to cover in one day's march. It varied from 9.6 to 18 or 24 kilometers.

7. Jpn. ri: 4 kilometers.

8. **Arhat** (Skt.): designates the one who has arrived at the highest of the four stages that a hearer-student (Skt. shravaka) aspires to attain in practicing the Hinayana teachings. Originally, arhat was a term synonymous with Buddha, but with the development of Mahayana Buddhism it ended up designating solely the saints of Hinayana Buddhism.

57

1. **Abhidharma** ("Toward the Law"): doctrinal study of the sutras. After Shākyamuni's death, repeated schisms were produced

within the Buddhist community, which ended up giving birth to eighteen or twenty schools. Certain of these strove to systematically interpret the sutras, and the results of their studies were gathered together in the works of the Abhidharma.

59

1. **Jōfukyō:** 20th chapter of the Lotus Sutra, dedicated to the Bodhisattva Jōfukyō.

60

1. Jpn. Sendanrin.
2. The lion dance (Jpn. shishimai) takes place on January 1 and certain festival days. A man wears a red mask in the form of a lion's head and two or three others under a cloth make up the body. This lion is supposed to chase away demons and bring health and prosperity to families and villages.
3. All the activities of a Zen monastery are announced or accompanied by percussion notes struck on wood or metal. Sound has a great importance in Zen; it defines silence. Numerous masters were awakened by a simple sound. The instruments are numerous: the large exterior bell is called gyōshō and one strikes its outside with a large hanging log. There are also taiko, the big drum and mokugyo, the wooden drum in the form of a round fish that one strikes with a mallet with a padded head.

61

1. *Nehangyō*: Nirvana Sutra—all the sutras containing Shākyamuni's teaching prior to his death or describing events relative to his entry into nirvana.

62

1. **Tendai school:** Japanese version of the Chinese T'ien-t'ai school. It was introduced into Japan in the eighth century by Saichō, who studied the doctrine in China. Its doctrine is based on the Lotus Sutra. It teaches the universality of buddha-nature, basing itself on the principle of the Three Truths: (1) Phenomena are empty. (2) They have an apparent and limited existence in time. (3) The whole and the parts make only one: identity of phenomena and the Absolute. In the ninth century, esoteric teachings were incorporated into the Tendai doctrine (mudras, mandalas).

63

1. *Shōman-kyō* (Skt. *Shrimālādevi-sutra*) Lit. "Princess Shrimala's Sutra" Mahayana sutra translated into Chinese in 435. It played an important role in the first days of Buddhism in Japan. It sets forth the doctrine of the one vehicle and that buddha nature is inherent in all sentient beings.
2. **Hishiryō:** state of awareness during zazen. Thinking beyond thinking. "rationally incommensurable."
3. **Jiun Sonja of Katsuragi** (1718–1804): Shingon monk, philosopher, and specialist in Sanskrit.

64

1. The daughter of the dragon: daughter of "Sagura, king of the dragons," she is said to have attained Awakening at the age of eight by listening to Manjushri. (see 12th chapter of the Lotus Sutra)
2. **Manju** or **Manjushri** (Skt. Manjushri): Bodhisattva who appears in the sutras and one of the principal figures in the Buddhist

pantheon. Considered to be the symbol of the perfection of wisdom, he is generally depicted at the left of the Buddha, seated on a lion. His attributes are the sword of wisdom and a book of sutras.

3. **Zenshō** (Chn. Shan-hsing, Skt. Sunakshatra): disciple and son of Shākyamuni, fathered before he renounced the world. He would have been a scholar but, influenced by bad friends, he became a nihilist and proclaimed that there were neither Buddha, Dharma, nor nirvana. He's said to have fallen living into hell.

66

1. **Nagārjuna:** Mahayana man of letters in South India who lived between 150 and 250 CE. He is the fourteenth patriarch in the Indian lineage of successors to Shākyamuni. Born into a brahman family, he first studied Hinayana Buddhism, but later converted to the Mahayana. He wrote numerous commentaries and organized the theoretical bases for Mahayana thought. His treatises were translated into Chinese around the year 400 CE by the excellent Kumārajiva. He is particularly known for his systemization of the principle of emptiness (Jpn. ku) His philosophy was called the Madhyamika ("Middle") doctrine.

67

1. This refers to the "hearers" (Skt. shravakas) or "buddhas-for-self–alone" (Skt. pratyekabuddhas) as opposed to the Bodhisattva, who represents the Mahayana ideal (the Great Vehicle).
2. **sei-ji:** "assistant."
3. **sei-dō:** "guest lecturer."
4. **Zagu:** piece of cloth that one unfolds before oneself to do sanpai

(three prostrations). It serves to protect the o-kesa by preventing it from touching the ground.

5. **Fusuma:** partition or sliding door covered with opaque paper.

6. **Sanpai:** three prostrations before the Buddha, or before the master, forehead against the ground, hands on either side of the head, slightly raised, with the palms facing up toward the sky. Symbolically, a mark of respect toward the Three Treasures: Buddha, Dharma, Sangha.

7. **Tenjiku Tokubei:** See Chapter 20, note 14.

68

1. **Saigyō** (1118–1190): poet at the end of the Heian era. He was born into a family of warriors. At the age of twenty-two, he left his family, became a monk and traveled throughout Japan. His simple and direct poems are expressions of his own emotions and experiences. The principal collection of his poetry, the Sanka-shū (House on the Mountain) contains 1,552 poems.

2. **Skandha:** see Chapter 4, Note 1.

3. **Twelve links** (Skt. nidana, "links"): one of the foremost Buddhist theories, showing the causal relation that exists between ignorance and suffering. Shākyamuni is said to have taught it in response to the question concerning why beings suffer old age and death. The twelve links are: (1) ignorance, (2) activity, (3) awareness, (4) name and form, (5) the six sense organs, (6) the contact of the senses, (7) sensations and feelings, (8) desires, (9) attachment, (10) existence, (11) birth, (12) old age and death.

4. **Eighteen worlds:** the eighteen domains of empirical awareness (the 6 sense organs, 6 objects of the senses, 6 perceptions or awarenesses)

69

1. Cf. *Hannya shingyō*: "go-on-kai-kū-do-issai-kū-yaku. "
2. **Manzan Oshō:** see Chapters 20, 47.

70

1. **Takayama Chogyū** (1871–1902) : man of letters, philosopher, critic, and founder of the review Taiyō.
2. *Kanmuryōjugyō* (Sutra on the meditation on the Buddha of Infinite Life): one of the basic sutras of the Pure Land School. At the request of Bimbasara, who was distressed by the evil actions of his son Ajase, Shākyamuni used his mystic powers to show him the various pure lands, including the Pure Land of Amida's perfect bliss.
3. **Ajase** (Skt. Ajātashatru): (see also Chapter 3, Note 3).
4. **Devadatta:** son of King Amrita, elder brother of Ananda, and Shākyamuni's cousin. In his youth, manifested his hostility to the latter by entering into rivalry with him over the hand of Yasodhara (wife of Shākyamuni before he renounced secular life, and mother of his son, Rahula). Later, he became a member of the sangha. Proud and jealous of the Buddha's ascendancy, he made many attempts on his life and provoked a schism in the sangha by taking a position in favor of a rigorous ascetism, reproaching the Buddha for leading a soft life.
5. **Furuna** (Skt. Pūrna): one of Shākyamuni's principal disciples, renowned for being the greatest preacher of the Dharma.

72

1. **Three worlds:** domains inhabited by unawakened beings that transmigrate in the six realms.

2. **Four continents** (Jpn. shishū): continents respectively situated at the east, west, north and south of Mt. Sumeru, according to the ancient Indian conception of the world. In the south, Nanzen-shū; in the east, Tōshōshin; in the west, Sugoka, in the north Hokukuro.

3. **Four bad paths** (Jpn. shiakushū): Hell, greed, animality, anger. One calls them bad because they are states of suffering.

4. **Six heavens of the world of desire** (Jpn. rokuten): According to the ancient Indian conception of the world, six heavens existed between the earth and the heaven of Brahma. These are: the heaven of four celestial kings (Jpn. shioten); the heaven of the thirty-three gods (Jpn. sanjusanten); the heaven of Yama (Jpn. yamaten); the heaven of satisfaction (Jpn. tosotsuten); the heaven where one is born in joy (Jpn. kerakuten); the heaven of Māra (Jpn. takeijizaiten). Māra is the demon king. The world of desires is called thus because man is subject to desires that prevent the attainment of Awakening.

5. **Four zen heavens of the world of form** (Jpn. shikikai no shizenten): Four stages of concentration (Skt. dhyana): (1) abolition of desires (2) calming of thoughts and reflection (3) absence of feeling and awareness of well-being (4) impassiveness and sharpness of mind.

6. **Four domains of the world of no-form** (Jpn. mushikikai no shijo): (1) emptiness without limits (Jpn. kū muhen jo), (2) awareness without limits (Jpn. shiki muhen jo), (3) non-existence (Jpn. mu sho u jo), (4) neither thought nor non-thought (Jpn. hisō hi hisō jo).

7. **Mondō** (lit. "question-answer"): the disciple poses a question concerning an existential problem that troubles him profoundly. Avoiding all theory or logical reasoning, the master responds in a

manner so as to provoke in his questioner a response coming from the depths of his being. Numerous mondō were afterward taken up again in kōans.

8. **Parable of the burning house:** 3rd chapter of the Lotus Sutra. Parable told by Shākyamuni to demonstrate that the sole purpose of the coming of the Buddha is to allow all beings to attain the state of Buddha. Imagine, he says, a rich man who has an incalculable number of children. A fire breaks out in his vast dwelling. His children, absorbed in their games, don't notice that the house is in flames and are unheeding of his cries of warning. He resorts to a stratagem to get them to leave. He shouts to them that he's placed outside three chariots that they've wanted for a long time. Immediately, the children rush toward the door. The house represents the three worlds, the flames, suffering, and the three chariots the means to become Buddha.

9. **Seal of the Dharma** (Jpn. Hōin): the seal that expresses the immutability of the Dharma and its transmission from one Buddha to another Buddha.

73

1. **Nihon-gaishi** (Unofficial history of Japan): historical work composed by Rai San'yo (1782–1823), which sets forth the destiny of the warrior class during the period of the wars between the Minamoto and Taira up to the Edo period.

2. **Fujiwara:** the Fujiwara clan had a powerful hand in the entire central administration of the Heian period, thanks to marriage alliances with the imperial household. They were jealously on the lookout to maintain their privilege of being grandfather to the crown prince or to the emperor. Chance happenings, epidemics,

and the hazard of births brought about their decline at the end of the eleventh century. In 1068, they were forced to allow Emperor Go-Sanjō, born of a princess who was not a Fujiwara, to mount the throne.

3. **Obaku Oshō** (Chn. Huang-po Hsi-yun, died 850): one of the great Ch'an masters. He was the master of Lin-chi (Jpn. Rinzai). His biography describes him as a man more than two meters tall with a protuberance on his forehead and a sonorous voice. His words and sermons have been preserved. (Cf. Patrick Carré: Les Entretiens de Huang-po, Paris, 1985).

4. **Jōshū Jūshin** (Chn. Chao-chou Ts'ung-shēn): see Chapter 2, Note 13. Dōgen, who was severe with regard to Zen masters, called him respectfully "Jōshū, the old Buddha." Jōshū always repeated that Awakening is only the beginning of true progress on the way of Zen. He passed his life in thoroughly investigating the Way; it was only at the age of eighty that he installed himself in a little monastery where he guided some students on the Way. He died at the age of one hundred and twenty.

5. One day a monk asked Chao-chou (Jpn. Jōshū): "Does a dog really possess the buddha nature or not?" Chao-chou answered "Wu!" (Jpn. mu; nothing, does not exist, without, not a single thing.) The task of the student consists in penetrating, without the intervention of intellect, the profound meaning of mu. This kōan is often the first one that a Rinzai Zen master gives his students to deeply investigate.

6. **Naniwa-bushi**: this popular music executed by a single performer consisted of a modulated recitation accompanied on the shamisen. It tells stories of great-hearted heroes, loyal servants, virtuous women who always remain faithful to the sentiment of duty (Jpn.

giri) no matter what the vicissitudes. These songs have been in decline since World War II.

7. *Jōruri*: modulated recitation with musical accompaniment on the shamisen, accompanying action by puppets. Jōruri became a theatrical genre with the advent of the present Bunraku Theatre in Osaka. The success of Jōruri during the Edo period promoted the appearance of numerous singers, shamisen players, puppeteers and remarkable authors.

8. **Hōtan Oshō:** (1654–1738) monk of the Kegon School, which he tried to restore.

74

1. **Okazaki Masamune:** celebrated master forger of swords during the Kamakura period.

75

1. *Yuimagyō* (Skt. *Vimalakirtinirdesa,* The Teachings of Vimalakirti): Cf. translation by Étienne Lamotte: "The Vimalakirtinirdesa is perhaps the jewel of Mahayana Buddhist literature. Quivering with life and full of humor, it has neither the wordy tediousness of the other Mahayana sutras nor the technicality of the Buddhist shastras, with whom, however, it shares science and information. Far from losing itself in the desert of abstract and impersonal doctrines, its author reacts at every turn before the depth of the Buddha Dharma, that he spares neither criticisms nor sarcasm. He's a virtuoso of paradox who pushes independence of spirit to the point of irreverence. Doesn't he claim to search for deliverance in the sixty-two false views of the heretics and doesn't he counsel plunging oneself into the sea of passions to arrive at omniscience?

Perhaps he scandalized the Indians. In any case, he amused and charmed the Chinese who, beginning with the fifth century, read him in Kumārajiva's excellent translation . . ."

This text is particularly appreciated in Zen. It dates from the second century CE. Vimalakirti was a rich merchant who, though living in this world, succeeded in following the way of the bodhisattvas.

2. **Upali:** one of the great disciples of Shākyamuni. At the outset, Upali was the barber for the Shāka princes. His old profession earned him appointment as head shaver for the monks. Tradition considers him to be the specialist in questions of discipline and rites.

3. **Daichidoron:** see Chapter 13, Note 3. It explains the notions of wisdom and emptiness (Jpn. ku). It sets forth what comprises the ideal of the bodhisattva and the six perfections (Skt. pāramita). It constitutes an essential text for Mahayana thought.

4. See Chapter 70, Note 4.

5. **Miso:** fermented soybean paste.

6. Notion of the gift in Buddhism (see the *Vinayapitaka Sutra* of the *Dharmaguptaka*): A good action that represents a gift of food to the Buddha is going to produce "fruits" in virtue of the great universal law of the "ripening" of deeds. Thus, when two merchants offered honey and flour to Shākyamuni, they said, "Accept these out of compassion for us." It's thus not the donor who gives proof of compassion, but he who receives. By accepting the offering, Shākyamuni permitted the two merchants to obtain the "fruits" of their good actions.

7. **Nyojō Zenji** (Chn. Ju-ching, 1163–1228). Ch'an master of the Ts'ao-tung (Jpn. Sōtō) school—Dōgen's master at the time of his sojourn in China.

8. **Hyakujō Ekai** (Chn. Pai-chang Huai-hai, 720–814) One of the great Ch'an masters. He started a monastic tradition that remained vigorous from then on. Up until then, Ch'an masters were received as "visitors" in monasteries of other Buddhist schools, whose rules of communal life they had to observe. From the time of Pai-chang, autonomous Ch'an monasteries developed, adapted to the demands of training in the way of Ch'an. Pai-chang insisted upon the importance of the link between zazen and daily labor carried out in the monastery or in the fields. It is to him that we owe the celebrated Zen saying: "A day without work, a day without eating." Unlike the other Chinese monks who, conforming to the Indian tradition, lived by begging or through gifts, the Ch'an monks drew their subsistence from the labor of their hands. The tradition of begging (Jpn. takahatsu) was conserved as a method of intellectual formation. He left one of Zen's fundamental writings, The Sudden Awakening (Jpn. Tongo) and a collection of remarks, Collected Words of Hyakujô (jpn. Hyakujō-roku).

76

1. **Keizan Jōkin** (1268-1325), See Chapter 1, Note 15. The most important monk of Japanese Sōtō Zen, after Dōgen. He composed a collection of anecdotes on the transmission of the Dharma, the Denkōroku (Writings of the monk Keizan on the transmission of the light.)
2. **Nyojō Zenji**: See Chapter 75, Note7.
3. Cf. *Hannya shingyō*: a-noku-ta-ra-san-myaku-san-bodai.

77

1. **Sanmai** or **zanmai** (Skt. samādhi): (1) Total absorption of the

mind during zazen (2) Perfect calm of heart and mind. (3) Perfect ease and mastery in action.

78

1. See Chapter 8, Note 3.

2. **Jōdo shin shū:** lit. "true school of the Pure Land," abbreviated as Shin shū. Japanese school of Buddhism founded by Shinran (1172–1262) and organized into a school by Rennyo (1415–1499). The essential doctrine is contained in the formula of adoration to Amida, namu amida butsu ("Homage to Amida Buddha"). The recitation of this formula permits the faithful to be reborn in the Pure Land even if they have bad karma. The fundamental religious element resides in an unshakeable faith in the power of Amida Buddha. The Jōdō-shin-shū represents the extreme form of the "easy" way. No effort is demanded for the purpose of Awakening, solely faith and surrender to Amida can provide salvation.

Disciples of Kōdō Sawaki with Great Influence in the West

Kōshō Uchiyama (1912–1998)

Dharma heir and successor to Sawaki at Antaiji temple Uchiyama Roshi has been particularly influential in the United States due to the translation of his popular books, Opening the Hand of Thought, edited by Jisho Cary Warner, as well as his commentary on Dōgen's Bendōwa in The Wholehearted Way, translated by Taigen Leighten and Shohaku Okumura, and his commentary on Dōgen's Tenzokyo-kun in Refining Your Life, translated by Thomas Wright.

Uchiyama's clarity and his insistence upon the value of shikan-taza (just sitting), and his championing of zazen as the sole and central element of authentic practice have had a major impact upon Sōtō Zen Buddhist practice in the United States, partly through the efforts of his dharma heir, Shōhaku Okumura. Rev. Okumura, Sawaki Roshi's dharma grandson, is a gifted scholar of Dōgen, and his translation, with Taigen Leighten, of the Eihei koroku (Dogen's Extensive Record) is a major accomplishment, along with his own books of commentary, Realizing Genjōkōan and Living by Vow. Abbot of the Sanshin Zen Community in Bloomington, Indiana, Rev. Okumura continues to translate Uchiyama's writings, including his comments on Sawaki

Roshi, which appeared in the fall of 2014 in a new translation of Sawaki's collected sayings titled The Zen Teaching of "Homeless" Kōdō.

Taisen Deshimaru (1917–1982)

Long-time student of Sawaki, ordained by him just prior to Sawaki's death, received dharma transmission from Reirin Yamada Zenji, 75th Abbot of Eiheiji. Alone, with no money and no knowledge of the French language, Deshimaru arrived in France in 1967. His concentration upon the pure and authentic practice of zazen provided a needed antidote to the orientalism of European intellectuals of that period. He gave lectures in France and other European countries, led sesshin and published his first book, True Zen. In 1970, he established l'Association Zen d'Europe, which in 1979 became l'Association Zen Internationale, today a powerful association of zendos and centers across Europe.

Master Deshimaru's wish was to bring tradition and modernity together into a coexistence that embraced both ancient Asian roots and contemporary Western sensibility and philosophy. Through the different forums of books, lectures and sesshin, his teaching always reflected his grounding in the teachings of Kōdō Sawaki. Today, through l'Association Zen International as well as at Gendronnière, the temple Deshimaru founded, this work continues, with a presence in the United States as well.

Gudō Wafu Nishijima (1919–2014)

Nishijima, with a long career within Japanese financial institutions, began to study with Kōdō Sawaki in 1940 and in 1973 was ordained by Niwa Rempō Roshi, from whom he later received dharma transmission. He lectured for many years on Buddhism and Zen in

English, founding the Dōgen Sangha in Tokyo. His translation work has had a major impact within the English-speaking world, primarily through his complete translation, with Chodo Cross, of Eihei Dōgen's masterwork, Shōbōgenzō, as well as through the work of his disciples, author Brad Warner (Hardcore Zen, Sit Down and Shut Up and other books), and teacher Jundo Cohen (Treeleaf Zendo, an internet zen community).

Suggested Reading

Yōka Genkaku (Yung-chia Hsuan-chueh).

Zen's Chinese Heritage, Andy Ferguson, Wisdom Publications, 2000.

The Roaring Stream, edited by Nelson Foster and Jack Shoemaker, The Ecco Press, 1996.

Translations of *The Song of Awakening* (Cheng-tao ke)

Norman Foster in *The Roaring Stream,* The Ecco Press, 1996.

D.T. Suzuki, *Manual of Zen Buddhism,* Grove Press, 1978.

Master Sheng-yen, *The Poetry of Enlightenment: Poems by Ancient Chan Masters*, Dharma Drum Publicatons, 1987.

Nyogen Senzaki and Ruth McCandless, *Buddhism and Zen*, North Point Press, 1987.

Lu K'uan Yu, *Ch'an and Zen Teachings*, series 3, Rider & Company, 1962.

Kōdō Sawaki Roshi

Living and Dying in Zazen: Five Zen Masters of Modern Japan, Arthur Braverman, Weatherhill, 2003.

The Zen Teaching of Homeless Kodo, by Kosho Uchiyama Roshi, translation and commentary by Shohaku Okumura, Wisdom Publications, 2014.

Eihei Dōgen Zenji

Master Dōgen's Shobogenzo, Vols. 1–4, trans. by Gudo Nishijima and Chodo Cross, Windbell Publications, 1994.

Treasury of the True Dharma Eye: Zen Master Dōgen's Shōbōgenzō, Vols. 1 & 2, trans. by Kazuaki Tanahashi, Shambala, 2010.

Moon In a Dewdrop: Writings of Zen Master Dōgen, edited by Kazuaki Tanahashi, Northpoint Press, 1995.

Dōgen's Genjo Koan: Three Commentaries, by Eihei Dogen, Nishiari Bokusan, Shohaku Okumura, Shunryu Suzuki, Counterpoint Press, 2011.

Realizing Genjō Kōan, by Shohaku Okumura, Wisdom Publications, 2010.

Dōgen Kigen, Mystical Realist, by Hee-Jin Kim , Wisdom Publications, 2000.

Dōgen's Extensive Record, A Translation of the Eihei Koroku, by Taigen Dan Leighton and Shohaku Okumura, Wisdom Publications, 2004.

The True Dharma Eye, Zen Master Dōgen's Three Hundred Koans, by John Daido Loori and Kazuaki Tanahashi, 2009.

The Heart of Dōgen's Shōbōgenzō, by Norman Wadell and Masao Abe, State University of New York, 2002.

Dōgen's Formative Years in China, by Takashi James Kodera, Prajna Press, Great Eastern Book Co., 1980.

Dōgen's Pure Standards for the Zen Community, A Translation of Eihei Shingi, by Eihei Dogen, Taigen Daniel Leighton, and Shohaku Okumura, State University of New York Press, 1996.

Impermanence is Buddha-Nature, Dōgen's Understanding of Temporality, by Joan Stambaugh, University of Hawaii Press, 1990.

Kōshō Uchiyama Roshi

The Wholehearted Way, a translation of *Dogen's Bendowa*, with commentary by Kōshō Uchiyama Roshi, translated by Shohaku Okumura and Taigen Daniel Leighton, Tuttle Publishing, 1997.

How to Cook Your Life: From Zen Kitchen to Enlightenment, by Eihei Dōgen and Kōshō Uchiyama Roshi, Shambala, 2005.

Opening the Hand of Thought: Foundations of Buddhist Practice, by Kōshō Uchiyama Roshi, tr. Tom Wright, Jisho Warner and Shohaku Okumura, Wisdom Publications, 2004.

Master Taisen Deshimaru

Questions to a Zen Master: Practical and Spiritual Answers, by Taisen Deshimaru and Nancy Amphoux, Penguin Arkana, 1991.

Sit: Zen Teachings of Master Taisen Deshimaru and Philippe Coupey, 1996

The Ring of the Way: Testament of a Zen Master, by Taisen Deshimaru, 1987

Mūshotoku Mind: The Heart of the Heart Sutra, by Taisen Deshimaru and Richard Collins, Hohm Press, 2012.

Table of Kōdō Sawaki's Commentaries

About the Translator

Tonen Sara O'Connor, a dharma-transmitted American Sōtō Zen Buddhist priest and *nitokyoshi* within the Japanese system, is Resident Priest Emerita at the Milwaukee Zen Center. She has served as President of the Sōtō Zen Buddhist Association, the national U.S. organization, and has translated numerous French plays for professional production.